$$\frac{6\overline{5}\,40}{4\,\overline{1}\,5}$$

HOLY COMMUNION AND HOLY SPIRIT

Holy Communion and Holy Spirit

A Study in
DOCTRINAL RELATIONSHIP

by

J. E. L. OULTON, D.D.

Regius Professor of Divinity in the University of Dublin
Chancellor of St. Patrick's

LONDON

S · P · C · K

1954

First Published - - - 1951
Reprinted - - - - 1954

PREFACE

IT WOULD not be difficult to find, scattered here and there in theological works, expressions of the opinion that there is a connection between the doctrine of the Holy Communion and that of the Holy Spirit. But I am not aware that hitherto any book has been written on this subject alone. The present work, therefore, is intended to supply this need, and at the same time, it is hoped, to lead to further study along these lines. It is mainly concerned with the teaching of the New Testament; but reference is also made, chiefly by way of illustration and amplification, to the doctrine and the liturgical practice of the early Church.

My aim in treating of the doctrine of the Holy Communion has not been controversial, but rather to show that when we place the sacrament within the wider context of the life and worship of the Church we shall find agreements underlying what we thought were differences. Perhaps at no other time in the history of the modern Church has there been a greater need for, and a greater willingness to discover, such agreements.

I have not thought it necessary to discuss the doctrine of the Holy Spirit before the Incarnation. Nor do I touch directly in this book upon recent controversies concerning Christian Initiation or the content of the term *Baptisma*.

In preparing this book for the Press, I have received the help of kind friends, to whom my grateful thanks are tendered. Canon W. C. de Pauley read through the entire work when it was in manuscript, and talked over many points with me, to my great advantage. Canon J. Purser Shortt performed a like office in respect of Chapter II. And a former pupil of mine, the Rev. R. F. Hipwell, gave me his ready and helpful assistance in correcting the proofs.

J. E. L. O.

Trinity College,
  Dublin.
December, 1949.

1

ACKNOWLEDGEMENTS

My acknowledgements are due to the Very Rev. the Dean of St. Paul's, Dr. W. R. Matthews, for kind permission to quote from an unpublished lecture of his (p. 180); and to the publishers and the editors of *The Expository Times* for like permission to reproduce, in Chapter VI, an article of mine which had appeared in it. My acknowledgements are also due to the following publishers and individuals for permitting me to quote from the works indicated: Geoffrey Bles, Ltd. (S. Bulgakov, *The Orthodox Church*); The Clarendon Press, Oxford (R. H. Connolly, *Didascalia Apostolorum*); The Rev. Dom G. Dix, O.S.B., and Dacre Press (*The Shape of the Liturgy*); William Heinemann, Ltd. (A. Symons, *Images of Good and Evil*); Macmillan & Co., Ltd. (A. S. Pringle-Pattison in *The Spirit*, ed. B. H. Streeter; H. B. Swete, *The Holy Catholic Church*); Methuen & Co., Ltd. (J. F. Bethune-Baker, *An Introduction to the Early History of Christian Doctrine*; W. R. Inge, *Christian Mysticism*); Messrs. John Murray (R. C. Moberly, *Atonement and Personality*); James Nisbet & Co., Ltd. (O. C. Quick, *The Christian Sacraments*); the executor of the late Miss Evelyn Underhill, and Messrs. Methuen (*Mysticism*).

ΤΑ ΑΓΙΑ ΤΟΙΣ ΑΓΙΟΙΣ

In thy light shall we see light.
Psalm 36. 9.

Tu ne me chercherais pas, si tu ne m'avais trouvé.
Pascal, *Pensées* VII

CONTENTS

*Ubi Ecclesia, ibi et Spiritus Dei ; et ubi Spiritus Dei,
illic Ecclesia, et omnis gratia.*

IRENÆUS.

CHAPTER I

THE FELLOWSHIP OF THE UPPER ROOM

WRITERS who treat of the scene which took place in the Upper Room, as it is described for us by the Evangelists, tend to be concerned solely or mainly with the words and actions of our Lord himself. What he did and said then is indeed all-important. But we must remember that the scene was a Supper. It was a social meal, a social gathering. Had the Sacrament never been instituted, or had it not been instituted on that occasion, the holding of the Supper simply by itself testified to a relationship already existing, and hereby emphasized, between the Saviour and his disciples. It is the purpose of this chapter to point out how clearly and emphatically all the Evangelists witness to that relationship. Later on, when the doctrine of the Sacrament comes up for consideration, the relevance of this relationship will become apparent.

In *Matthew*[1] and *Mark*[2] the initiative in the matter of holding the Paschal Supper is ascribed to the disciples, who "came to Jesus, saying, Where wilt thou that we make ready for thee to eat the Passover?" In *Luke*[3] it is Jesus who takes the first step. "And the day of unleavened bread came, on which the Passover must be sacrificed. And he sent Peter and John, saying, Go and make ready for us the Passover, that we may eat." Then follows the question of the disciples, as in *Matthew* and *Mark*, concerning the place where the meal should be held. Either of these accounts of the matter is convincing, because both seem equally natural, as testifying to the mutual desire and expectation of our Lord on the one hand and of his disciples on the other to partake of this meal together. The Passover was the great family meal of the Jews. The Biblical account of its institution spoke of the household as the normal unit for those who gathered together to eat it.[4] And this aspect of the feast was in our Lord's day emphasized by the Pharisees, for whom the Passover was essentially a home feast

[1] Matt. 26. 17.   [2] Mark 14. 12.   [3] Luke 22. 7, 8.
[4] Ex. 12. 3.

at which the father of the house acted as a kind of priest.[1] The
Lord's mother was then in Jerusalem,[2] and presumably his brethren[3] also; but he did not join in the Paschal Supper with them. The
"family" meal is shared instead with his disciples. And thus at
the end of the ministry he gives effect to words spoken by him at
an earlier stage: "Who is my mother? and who are my brethren?
And he stretched forth his hand towards his disciples, and said,
Behold my mother and my brethren! For whosoever shall do the
will of my Father which is in heaven, he is my brother, and sister,
and mother."[4] The Lord's brethren, as well as his mother, are
indeed found in company with the Apostles in the interval between the Ascension and Pentecost.[5] But it seems probable that
their disbelief[6] in him, manifested during part at least of his
ministry, remained until after the Resurrection. It may be that
one of them—James, subsequently named the Just—was already
a believer in him before his death. The apocryphal Gospel according to the Hebrews tells a story which seems to imply that he was
present at the Last Supper. The Lord after his resurrection
appeared to James, who had sworn that he would not eat bread
from the hour in which he had drunk the cup of the Lord[7] till he
saw him risen from the dead. Jesus therefore "took bread and
blessed and brake it and gave it to James the Just, and said to him,
My brother, eat thy bread, for the Son of Man has risen from the
dead."[8] But we cannot appeal with confidence to this tradition,
and there may in any case be a confusion between James the Just
and James the son of Zebedee.[9] We are on firmer ground when we
see in the appearance of the risen Christ to James,[10] as recorded by
St. Paul, an indication that in one at least of his brethren there
was a germ of faith which the revelation of the Resurrection
could quicken into fuller life. But it is of the Twelve and of
them alone that the Synoptists speak as sharing with our Lord the
Last Supper.[11]

[1] G. H. Box, *Judaism in the Greek Period*, p. 54. It is clear that our Lord,
though criticizing much of Pharisaism, accepted some of the ideas and doctrines
associated with it—e.g., belief in a resurrection; and he may have also accepted
its view of the Passover.　　　　　　　　　　　[2] John 19. 25-27.

[3] In John 7. 10 they are at Jerusalem for the Feast of Tabernacles.

[4] Matt. 12. 48-50; cp. Mark 3. 33-35.　　[5] Acts 1. 14.　　[6] John 7. 5.

[7] Lightfoot reads " in which the Lord had drunk his cup".

[8] Mayor, *Epistle of St. James*, xxxvii.

[9] See H. B. Swete, *Appearances of our Lord after His Passion*, 89.

[10] 1 Cor. 15. 7.　　[11] Matt. 26. 20; Mark 14. 17, 20; Luke 22. 14, 30.

The partaking of the Paschal Supper with his disciples cannot, therefore, be regarded as a merely formal act, whether we look upon that Supper in the light of what Scripture or tradition held concerning it, or from the point of view of the solemn circumstances under which it was held. A few days before, in reply to the churlish criticism that was made concerning the costly gift lavished by Mary of Bethany upon our Lord, he had said: "But me ye have not always."[1] They were words of tragic foreboding which must have fallen like lead upon the hearts of the disciples. The predictions of a terrible catastrophe, hinted at in days gone by when they were afraid to inquire further,[2] could now no longer be wholly misunderstood. And as children count minute by minute of joys they cannot retain, so Christ's friends felt the inexorable day—whatever it might bring forth—stealing on apace. And the sharing of the Paschal Supper with them at such a time, when the sands of opportunity for their intercourse were almost run out, testified to the existence of a fellowship, a union of heart and will between him and them, which removed the ritual act far above the region of merely customary observance.

Moreover, it is probable that the Last Supper was not the actual Passover meal at all, as the Synoptists reckon it to be,[3] but rather a meal held, as the Fourth Gospel implies,[4] on the day before the Passover. The words of St. Paul, too, "Our passover also hath been sacrificed, even Christ"[5] have been taken to imply that the Apostle followed the Johannine tradition that Christ had been crucified on the 14th of Nisan. Many, but not all, modern scholars hold with St. John on this point for the following reasons among others.[6] The chief priests and the scribes decide that they will *not* arrest Jesus during the feast, lest a tumult arise among the people.[7] Yet according to the Synoptists this is exactly what they did do. We read of Peter carrying a sword,[8] of Joseph of Arimathæa buying linen,[9] and of the Jews generally being out of doors, during the twenty-four hours beginning with the evening of the Last Supper: all of which appear to be contrary to Jewish law and tradition concerning the

---

[1] Mark 14. 7. [2] Cp. Mark 9. 32, "they were afraid to ask him."
[3] Matt. 26. 18; Mark 14. 16; Luke 22. 13. [4] Cp. John 13. 1, 29; 18. 28.
[5] 1 Cor. 5. 7.
[6] Cp., e.g., A. H. McNeile, *Matthew*, 377f.; R. H. Kennett, *The Last Supper*, 5ff. [7] Matt. 26. 5. [8] John 18. 10. [9] Mark 15. 46.

observance of the Passover.[1] The customary release of a prisoner[2] would more naturally be made at the beginning of the festival, not when its most important point of observance was ended. Further there is, in fact, nothing recorded by the Synoptists with regard to the actual meal which is peculiar to the Passover. No lamb is spoken of, or unleavened bread, but bread and wine only, the constituents of any ordinary repast.

How precisely this conflicting tradition concerning the Last Supper arose, it is not now possible to determine. But if it was the Lord's deliberate intention to substitute for the Passover meal a farewell meal with his disciples on the night before the day of his death, it is not very difficult to suppose that later on in the minds of Christian disciples the farewell meal would be regarded as having taken place on the actual day of the Feast, whereas it was merely anticipatory. This not unnatural confusion may have been assisted by a misinterpretation of something our Lord had said at the Supper itself: "With desire I desired to eat this Passover with you before I suffer."[3]

The saying immediately arrests our attention by the phrase "With desire I desired", which is as un-English as the Greek which it translates, ἐπιθυμίᾳ ἐπεθύμησα, is un-Greek. In all likelihood we have here an attempt to translate a common Hebrew idiom, according to which, when it is wished to define more accurately or strengthen the idea of a verb, the infinitive absolute of the verb is placed before a finite tense.[4] The same kind of construction occurs but with much less frequency in Aramaic.[5] Thus the meaning in this case is "I *earnestly* desired to eat this Passover with you—but my death will come first." The words "this Passover" came to be understood as "this meal on the table" instead of "this Passover which is to be celebrated to-morrow".[6] They express an unfulfilled wish. But both A.V. and R.V., by translating "I have desired", encourage English readers to fall into the very misinterpretation which on this assumption was prevalent in the infant Church.

If, then, the Last Supper was not the actual Paschal meal, but a

---

[1] Cp. Ex. 12. 22.   [2] John 18. 39.   [3] Luke 22. 15.

[4] Cp. Gen. 31. 30 (LXX): ἐπιθυμίᾳ γὰρ ἐπεθύμησας εἰς τὸν οἶκον τοῦ πατρός σου ἀπελθεῖν: R.V. "thou sore longedst after thy father's house".

[5] J. H. Moulton, *Grammar of New Testament Greek*, ii. 443.

[6] R. H. Kennett, *id.* 8.

farewell meal arranged by our Lord and his disciples for a special purpose, it emphasizes all the more clearly the fellowship that existed between him and them, all notions of what was merely customary or formal being excluded from the holding of it.

Recent writers[1] have spoken of the Last Supper as being of the type of the *Haburah* meal of the Jews. The word *Haburah* suggests an associate, a companion, and may be used to imply likeness in character; and in the plural *Haburoth* it can be employed to indicate members of a guild associated for purposes of worship. Oesterley[2] goes as far as to say that *Haburah* means "fellowship", almost "love". *Haburoth* or meals of a social and religious character came into use among the Jews at some period after the exile, and at any rate before the Christian era. The meal was held at the home of one of the members, usually on a Friday, and beginning in the afternoon was drawn out by conversation and discussion of a predominantly religious character until dusk.

The evangelical accounts of the Last Supper answer in some respects to what we know of the *Haburah*. For our present purpose it is sufficient to note that two leading thoughts stand out in these accounts as concerning the persons who took part in the meal. The two are very closely connected: *loyalty* and *fellowship*. The loyalty of the disciples is indicated both indirectly and directly. Indirectly, by the singling out of the traitor from among them, who are thereby contrasted with him. When the Lord announced at Supper "Verily I say unto you, One of you shall betray me, even he that eateth with me",[3] it was the one thing that could darken with deeper tragedy the clouds which already hung over the disciples. They had been often accused in the past of dullness, faintheartedness, lack of faith. But that one of their number was a traitor was the most horrible accusation that could be launched against them. They began to be sorrowful, or, as *Matthew* has it, exceeding sorrowful. They had assembled in anxious foreboding: they were now plunged into grief. And, though his words might not be gainsaid, they began, one by one, to repudiate the possibility of personal guilt, as men will do whose conscience is clear. "Lord, is it I?" That means, "Lord, surely it isn't I?" Their ignorance, too, of the identity of the traitor is a further indication of their integrity. Judas had kept

[1] e. g., F. L. Cirlot, *The Early Eucharist*, 14, 44.
[2] *The Jewish Background of the Christian Liturgy*, 204.   [3] Mark 14. 18.

his vile intention from the knowledge of the rest. There was among the Eleven none who would tolerate even the suggestion of what he had actually planned to do.

The loyalty of the disciples to their Lord is directly indicated in so many words in the saying recorded in *Luke*: "Ye are they which have continued with me in my temptations; and I appoint unto you a kingdom, even as my Father appointed unto me."[1] Plummer's apt comment on the opening words of this saying is as follows:[2] "The idea of *persistent loyalty* is enforced by the compound verb, by the perfect tense, and by the preposition";[3] and he paraphrases thus: "who have perseveringly remained with me and continue to do so". There is no essential inconsistency between this testimony and the frequent failures of the Apostles during the days of their Lord's ministry, or even their contentious self-seeking at the Supper itself, or the worse than this which was soon to follow[4] in Peter's denial and in the defection of them all. The Lord himself went to the root of the matter in the saying "The spirit indeed is willing, but the flesh is weak".[5] In the past the Eleven had given many indications that they shared in the frailty and imperfections of human nature; but insincere or disloyal they had not been. It is this distinction which creates a great gulf between a Peter and a Judas. And in human relationships it is fundamentally important to be able to discriminate between the weak but honest man and the person of whom we are at last obliged to say that we cannot trust him. The former may be taken into fellowship, and may play a useful part in it. The latter is useless as a member of society, for everything he does is vitiated by the lack of essential straightforwardness: "unless the vessel be clean (*sincerum*), everything you pour into it turns sour."[6]

Further, "the covenant"[7] in his Blood, which the Lord made with his disciples at the Last Supper, presupposed their loyalty as the ground on which it was possible to make it. The co-ordination of the words "covenant" and "blood" at once suggests a reference to the incident recorded in Exodus 24. 7, 8, in which for our present purpose the italicized words are especially sig-

---

[1] 22. 28, 29.   [2] *I.C.C., ad loc.*   [3] οἱ διαμεμενηκότες μετ᾽ ἐμοῦ.
[4] The sheep might be scattered, but they still remained the Shepherd's flock: Matt. 26. 31.   [5] Matt. 26. 41.   [6] Horace, *Epistles* I. 2. 54.
[7] Matt. 26. 28.

nificant: "And Moses took the book of the covenant, and read in the audience of the people: and they said, *All that the Lord hath spoken will we do, and be obedient*. And Moses took the blood, and sprinkled it on the people, and said, Behold the blood of the covenant, which the Lord hath made with you concerning all these words."

The words of St. Luke quoted above, "Ye are they which have continued with me in my temptations", suggest the picture of a faithful remnant which remained, sifted out by every kind of test from a once larger company of disciples. That there was an outer circle of followers, who stayed with our Lord to the end with greater or lesser faithfulness, we need not doubt; and some of these may also have been of the number of his followers from the beginning. But it is clear that as the ministry proceeded, there were defections. The stern conditions which the Synoptists represent our Lord as laying down for discipleship suggest this.[1] *Matthew* and *Luke*,[2] following Q, briefly record the incidents of "divers who would follow him, but upon conditions".[3] And the Fourth Gospel says plainly that after the discourse at Capernaum on the bread of life "Upon this many of his disciples went back, and walked no more with him";[4] and that when at this critical moment Jesus addressed to the Twelve the question "Would ye also go away?" Simon Peter bravely answered for them all in the words "Lord, to whom shall we go? thou hast the words of eternal life".

That the Twelve maintained their solidarity to the end is noteworthy in view of the different types to be found among those who formed the little company. Several of them are mere names to us, upon whom neither Scripture nor reliable tradition has thrown light as concerning their characteristics. But others stand out more clearly, even if quite briefly sketched; and variety among them becomes apparent. The "Sons of Thunder"[5] —whatever may be the exact significance of the *sobriquet*—provided an element which could scarcely make for undisturbed companionship. Over against the impetuous, sanguine Peter there is placed as a foil the cautious and despondent Thomas.

[1] Matt. 10. 38; 16. 24: Mark 8. 34: Luke 9. 23; 14. 25-33.
[2] Matt. 8. 19-22; Luke 9. 57-62.
[3] Chapter heading in A.V. of Luke 9. 57.　　　　[4] John 6. 66.
[5] Mark 3. 17.

The practical, matter-of-fact, common sense of Philip may be contrasted with the mystical insight and reflective powers of at least one of the Twelve. And an Irishman may be permitted to wonder what sort of coming and going there was between Simon, the perfervid nationalist, and Matthew, former agent of the hated foreign government. Yet this heterogeneous company had kept together, and, in spite of disputes maintained among themselves to the very end,[1] brought to the farewell Supper in the Upper Room a loyalty and a fellowship which the eleventh-hour treachery of one of them only served to throw into the greater relief. In them was to be seen an adumbration of the unity in diversity which was afterwards exhibited in the fellowship of the Church, styled by St. Paul a "body" for this very reason—namely, that God had distributed among its members different gifts and functions and points of view.[2]

The evidence of the Fourth Gospel for the purposes of this chapter is complicated by the fact that certain commentators regard the discourses of the Lord recorded in chaps. 14-17, or certain portions of them, as definitely eucharistic in character, having been delivered immediately or at some interval after the Institution of the Sacrament; whereas we are at the moment concerned with the fact of fellowship prior to the Sacrament. Thus, for example, Bernard holds[3] that the point in the narrative of this Gospel at which the Institution took place is John 13. 30 (the departure of Judas from the Upper Room), and that immediately afterwards the Lord spoke the allegory of the vine and the branches, the original order of the Gospel having been ch. 13. 1-30, ch. 15, ch. 16, ch. 13. 31-38, ch. 14, ch. 17. Hoskyns, who does not find it necessary to postulate dislocation in the text, or speculate as to the point of time of Institution, nevertheless remarks that "the immediate background" of the vine and its branches "is the tradition of the Last Supper and in particular the words concerning the Cup, including the promise to the disciples that they would drink of the fruit of the vine in the Kingdom".[4]

In any case, the record contained in John 13. 1-30 is relevant, and it emphasizes as emphatically as do the Synoptists the close relationship existing between the Lord and his Apostles prior to

[1] Luke 22. 24.   [2] Cp. 1 Cor. 12; Rom. 12. 3ff., 14. 1ff.
[3] I.C.C., St. John, ii. 458.   [4] The Fourth Gospel, ii. 559.

the actual Institution of the Sacrament. I have already noted that on the Johannine dating of the Last Supper that meal is even more significantly an act of fellowship than if it were the traditional Paschal meal. The opening verse of the thirteenth chapter, which forms an introduction to the record which follows, and indicates its inner significance, states that Jesus, "having loved his own which were in the world, loved them unto the end"—i.e., he loved them completely and finally, to the uttermost, unto death.[1] Then, after a brief mention of the traitor, the narrative of the feet-washing follows. This incident took place "during supper" (R.V.), and not "supper being ended", as the A.V., following the received text, misleadingly states. It might be supposed superficially that it constituted symbolically a new relationship between the Master and his disciples, especially if his words to Simon Peter "If I wash thee not, thou hast no part with me" are read without due regard to their significance. But this is a reply to Peter's emphatic statement "Thou shalt *never* wash *my* feet", in which *never* and *my* are emphatic. The Lord rejoins that this refusal on the part of the disciple "was really to reject that principle of the dignity of ministry and service which was behind the work of Jesus" (Bernard). To "have part" with Jesus is to share in his work of love, involving an adoption of his methods and the spirit by which they were inspired. He who would accept Jesus as his Master must accept his humiliation in the eyes of men. But "it was not said affirmatively that he whom Jesus washed was thereby recognized as his partner; for the feet of Judas were washed by him, and he knew Judas for a traitor" (Bernard). The feet-washing, then, did not betoken a *new* relationship between Master and disciples: it was rather a more advanced lesson[2] on the meaning of discipleship to those who had already been "with him"[3] and had marked his ways; and it was a preparation for the still more difficult lesson that was soon to be set before them—to see the glorification of Jesus in the humiliation of the Cross.

After this incident comes, appropriately, the departure of the traitor from the midst. (St. John is the only Evangelist who says expressly that Judas left the room.[4]) The pressure of loyalty had expelled him, and the fellowship of Jesus and the Eleven is there-

[1] Hoskyns, *op. cit.* ii. 510. [2] Cp. the earlier lesson in Matt. 18. 1-4 and parallels. [3] Mark 3. 14. [4] 13. 30.

by reaffirmed, and the way prepared for the action which was to symbolize with still greater emphasis the union between him and them. It is true that St. Luke's account implies that the traitor was present at the Institution of the Sacrament, and that he received the bread and the cup.[1] And this tradition is followed by the Book of Common Prayer, which warns intending communicants of the need of repentance, "lest, after the taking of that holy Sacrament, the devil enter into you, as he entered into Judas, and fill you full of all iniquities, and bring you to destruction both of body and soul".[2] But the Lucan account is admittedly puzzling in respect of the order of its events, as it is uncertain in the matter of text. And if we have to choose between it and the rest, many will decide that the order as given in *Mark* and *John* is more natural and convincing. Bernard, who adopts this order, goes so far as to say that these accounts "probably rest respectively on the reminiscences of Peter and of John the son of Zebedee, both of whom were present at the Supper".[3]

Nevertheless, the fact remains that the Fourth Gospel contains no account of the Institution of the Sacrament, and that the discourse and prayer in chapters 14-17 follow without more ado the incident of the departure of the traitor from the room. A change of scene is indicated in the enigmatic words "Arise, let us go hence" at the end of chapter 14, which would appear to suggest—if taken in their literal force—that chapters 15-17 were spoken while on the way from the Upper Room through the streets of the city to the garden of Gethsemane. The various expedients to which commentators have had recourse in order to avoid this difficult conclusion may be read in Hoskyns.[4] They only serve to indicate the kind of problem that occurs elsewhere in the Fourth Gospel—namely, that the Evangelist insists on placing in a certain historical situation discourses which appear altogether to transcend it. We might have expected at the Last Supper a discourse on the bread of life: but that is placed much earlier in the ministry by the Evangelist in an entirely different situation, save for the fact that in both cases the feast of the Passover was at hand. It has been suggested that chapters 14-17 would appear more appropriately in a post-Resurrection setting;

[1] 22. 19-23.
[2] First Exhortation in Communion Office.
[3] *St. John*, ii. 458.
[4] Vol. ii. 547, 548.

and in fact not only in the Anglican Communion but also in the Latin, Greek and Syrian Churches portions of these chapters are read as the liturgical Gospels during the Sundays after Easter. Such considerations may cause us to hesitate before concurring with the view of some commentators that the allegory of the vine and its branches (ch. 15) is to be given a precise historical situation—namely, immediately after the Sacrament had been instituted. Bernard actually transposes it to that point in the narrative (13. 30) when he supposes the act of Institution to have taken place. Sacramental in its imagery this allegory undoubtedly is; yet it is based ultimately on that conception of Israel as a vine which is found in several passages of the Old Testament—e.g., Isaiah 5. 1-7; 27. 2-6: Jeremiah 2. 21: Ezekiel 19. 10-14; 15. 2-6; 17. 5-10: Psalm 80. 8-16. And as its position in the Gospel forbids us to affirm that the discourse in chapter 6 refers primarily to the Holy Communion when it speaks of Christ as the bread of life, so the absence of reference to the Institution of the Sacrament is against an exclusively eucharistic interpretation of the vine and its branches. And it may be that the soundest interpretation of this and the discourse of which it forms part is simply to take it as it stands without seeking to relate it to a background derived from the Synoptic Gospels.

Indeed, the term "friends" which is applied to the disciples by the Lord in this chapter[1] indicates a relationship between them and him which was of no recent or spontaneous growth, but had gradually developed and ripened since the days when he first called them to be of the number of his company. Friendship with him, he says, involves two things: obedience to his commandments and an understanding of his mind. In both of these they had already made a beginning. In the earily days of the ministry he had "looked round on them which sat round about him", and said, "Behold, my mother and my brethren! For whosoever shall do the will of God, the same is my brother and sister and mother."[2] Again, to the disciples privately he had expounded "the mysteries of the kingdom of heaven", which were hidden from "them that are without".[3] Further, in the discourse which immediately follows the allegory of the vine, the Lord refers definitely to the

[1] John 15. 13-15: these words were especially suitable at a *Haburah*, if, as many suppose, the Last Supper was such.
[2] Mark 3. 34, 35.   [3] Matt. 13. 11; Mark 4. 10-12.

17

first calling of the disciples: "Ye did not choose me, but I chose you, and appointed you, that ye should go and bear fruit, and that your fruit should abide."[1] It might be said, indeed, that as yet they displayed but little of the "fruit" of which he spoke as the outward and visible sign of their calling: "full proof" of their "ministry"[2] they had not yet made. Nevertheless, "in the days of his flesh"[3] they had not been idle nor wholly blind. Never-to-be-forgotten lessons about him and about themselves had been learned. The foundation of loyal love to the Lord had been well and truly laid. Above all, it was in those early days that their relationship with him began; and it was initiated not by them but by him. All the fruit that they were afterwards to show was to be traced back ultimately to his deliberate choice, as he went in and out among them calling now one and now another to be of the number of his disciples.

The last discourse, as recorded in the Fourth Gospel, speaks also, with a definiteness not to be found in the Synoptists, of the gift and function of the Holy Spirit, who was to be to the disciples "another comforter"[4]—that is, to be to them all that Jesus himself had been. This gift, this presence, did not begin for them in the Upper Room: it had been with them "all the days".[5] It was to be with them in the future, so that when Jesus was gone from their visible sight they would not be as "orphans".[6] No other word could more clearly express the fact that in the Upper Room the whole period of discipleship was consciously summed up. The sorrow of the orphan is the sorrow of the child who experiences the loss of one who has been with him ever since he can remember what it is to be a member of a family. In the history of the new family of Jesus Christ, the Upper Room seemed to write *finis* to all that had gone before. It was the message of the Lord to assure his sorrowful children that in the Holy Spirit he would himself be with them as in the days of yore.

[1] John 15. 16. [2] 2 Tim. 4. 5. [3] Heb. 5. 7.
[4] John 14. 16. [5] Matt. 28. 20. [6] John 14. 18.

CHAPTER II

THE INSTITUTION OF THE SACRAMENT

IN the preceding chapter we have indicated how close was the relationship to the Lord of the disciples who associated with him in the Upper Room for the Last Supper. It follows, therefore, that the Sacrament when instituted and partaken of by the Apostles did not of itself inaugurate that relationship, but found it already existing; and we shall do well to carry this thought with us when we come to consider the evidence of the other books of the New Testament. As regards the point in the Supper at which the Institution took place, *Matthew* and *Mark* say, "*As they were eating*, Jesus took bread . . ."[1] The most natural interpretation of these words is that the Supper was in progress when the incident occurred, or, in other words, that the Sacrament was, so to speak, a meal within a meal. It is difficult to accept the view of F. L. Cirlot[2] that *as they were eating* need not mean more than that the sacramental action was *part* of the meal and might have taken place at or very near its beginning. Gregory Dix is even less satisfactory on this point, for he appears to ignore the evidence of *Matthew* and *Mark* altogether, and at least four times[3] speaks, without more ado, of the sacramental bread as being broken at the beginning of the meal. The facts are that in the Marcan tradition, followed by *Matthew*, our Lord sat down[4] with the Twelve, and as they were eating told them that one of them would betray him. (Bread would be blessed by him according to custom, after they had reclined, at the beginning of the meal; but this is assumed, not referred to.) Then, after this, *as they were eating* (the second occurrence of the phrase) he took bread and blessed and brake it, and said to them, "Take, this is my body".

This fact is significant. The blessing of the sacramental bread

---

[1] Matt. 26. 26; Mark 14. 22.
[2] *The Early Eucharist*, 146; cp. 164-165; but see also p. 24.
[3] *The Shape of the Liturgy*, 54, 55, 59, 67.
[4] i.e., "reclined", the meal then formally beginning (see Cirlot, *op. cit.*, 10).

took place during the meal. F. L. Cirlot and Gregory Dix, unduly anxious to make the procedure at the Last Supper correspond at every point with that of a *Haburah*, transfer this blessing to the beginning of the meal; and indeed Gregory Dix is insistent that our Lord at that Supper "commanded nothing new to be done, but reinterpreted what he could be sure would go on in any case".[1] But the Marcan tradition does suggest that this Supper as observed by our Lord was not without distinctive action. It was a rule at such Jewish feasts that "no article was ever blessed more than once at the same meal"; so that, for example, "if more bread were brought it would not require another blessing".[2] But here our Lord, in the midst of a meal at which bread must have been blessed for use at its beginning, took a loaf *and blessed it*. This fact, and the words "This is my body" which accompanied the distribution of portions of the loaf, singled his action out for the disciples and made it memorable. Further, the cup-blessing which came at the end of the Supper—for we may accept St. Paul's testimony[3] to the tradition that it came in this place—was not without special significance; for it did not invariably follow that the meal would end in this way. "On special, joyous, or festival occasions, however, and hence probably at every *Haburah* meal, this grace-after-meals would be said over a special common cup, blessed by one leader for the whole group."[4] The saying of it, therefore, apart from the accompanying words "This is my blood", denoted that this fellowship meal was of a particularly solemn character.

Further, those who maintain, contrary to the Marcan tradition, that the blessing of the sacramental bread came at the opening of the meal, take up the position that a long interval—perhaps of some hours—separated that blessing from the blessing of the sacramental cup. This seems most unnatural, and contrary to the impression left by all the Evangelists who record the scene; for they bring the two blessings into juxtaposition. The broken bread and the wine poured out symbolized his body broken and his blood poured out upon the Cross; and as these happenings to him took place at one and the same time, so also it was fitting that the symbolic actions should not be unduly separated. The whole

---

[1] *Op. cit.*, 59.   [2] F. L. Cirlot, *ib.*, 10, note 2, 11.   [3] 1 Cor. 11. 25.
[4] F. L. Cirlot, *op. cit.*, 12. G. Dix (p. 57) assumes, it would seem unwarrantably, that it was said at every *Haburah*.

of the meal was indeed solemn, and an appropriate occasion in any part of it for solemn action; but the closing stages of a *last* Supper must have been particularly so, and especially in view of the events that were to follow. In these stages it seems natural to place the Institution of the Sacrament in both its parts. And perhaps, indeed, St. Paul indicates that the blessing of the sacramental bread took place when the Supper was well advanced, when he says: "I received of the Lord that which also I delivered unto you, how that the Lord Jesus, in the night *in which he was being betrayed*, took bread" etc.[1] The picturesque imperfect may suggest that the earlier stages of the meal were over, and Judas had already departed and was already engaged upon his treacherous errand, when the Institution of the Sacrament began.

The order of events here indicated would seem to be consistent with St. Paul's reference to the sacramental observance as it was conducted in the Corinthian Church.[2] Much, indeed, in that reference is obscure to us, because we have no inside knowledge of the events. The one point of order on which we may feel fairly confident is that the blessing of the sacramental wine came at the close of the proceedings, in accordance with the tradition that the Lord after Supper blessed the cup.[3] When did the blessing of the sacramental bread take place? Clearly not at the beginning of the common meal. For it would appear that the members of the Church did not arrive for it all together. Some came early and took their Supper before the rest. Others, the poor more especially, would have work to do, and arrived later, when there was little left to eat. In these circumstances there could have been no opportunity during the early stages of the proceedings for a leader or president to break the sacramental bread on behalf of all.[4] That must have come later, and at a point—we should imagine—not far distant from the blessing of the sacramental cup. In any case, the eating of ordinary food, as well as the drinking—sometimes to excess—of wine, had been going on before the bread was blessed to be the means of "joint participation of the body of Christ";[5] so that when the sacramental loaf was consecrated, some of the Corinthians were unable to "discern" in it

---

[1] 1 Cor. 11. 23, 24.   [2] 1 Cor. 11. 17-34.   [3] 1 Cor. 11. 25.
[4] It is difficult to see how Cirlot arrives at the statement (*op. cit.*, 45): "In 1 Cor. 11. . . . the body of Christ is at the beginning, the common meal follows, and the blood of Christ is at the end."   [5] 1 Cor. 10. 16.

the (Lord's) body.[1] This, on the whole, appears to be the most natural interpretation of the order of events that we may deduce from St. Paul's not always luminous account of them; and we may infer that the Supper of the Corinthian Church followed, or was intended to follow, the Last Supper in its general outlines. This would *a priori* be probable, since St. Paul doubtless received his tradition concerning it from the Jerusalem Church.

The Lucan account contains well-known difficulties concerning the order of proceedings, both in itself and also when we try to harmonize it with the Marcan tradition preserved in the first two Gospels. In the first place, the Institution of the Sacrament is placed at a point previous to the announcement of the traitor, and it is implied that he received the sacramental bread and wine. To many this has not seemed a convincing arrangement;[2] but some have supposed that Luke's intention was, first, to recount the Institution of the Sacrament, and then merely to indicate certain topics that had been discussed at the Supper. On this supposition no chronological order or arrangement would attach to Luke 22. 21-38. But more remarkable in the Lucan account is the reference to the two cups. At the beginning of the Supper, after he had sat down, and the Apostles with him, he "received a cup, and when he had given thanks, he said, Take this, and divide it among yourselves". Then follows, apparently, the Institution of the Sacrament, first of the bread, and secondly of the cup: but the "Western" text omits the words relating to this cup, thus suggesting that the first cup was the sacramental cup, although the eucharistic words "This is my blood" or "This cup is the new covenant in my blood" are in this place absent. There is much textual confusion in the Lucan account as it has been transmitted—a matter which will be discussed more fully in a later chapter. And Luke has followed a different tradition from that of Matthew and Mark. If the reference to a first cup in addition to the sacramental cup is historical, it may be connected with a custom still observed to this day among the

[1] 1 Cor. 11. 29.

[2] I am unable to follow the argument by which Hoskyns (ii. 506, 507, 518) seeks to prove that the Johannine follows the Lucan order on this point. Bernard (ii. 458) places the institution of the Eucharist at a point in the narrative of *John* subsequent to the departure of Judas from the room.

Jews of passing round a preliminary cup of wine for each of the company to sip, before they sit down and the meal proper begins. The words "Take this, and divide it among yourselves" are consistent with this. On the other hand, Luke says that they had sat down before this cup was passed round, and that the Lord gave thanks over it: that is to say, it seems to have formed part of the meal proper.[1] If the shorter text of *Luke* is correct, and the first cup is actually the sacramental cup, then his tradition was one which placed the eucharistic cup before the bread: for which there is apparently support in the *Didache* ch. 9: "First concerning the cup, 'We give thanks to thee, our Father . . .' And concerning the broken bread: 'We give thanks to thee, our Father . . .' " On the whole, I am inclined to hold that in the original Lucan account there was reference to two cups. The first of these was the customary cup of the preliminary course, partaken of in this case just after the company had sat down to supper. At the end of the meal, or at any rate during the course of it, the Lord blessed the sacramental bread, and, after supper, the sacramental cup, and uttered the words of mysterious import concerning them. Subsequently, scribes, not perceiving the merely conventional significance of the first cup, and supposing it to be a sacramental cup, omitted the words relating to the second cup. The tradition preserved in the *Didache* may be connected with the tradition contained in the shorter text of *Luke*, or it may be an independent tradition based on something of which we have no certain knowledge.

St. Paul says, as we have already noted, that the Lord Jesus consecrated the sacramental cup *after supper*.[2] If these words are to be given their precise significance, they would appear to indicate that this cup corresponded to the final cup at a *Haburah*, over which the grace-after-meals is pronounced by the leader, and partaken of by all after the meal has ended. Only this grace or blessing would normally be said over it: hence St. Paul appropriately styles it the cup of blessing.[3] It is to be distinguished from the Paschal cup of blessing, which in the Passover

---

[1] Unless Luke's word for "sat down" (ἀνέπεσε) is intended to indicate a less formal posture than the usual "recline" (ἀνέκειτο). At the preliminary course each person blessed the article of food or drink for himself, and not the leader for all.

[2] 1 Cor. 11. 25.   [3] 1 Cor. 10. 16.

feast was the third cup, preceded by part of the Hallel, and followed by a fourth cup and the remainder of the Hallel.[1] The Pauline tradition, therefore, suggests that an interval, though not necessarily a long one, separated the Lord's blessing of the bread from his blessing of the cup, the former taking place during, the latter at the conclusion of, the meal.

The words used of this blessing by the Evangelists are "blessed" (εὐλογήσας: *Matthew* and *Mark*, of bread; Paul, of cup), and "gave thanks" (εὐχαριστήσας: *Matthew* and *Mark*, of cup; *Luke*, of bread and cup; Paul, of bread). The two words are in this connection practically synonymous, the blessing being in fact a form of thanksgiving. We are not told in what terms the Lord "blessed" or "gave thanks over" the elements, and the reason for this may well be that there was nothing remarkable in the words employed, which were simply a customary Jewish grace. The following forms, quoted from present-day Jewish Prayer Books, are probably not dissimilar from those employed by our Lord on this occasion. "Blessed art thou, O Lord our God, King of the universe, who bringest forth bread from the earth." "Blessed art thou, O Lord our God, King of the universe, who createst the fruit of the vine."[2] It is to be noted that a Jewish blessing does not ask God to bless the food, but it blesses God for the food; and the thing for which thanks are given is mentioned in a relative clause. Hence, as we have noted, the indiscriminate use of "blessed" and "gave thanks" in the evangelical accounts of the eucharist. Actually, in Matthew 26. 26 the Sinaitic Syriac version has "blessed (*sc.* God) over it". And Justin Martyr speaks of the bread and the wine and water for which thanks have been given.[3]

After the Lord had given thanks for the bread, he broke it (ἔκλασεν: all accounts), gave a portion to each of the disciples present and said "This is my body"—either this alone, or with some of the additions given in our sources. *Mark*: "Take, this is

---

[1] A. H. McNeile, *St. Matthew*, 384.

[2] But if, as is probable, the Sacramental Cup at the Last Supper corresponded to the final cup of a *Haburah*, there would be no wine-blessing, as above, pronounced over it (unless there had been no wine served earlier in the meal), but instead a much longer "grace-after-meals", the text of which is quoted by Cirlot, pp. 3, 4, and G. Dix, pp. 52, 53.

[3] *Apol.* i. 65, τοῦ εὐχαριστηθέντος ἄρτου καὶ οἴνου καὶ ὕδατος. Cp. *id.*, 67, τῶν εὐχαριστηθέντων.

my body." *Luke*: "This is my body (which is given for you: this do in remembrance of me)." *Matthew*: "Take, eat, this is my body." *Paul*: "This is my body which is (broken) for you: this do in remembrance of me."

Similarly, having taken and given thanks for the cup, the Lord gave it to them all to drink, saying, it would appear, not merely "This is my blood", but also some words in addition which included the word "covenant". The variations in this saying are even greater than in the case of the bread. *Mark*: "This is my blood of the covenant, which is poured out for many." *Luke*: "This cup is the new covenant in my blood, which is poured out for you." *Matthew*: "This is my blood of the covenant, which is poured out for many unto remission of sins." *Paul*: "This cup is the new covenant in my blood: this do, as oft as ye drink it, in remembrance of me."

It is remarkable how much the "words of institution", as they are called, differ among themselves in the four accounts. In fact, there is only one clause upon which all agree—"This is my body" —and even here there is a difference of order in the Greek words ($τοῦτό ἐστιν τὸ σῶμά μου$: *Mark, Luke, Matthew*; $τοῦτό μού ἐστιν τὸ σῶμα$: *Paul*). In general significance, however, if not in detail, there is substantial agreement. But the impression conveyed by a careful study of the evangelical and Pauline accounts differs in some respects from the impression formed by familiarity with the Prayer of Consecration as set forth, for example, in an Anglican Liturgy. The following points are noteworthy.

(1) The sacramental meal in the Upper Room was a portion only of the Supper: it was a meal within a meal. In 1 Cor. 11. 20, "Lord's Supper" ($κυριακὸν δεῖπνον$) probably refers to the whole action: the purely social meal, or agape, followed by the eucharistic meal. But now that the agape has fallen into disuse, a celebration of the Holy Communion must fail to reproduce in its entirety the significance of the scene in the Upper Room. In the Orthodox Church, after the liturgy is over, blessed bread (*eulogia*, $ἀντίδωρον$) is distributed by the priest among the congregation, who come up severally to him to receive it. The partaking of it signifies communion in the Church and with one another, and, having a social significance, is reminiscent of an agape. The name $ἀντίδωρον$, however, shows that the bread

25

is regarded *as a substitute* for the eucharistic bread, which the food partaken of at the Love-feast never was. But we shall see later on that when the doctrine of the Holy Communion is placed against the theological background in which we find it in the New Testament, the conception of a meal within a meal is preserved.

(2) The words of blessing, consecration, or setting apart, of the bread and wine have not been told us. They were probably some well-known form of grace as used by the Jews. No liturgy now in use has attempted to reproduce them; but the *Didache* preserves a giving-of-thanks for the cup and the bread which brings us back close to primitive Jewish forms, the wine-blessing being placed before the bread-blessing.

(3) An interval of time, probably, separated the blessing of the sacramental bread from the blessing of the sacramental cup, if we are to suppose that the former took place in the course of the supper and the latter (as St. Paul states) at its conclusion. So far as I know, no liturgy has attempted to reproduce this feature, and it would seem to be impossible to do so effectively. It adds, however, to the significance of the scene in the Upper Room, if we remember that just before the party broke up for the walk across the ravine of Kidron and for the first stage of his Passion in Gethsemane, the Saviour had spoken of the wine as the symbol of the Blood that was about to be poured out for men upon the Cross.

(4) The words "This is my body", "This is my blood", were not words of consecration spoken immediately after he had blessed the bread and the wine; they were words of administration spoken as he was delivering to the disciples the fragments of the broken bread and the cup, or after he had delivered to each his portion and had passed the cup round to all. Actually, St. Mark says of the cup[1]: "And he took a cup, and when he had given thanks, he gave to them: and they all drank of it.[2] And he said unto them, This is my blood of the covenant, which is shed for many." If taken in its precise meaning, this would imply that the words "This is my blood" by no means followed immediately the blessing of the cup. It is going too far to say, as Vincent Taylor does,[3] that, in contrast to this, in the

---

[1] 14. 23, 24.   [2] *all* is emphatic: καὶ ἔπιον ἐξ αὐτοῦ πάντες.
[3] *Jesus and His Sacrifice*, 128.

corresponding passage concerning the bread the explanation *accompanied* the distribution. The words "having taken bread and blessed, he brake it, and gave to them, and said, Take ye; this is my body" *may* mean that the explanation in this case also followed the distribution.[1] But if a distinction in this respect is intended as between the bread and the wine, there is the practical consideration to be remembered—namely, that the delivery of the wine would take much longer than the delivery of the bread, and this fact might suggest the postponement of "This is my blood" until such time as all had drunk of the cup. Also, to Jewish ears the words would be so startling and disturbing, that the Lord may have prefaced them by an explanation relating them to the sacrificial character of his impending death. Hence Matthew's editing of them: "Drink ye all of it: *for* this is my qlood."

It seems to be not unnecessary to underline the point contained in the preceding paragraph, since the familiar prayers and actions and their sequence in the Book of Common Prayer tend so to substitute in our minds something different from the evangelical order that we are recalled to it with a measure of surprise. To show that this is not an overstatement, I venture to quote the following from a fairly recent work: "He took the bread that was before him; he called it his body; he gave thanks for it; he broke it; he gave it . . . How would the disciples think of those strange words, 'This is my body'? Inevitably they would see that as in that moment he treated the bread, so in that moment he was treating his body: 'He brake it and gave it.' He was offering a sacrifice; the victim was himself."[2] Clearly, this is not the sequence of words and actions that we find recorded in the Synoptists or St. Paul; it appears to be written from the point of view of a communicant to-day, who before he receives the elements has already heard in the Prayer of Consecration the words of mysterious import which the Lord used in delivering the bread and the wine. It is noteworthy that though the Evangelists (as we have seen) differ much among themselves in other details about the Institution of the Sacrament, they are

---

[1] Actually, the Latin MS. k has in this place: "and gave to them: and they all ate of it. And he said unto them, This is my body."

[2] W. Temple, *Thoughts on Some Problems of the Day* (1931), 142. See also 144, 158. Cp. the same writer's *Christian Faith and Life*, 118.

agreed that at its most significant moment the Lord's actions were in the following order: (1) He took the bread (or the cup) into his hands; (2) He blessed it; (3) He brake (the bread); (4) He gave the bread and the cup to the disciples; (5) He said "This is my body", or (in some form or another) "This is my blood of the covenant".

The eucharistic[1] prayers in the *Didache*, as we have noted, approach more closely than do any other extant liturgical prayers to the forms of blessing of the bread and the wine which we may suppose the Saviour to have used at the Last Supper. Their primitive and Jewish character is evident, and in them we appear to have scarcely moved forward from their Jewish antecedents.[2] They are as follows[3]:

"First, concerning the cup: We give thanks to thee, our Father, for the holy vine of David thy child,[4] which thou didst make known to us through Jesus thy child[4]; to thee be glory for ever."

"And concerning the broken bread: We give thanks to thee, our Father, for the life and knowledge which thou didst make known to us through Jesus thy child; to thee be glory for ever. As this broken bread was scattered upon the mountains, and when brought together became one, so let thy Church be brought together from the ends of the earth into thy kingdom: for thine is the glory and the power through Jesus Christ for ever."

A remarkable feature of these prayers is the absence of reference to the act of institution; and at first sight they might seem to lack what is distinctively sacramental and to represent nothing more than a grace before meat. This impression, however, is corrected by the words that immediately follow: "But let none eat or drink of your eucharist, save only they who have been baptized in the Lord's name: for concerning this (*or* such a one)

---

[1] So I would hold. But some scholars question their eucharistic character, and would relate them rather to the Agape. For a *résumé* of views, see J. Norman, *Handbook to the Christian Liturgy*, 6-9.

[2] For this and for other reasons I am unable to subscribe to the view that the *Didache* as a whole is a faked work, belonging to a comparatively late date. It is difficult also to see how it could have been so widely revered in the ancient Church if it issued from a "backwater" or even sectarian community, as some modern writers would have us think.

[3] Chapter 9.   [4] Or "servant" (παιδός): cp. Acts 3. 13, etc.

the Lord said, Give not that which is holy unto the dogs." And a prayer which follows in the next section[1] speaks of the gift of "spiritual food and drink", and ends with the words: "Let grace come and let this world come to an end. Hosanna to the God of David. If any man be holy, let him come. If any man be not, let him repent. Maran atha. Amen." May it not be that in this ancient form, as in the Upper Room, the words "This is my body", "This is my blood", were not said until the delivery to the congregation of the sacramental food, thus emphasizing the solemn and sacred character of the act of communion?

Be that as it may, the words in question, concerning which there has been sad controversy among Christians, were originally said by the Lord to persons to whom he already stood in an intimate relation, and said when he was delivering, or had delivered, to them the elements. If in the action of the liturgy it has not been found practicable to follow the exact order of the Saviour's actions in the Upper Room, or if at any rate this has not in fact been done (except perhaps in the order contemplated in the *Didache*),[2] nevertheless certain forms of eucharistic prayer are closer to the evangelical records than are others. The Prayer of Consecration as found in the Book of Common Prayer of the Church of England from 1552 on labours under the defect of appearing to adopt "an extreme and even exaggerated acceptance of the scholastic view of consecration in its most exclusive form"[3]—namely, that the words *Hoc est corpus meum* are the form of consecration for the bread, and *Hic est calix sanguinis mei, novi et aeterni testamenti, mysterium fidei, qui pro vobis et pro multis effundetur in remissionem peccatorum* for the cup. On the other hand, an earlier clause in the prayer, "Grant that we receiving these thy creatures of bread and wine . . . may be partakers of his most blessed body and blood"—words that took the place in the Book of 1552 of the Epiclesis in the Book of 1549, and may be regarded as a kind of oblique Epiclesis, and were perhaps

---

[1] The opening words, "But after ye are 'filled'" ($\dot{\epsilon}\mu\pi\lambda\eta\sigma\theta\tilde{\eta}\nu\alpha\iota$), would suggest that the Eucharist was combined with a common meal.

[2] The MSS. of the East Syrian Liturgy (Nestorian) contain no recital of the Institution. G. Dix (*The Shape of the Liturgy*, 197f.) thinks that the Rite of Jerusalem in the fourth century, described by Cyril, lacked also a narrative of an Institution.

[3] W. H. Frere, *The Anaphora*, 201.

C

originally intended as *the* words of consecration—this clause brings the gift of the Sacrament into relation with the communicants. So also, in the ill-fated "Deposited Book" of 1927, following the 1549 Book, the Holy Spirit is invoked "to bless and sanctify both us and these thy gifts of bread and wine, *that they may be unto us*[1] the body and blood of thy Son, our Saviour, Jesus Christ, to the end that we, receiving the same, may be strengthened and refreshed both in body and soul." But the qualifying and relating words *unto us* are absent in, e.g., the Scottish Liturgy: "that . . . they may become the body and blood of thy most dearly beloved Son, to the end that all who shall receive the same may be sanctified both in body and soul, and preserved unto everlasting life." The wording of the English Books is more in harmony with the course of action in the Upper Room as it is described by the Synoptists, in which the words "This is my body" and "This is my blood" are brought into relation with persons.

The words concerning the cup (if not also the words concerning the bread) must have conveyed to the disciples a sacrificial meaning of some sort. Again, we have varying traditions of these. "This is my blood of the covenant, which is poured out for many": *Mark*; and also *Matthew*, who adds "unto remission of sins". "This cup is the new covenant in my blood": Paul; and also the longer text of *Luke*, who adds "which is poured out for you". The addition of *Matthew* "unto remission of sins" seems to lack sufficient authority; but the correlation of "blood" and "covenant", which appears in every version of the saying, would undoubtedly have a sacrificial sound for Jewish ears. The passage in Exodus 24. 4-8 has already been referred to.[2] "This unmistakably includes the thought of sacrifice, *i.e.*, the application of the victim's blood, which is its life, poured out, set free from its body, and available for the use of others."[3] The Blood of the new[4] covenant, spoken of in the Upper Room, was the Blood of Christ (τὸ αἷμά μου), and it was also the Blood of the covenant (τὸ αἷμα τῆς διαθήκης), inasmuch as it sealed and ratified it.

[1] Cp. the words of the Roman Canon: "Quam oblationem tu, Deus, . . . benedictam . . . facere digneris: *ut nobis corpus et sanguis fiat* dilectissimi Filii tui Domini nostri Jesu Christi."

[2] See p. 12f.   [3] A. H. McNeile on Matt. 26. 28.

[4] 1 Cor. 11. 25 (Luke 22. 20).

Though the Last Supper was not the Paschal Supper, that did not prevent thoughts of the imminent sacrificial feast being present as surely as if it were the actual day. The Last Supper was a Passover meal by anticipation. The Lord could not be hindered in his desire merely by the temporal fact that the exact day had not yet come. Whatever was on the table—even if it were merely bread and wine—could be eaten and drunk in memory of the great deliverance which God had long ago wrought for his people.

Accordingly, our Lord's intentions as well as his words during the Supper were sacrificial. He knew it to be his Father's will that he should die. He so interpreted the ancient sayings of the Old Testament.[1] To carry out his Father's will he was determined. When a word from him might have prevented the traitor from leaving the room on his fatal errand, he refrained from uttering it, and freely let him go. When Judas went out to set in motion the events which led to their culmination on the Cross, then indeed "was the Son of man glorified, and God glorified in him".[2] The supreme moment to which the whole of the ministry had been leading up was at hand, and now more immovably than ever was the Lord's will set toward it.

It does not follow, however, that, because our Lord conceived his death to be a sacrifice and spoke of it as such, he necessarily accepted or approved the sacrificial system as a whole as set forth in the Old Testament. Certain writers on the eucharist and its doctrine assume that the Lord's employment of sacrificial terms justifies us in interpreting that doctrine in the light of what animal sacrifices meant and symbolized in the *cultus* of the ancient Jewish Church. But in point of fact we find in the Old Testament itself a strong undercurrent of criticism of the sacrificial system, which at times breaks out into a fierce protest; and it is reasonable to suppose that the passages to which we are about to refer reflect the views not simply of their several writers but also of a large body of spiritually minded members of the Jewish Church.[3] The following list of passages makes no claim to be exhaustive, but rather to indicate merely that the sentiment in question is widely expressed: 1 Sam. 15. 22: Psalms 40. 6-8; 50. 7-15; 51. 16, 17: Proverbs 15. 8; 21. 3: Eccles. 5. 1:

---

[1] Matt. 26. 24; Luke 22. 37. [2] John 13. 31.
[3] See S. H. Hooke in *The Age of Transition* (ed. W. O. E. Oesterley), 258ff.

Isa. 1. 11-17; 61. 8 (R.V.ᵐ): Jer. 6. 20; 7. 21-23; 14. 12: Hosea 4. 11-14; 6. 6: Micah 6. 6-8: Ecclus. 34. 18, 19.

It is significant that these references contain the words not only of great spiritual leaders but also of obscure and anonymous individuals, and that they are taken from two of the three divisions of the sacred canon, and from the poetical and the sapiential no less than from the prophetical books. (Reference could also be made to the general attitude of Jeremiah, for example, and to the large silences in the matter of sacrifice that are to be found in many portions of the Old Testament.) It is true that a controversy, not yet settled, has arisen as to the exact significance of these passages. Is material sacrifice disparaged altogether, or is there merely a criticism of sacrifice when divorced from morality and penitence? The language of some of the passages is so strong that the first of these alternatives is the more natural. God, speaking through his prophet or other spokesman, declares that he neither needs nor takes pleasure in sacrifice. And even if the less drastic of the alternatives be adopted—that the denunciation is addressed solely against sacrifice when divorced from morality or penitence—it is clear that these passages at any rate embody the conviction that a sincere and contrite heart is a sacrifice independent of and superior to any of the sacrifices prescribed by the law, and further that the offering of a sacrifice without regard to moral requirements left the offerer in worse case and increased his condemnation before God.

It is an interesting question how much we may deduce from the Gospels as to the views of our Lord concerning the sacrificial system of his Church and people. It is commonly asserted that he must have approved of the system because he frequented the Temple. But this is a statement which calls for closer examination. The very word "Temple" is ambiguous, because it was a building or rather a group of buildings used for different objects and by persons with different aims in view. Our Lord is found as a boy of twelve in the Temple[1]—that is, on some terrace or in some chamber in the buildings, customarily used by the scribes for religious discussion and instruction. In this respect the Temple was for the Jews what the Agora was for the Greeks and the Forum for the Romans—a place where people met for social and intellectual converse, and, in the case of the Jews, with whom

[1] Luke 2. 46: ἐν τῷ ἱερῷ.

religious interests were paramount, for interchange of ideas on those doctrines concerning God and his covenant relation to Israel which made of the Jews at once a people and a Church. There is clear evidence that, when he grew up, Jesus continued to use the Temple precincts for this purpose. He was now a Rabbi himself, who, if looked upon with suspicion by the orthodox Rabbis, spake as man never spake, and commanded the rapt attention of the multitudes. He reminded those same multitudes, when their fickle heart was turned against him, that in the past they had had frequent opportunity to apprehend him, had they wished to do so: "I sat daily in the temple teaching, and ye took me not."[1] To the high priest Annas, when brought before him, he said: "I ever taught in the synagogue and in the Temple, where all the Jews come together."[2] The combination here of "synagogue" and "Temple" is significant as indicating his use of the Temple as a place of instruction, even as the synagogue was recognized to be by common consent. It is true that these sayings have special reference to the Lord's actions in Holy Week. But they cannot be limited to such. The Synoptists have nothing to say about our Lord's contact with Jerusalem in the earlier years of his ministry. But the Fourth Gospel, which supplies this deficiency, speaks also of other occasions when he taught in the Temple.[3]

On the other hand, the Gospels are silent as to his use of the Temple for worship. We cannot infer from this that he absented himself entirely from the morning and evening sacrifices, which were offered every day. But his recognition of the Temple as a house of prayer does not necessarily involve his presence at them. No doubt he approved the custom of many Jews of using the Temple as a place for offering their private petitions. He himself draws a picture of a Pharisee and a publican who went up to the Temple to pray concerning their personal needs (in the case of the Pharisee to congratulate himself before God that *he* was righteous). Nevertheless, the occasion on which he spoke of the Temple as a house of prayer was the very occasion on which he cleansed the Temple of the crowd of those who trafficked in the business connected with sacrifices, and drove out the sheep and

[1] Matt. 26. 55 (Mark 14. 49: Luke 22. 53). Cp. Mark 12. 35: Luke 19. 47; 20. 1; 21. 38.
[2] John 18. 20.   [3] 7. 14, 28; 8. 20.

the oxen.[1] And this incident has been interpreted[2]—and we believe rightly—as an attack upon the Jewish sacrificial system. His first conflict with the ecclesiastical authorities had been concerning the Sabbath and its observance. He now struck at the other key-stone of practical Judaism—namely, the regular carrying out of the prescribed sacrifices. This action made the breach between them and him complete. He was indeed a destroyer of the Temple, if not in the literal sense alleged by his enemies,[3] yet in the deeper and more fundamental sense that St. Stephen and after him St. Paul were able to perceive.

Two or three other passages in the Gospels have a bearing on this matter. In two places in *Matthew*,[4] Jesus quotes the words of Hosea 6. 6, "I desire mercy, and not sacrifice". If we do not take these words to mean an absolute repudiation of the Jewish *cultus*, we must at any rate see in them an adoption of the prophetical attitude which condemned sacrifice when divorced from ethical considerations. Our Lord's injunction to the leper whom he had healed, "Shew thyself to the priest, and offer for thy cleansing the things which Moses commanded, for a testimony unto them",[5] is not inconsistent with the view put forward above. He did not encourage an individual to disregard the regulations of the law, which in this case prescribed the offering of a sacrifice.[6] In fact, he wished the leper to make it known to the priests or the people generally that he had bidden the man obey it. This is probably the meaning of the words "for a testimony unto them". And on this interpretation these words significantly suggest that Jesus was under suspicion of teaching men to neglect the Mosaic observances. Even more significant is the passage Mark 12. 28-34, which if its setting in the Gospel is correct describes an incident which took place only a few days before the Last Supper. On the scribe's assertion that love to God and one's neighbour is much more than all whole burnt offerings and sacrifices, Jesus makes the comment, "Thou art not far from the kingdom of God". Our Lord's commendation of this man's spiritual insight and of his grasp of one of the fundamental principles of the Kingdom—

[1] Matt. 21. 12; John 2. 15.
[2] E.g., by W. O. E. Oesterley (*DCG* ii. 712[b]), J. H. Bernard and E. Hoskyns.
[3] Mark 14. 57-59.   [4] 9. 13; 12. 7.
[5] Mark 1. 44; cp. Luke 17. 14.   [6] Lev. 14. 1-32.

namely, the superiority of moral over ritual obligations,[1] was in fact an endorsement of the teaching of those Old Testament passages referred to above which disparage the sacrificial and ceremonial law.

In a context containing a quotation from one of these passages (Psalm 40. 6-8, *ap.* Heb. 10. 4-10) the author of the Epistle to the Hebrews hits upon a phrase which forms the best commentary upon the nature of the sacrifice which Jesus adumbrated to his disciples in the Upper Room: "In whole burnt offerings and sacrifices for sin thou hadst no pleasure: then said I, Lo I am come . . . to do thy will, O God. . . . By which will we have been sanctified through the offering of the body of Jesus Christ once for all." If we are to understand—however dimly—what it is that gives its perfection and completeness to the sacrifice upon the Cross, we shall find it, not by a laborious discussion and comparison of the different types of sacrifices under the old law, but by a realization of the union of will in Father and incarnate Son. The self-dedication and obedience of Jesus was absolute and unconditioned. The scribe who had seen in whole-hearted love to God and man the greatest of all commandments had been commended as "not far from the kingdom of God". The absolute surrender of Jesus at every point to the will of his Father was a manifestation, never before seen on earth, of the kingdom, the sovereignty, of God in human life: and this surrender reached its culminating point in his willingness to die. The author of *Hebrews* does not tell us in so many words how it is that the fruits of Christ's sacrifice are made available for us: what he says is that we are sanctified by being included in God's will to redeem us as manifested on the Cross. In the Upper Room, however, we are shown that through discipleship, sincere though weak and wavering, human wills can come into contact with the divine will and be strengthened by its redemptive power. "Ye are they which have continued with me in my temptations; and I appoint unto you a kingdom, even as my Father appointed unto me." "Take ye: this is my body . . . This is my blood of the covenant."

It is noteworthy that in this passage in *Hebrews* the author at one and the same time manifests that in which the efficacy of Christ's sacrifice lay and also emphasizes the inadequacy of the Jewish sacrifices, quoting from Psalm 40 one of the most tren-

[1] See H. B. Swete *ad loc.*

chant criticisms of sacrifice to be found in the Old Testament. This should help to dispel the fear, which some appear to entertain, that if we hold that Jesus shared in this disparagement of the Jewish sacrificial system, we are thereby making it impossible to read any sacrificial meaning whatever into those sayings of his about his death which *prima facie* suggest it, and are in fact denying the necessity of an objective Atonement. The fear is ungrounded. The author of *Hebrews* is not inconsistent when, on the one hand, he emphasizes the sacrificial nature of Christ's death, and, on the other, cites the Old Testament in disparagement of the Jewish *cultus*. For he places his finger just upon that point in the *cultus* where it was most obviously deficient. In the words of Vincent Taylor: "In Old Testament worship the idea of self-sacrifice was waiting to be born. . . . The main obstacle to a healthy development was the passive character of the Levitical offering; the worshipper faced the demand of identifying himself with that which could neither will nor experience the glory of vicarious sacrifice."[1] In contrast to this inadequacy the author of *Hebrews* sets the Cross of Christ as the perfect expression of that sacrifice which could never have been achieved under the old system. But it is difficult to follow Dr. Taylor when in the same context he asserts that the Jewish ritual provided at the time the only means where the idea of self-surrender to God could live in an ethical or spiritual form; or that "no Hebrew could think of offering himself as he was, frail and sinful, to a holy and righteous God, while the idea of a purely spiritual offering would have seemed to him abstract and meaningless". In view of the Old Testament passages depreciatory of sacrifices, to which reference has been made, we may believe that there were many in Israel—prophetical souls—who could grasp such an idea and give it noble expression. Not to mention passages already quoted, there is—to give one example—the wonderful elevation reached by the author of Psalm 51. 16, 17: "For thou delightest not in sacrifice; else would I give it: thou hast no pleasure in burnt offering. The sacrifices of God are a broken spirit; a broken and a contrite heart, O God, thou wilt not despise." It seems rather perilous in the supposed interests of the doctrine of the Atonement, or of eucharistic doctrine, to evacuate such passages of their obvious meaning; for by so doing a spiritual link between the Old and

[1] *Jesus and His Sacrifice*, 60.

New Testaments is severed. On the contrary, the offering of self to God in a purely spiritual manner is, we believe, a conception reached here and there in the revelation recorded in the Old Testament, and in such a way that, as the author of *Hebrews* believed, the sacrifice of the Cross was thereby prefigured in spiritual reality. Similarly, the faith of Abraham and other Old Testament heroes was more than a mere type of the faith of Jesus. His faith was not different in quality from theirs. Rather, he exhibited in its perfection that faith which they had partially manifested.[1]

It may be well to sum up now the conclusions reached in this chapter. The sacramental part of the Last Supper took place within the action of the Supper proper, which was perhaps of the nature of a *Haburah*, and in any case testified to the unity already existing between the Lord and his disciples. Though there is much divergence among the Evangelists as to the exact words spoken by the Lord at the Institution of the Sacrament, there is unanimity in *Matthew* and *Mark*, and perhaps also in *Luke*, concerning the order of his actions when instituting it. A noteworthy point in this order is that the words "This is my body", "This is my blood", were spoken in connection with the "taking" and the "eating" or "drinking" of the elements; that is to say, they are not isolated sayings, but sayings within the context of a relationship of an intimate kind, and sayings related to persons. This fact is not easily expressed in liturgical action, but is more successfully expressed in some liturgies than in others; and it may be that the *Didache* is worth examining afresh on this point. The Lord's words and actions at the Institution were of a sacrificial character, and this must have been to some extent plain to the disciples. But it does not follow that he thereby accepted the sacrificial *cultus* of his people, and still less that we are to interpret the sacrificial aspect of the eucharist by reference to the details of that *cultus*. The perfection of the sacrifice of Christ lay in its self-sacrifice and in the absolute identification of his will with the will of his Father.

[1] Hebrews 12. 2: "Jesus the . . . perfecter of faith."

CHAPTER III

THE ACTS OF THE APOSTLES

THE Fellowship of the Upper Room became from the Day of Pentecost onwards the Fellowship of the whole Church, and the bond of union was the Holy Spirit, who was to the Church what Jesus had himself been to the Twelve in the days of his visible presence. The Holy Spirit united from its very beginning the Church with the historic Jesus. He formed into one fellowship those who had known Jesus in the flesh and those who knew him only in the Spirit. The Apostles and the other original disciples could testify that the Spirit who dwelt in the Church was indeed the Spirit who had dwelt in the Lord when he was on earth—*the Spirit of Jesus*,[1] as he is once called. In fact, Christian tradition from the fourth century has identified the Upper Room as the place of Descent of the Pentecostal Gift, thus affirming not only an historical but also a local continuity.[2] Be that as it may, the second chapter of *Acts*, however we may interpret the details of a scene which transcended the powers of even a St. Luke to give it precise description, makes it clear that the Pentecostal Gift created a *visible* Church, with its roots in history, in the persons of those who could carry into the newly formed spiritual Society their *witness* to the Lord in the days of his flesh.

This historical witness is made all the more evident when we follow the natural interpretation of the account in *Acts* that the first bestowal of the Holy Spirit was shared by all the one hundred and twenty disciples assembled. It is true that for a long time there was a notion prevalent in the Church that the Holy Spirit then descended upon the Apostles only. Members of the Anglican Communion who have reached middle age will remember in their earlier days a Proper Preface for Whit-Sunday which spoke of the Holy Spirit "lighting" at Pentecost "upon the

[1] Acts 16. 7 (R.V.).
[2] H. B. Swete, *The Holy Spirit in the New Testament*, 69f. and refs.

Apostles, to teach them, and to lead them to all truth; giving them both the gift of divers languages, and also boldness with fervent zeal constantly to preach the Gospel unto all nations". But the reference to the Apostles, as well as to the gift of languages, has now disappeared in the new Preface which is to be found in varying forms in the Irish, English (1928), American, South African, Indian, and Ceylon Prayer Books, and also in the Scottish as an alternative Preface.[1]

On the other hand, *Acts* implies that those who were not in the privileged position of such eyewitnesses did not on that account lack a share in the Pentecostal Gift. True, we are not told in so many words that the three thousand persons who were baptized on that day[2] received the gift of the Holy Spirit, which St. Peter had promised; but the description of the life of the new fellowship, given in the following verses (Acts 2. 42-47), testifies as strongly as a precise reference could do to the Presence in their midst. "The closing verses of the second chapter of the Acts, with their picture of the simple, joyful, strenuous life of the newly baptized in the days that followed the Pentecost, reveal even more than the miracles of the Pentecost itself the nature of the Power which had come to dwell with the Church."[3] For the account goes on to show that so far from this sudden accession of members—amounting to twenty-five times the number of the original society—imperilling the unity of the whole or undermining the authority of its leaders, the sense of brotherhood and of order became all the more marked. The note of joy which runs through the early chapters of *Acts* is the token of a happy fellowship. "With one accord"[4] is St. Luke's favourite word to express it. "The multitude of them that believed were of one heart and soul."[5] Their unity was accompanied by a wave of communistic fervour, which expressed itself in a voluntary "pooling" of their goods and possessions. And this unity neither the hostile pressure of the Jews,[6] nor the sin of individual members of the Church,[7] was able to impair.

In this life of fellowship, formed and maintained by the Holy

[1] The Canadian Prayer Book alone retains the older form, but speaks of "the gift of *tongues*". [2] *Or* "at that season".

[3] H. B. Swete, *op. cit.* 80.

[4] 1. 14; 2. 46; 4. 24; 5. 12; cp. 15. 25.

[5] 4. 32. [6] 4. 23-31. [7] 5. 11-15; 6. 1-7.

Spirit, doubtless the Sacrament of the Upper Room found its place. But it cannot be said that any passage in *Acts* can be pointed to as absolutely requiring a reference to it. In 27. 35 St. Paul, on board ship, "took bread, and gave thanks to God in the presence of them all, and when he had broken it, he began to eat". But we can scarcely suppose that St. Paul would have celebrated the eucharist under such conditions and before an unbelieving audience. "Upon the first day of the week" the disciples "were gathered together to break bread" (20. 7). After the Eutychus incident, and after St. Paul "had broken the bread, and eaten, and had talked with them a long while, even till break of day, so he departed" (v. 11). Here a liturgical reference is probable, or at any rate the "breaking of bread" is placed in a liturgical setting; and there is much to be said for an interpretation of this passage which finds in it a celebration of the eucharist followed by an agape, or it may be an agape followed by a celebration of the eucharist.[1] Much discussion has arisen around 2. 42, 46: "And they continued stedfastly in the apostles' teaching and fellowship, in the breaking of bread and the prayers. . . . And day by day, continuing stedfastly with one accord in the temple, and breaking bread at home, they did take their food with gladness and singleness of heart." Thus punctuated, and omitting with the R.V. *and* before *in the breaking of bread*, verse 42 co-ordinates this phrase with *the prayers*, and so a liturgical significance is suggested.[2] But this is not so clear in the rendering *in the apostles' teaching and in fellowship*, (*and*) *in breaking of bread, and in prayers*; and still less clear is it when we compare these words with the phrase in v. 46, *breaking bread at home they did take their food* (τροφή) *with gladness and singleness of heart*, where the natural reference would be to the partaking of ordinary food. Nevertheless, though we should come to the conclusion that the phrase *to break bread* in Acts 2 and 20 does not necessarily by itself carry a sacramental significance, we may not leave out of account the fact that it is used by St. Luke, who cannot have been ignorant of the sacramental associations of the common meal as taught by

---

[1] κλάσας τὸν ἄρτον καὶ γευσάμενος: the phrase does not determine which came first.

[2] The "Western" (Bezan) text has "in the fellowship of the breaking of bread": cp. Vulgate "communicatione fractionis panis". This is supported by the Peshitto and the Sahidic versions.

St. Paul.[1] Nor can we safely forget that, quite apart from the associations of the Last Supper, the primitive Church through its original members found in the breaking of bread at any time that which reminded it of one of the most characteristic actions of the Lord as indicated in the tradition handed down in the Gospels. We need not suppose that the Supper at Emmaus was a eucharist in the liturgical sense of the term; but the risen Christ *was known of* the two disciples *in the breaking of bread*[2]: what his mien and words did not accomplish, that his manner as he took the loaf and broke it significantly revealed. Here was the personal touch so familiar to them all in the old days of their discipleship; and by it they knew him for their Master and Friend.

In any case, whatever may be the precise connotation of the term "breaking of bread" as used in *Acts*, the social and religious element contained in it is clearly placed by the author in relation to the life of the Church as a whole. The sacramental observance —if it be such in the modern sense of the term—is a result not the cause of the inner unity of heart and mind which the gift of the Holy Spirit had brought to the disciples by his presence. It testified in a special way to their belief in the unseen Christ as the bond of union between them. Thus the Last Supper was reproduced on a larger scale. Corresponding to the Supper as a whole was the multiform unity of Church life expressing itself in the various religious and social activities as indicated in the early chapters of *Acts*; and part of that feast of good things of the Spirit were the sacred meals which brought them in touch, as perhaps nothing else did so vividly, with the Author of all their strength and joy. The Sacrament was a "meal within a meal"; it was placed in a context from which it could not be separated, and from which the infant Church had no thought of separating it.

But a sacramental meal suggests by its very nature and symbolism a relation with the unseen Host of an intimate, mystical character. And it has been stated that in *Acts* the conception of the Spirit in his relation to the life of the Church and of the individual Christian is different from the conception of the indwelling Presence, so plainly taught by St. Paul and St. John, as we shall see in the chapters which follow. We have, therefore,

[1] But this argument will carry no weight with those who do not accept the Lucan authorship of *Acts*, because, among other things, of its *differentia* from the Pauline Epistles.   [2] Luke 24. 35.

to examine *Acts* more closely, in order to see if it finds a place for this continuous mystical experience in the Church, in relation to which we may set the experience of sacramental communion. A. H. McNeile says that "the writer [of *Acts*] remains at the Old Testament standpoint in thinking of the Spirit as an effluence, an *afflatus*, from God which 'comes upon' men. . . . But St. Paul's thought of the Spirit as an immanent power, the highest element in the Christian's personality, because it is the divine atmosphere in which his whole being lives, never finds expression."[1] It may be granted at once that St. Luke, however skilfully he could in a few strokes sketch a man's character (e.g., Acts 11. 24), had not that psychological interest which led St. Paul to give classical expression to the working of the Holy Spirit in a man's inner life. St. Luke wrote the Gospel and *Acts* for a more "objective" purpose—namely, to set forth for one who was perhaps not a believer the Christian life in its relation to the world of men. But it seems that McNeile's distinction between the Lucan and the Pauline conceptions of the Spirit's working is over-emphasized. It is true that in *Acts* the Holy Spirit is spoken of as coming on Christians on a particular occasion—e.g., 8. 17; 10. 44; 11. 15; 19. 6; or to deliver a particular message from God—e.g., 1. 16; 2. 4; 8. 29; 10. 19; 11. 12; 13. 2; 16. 6, 7; 20. 23; 21. 11; 28. 25. Again, men are "filled" ($\pi\lambda\eta\sigma\theta\acute{\epsilon}\nu\tau\epsilon\varsigma$) with the Holy Spirit on an occasion of particular crisis in order that they may meet it successfully—e.g., 2. 4; 4. 8; 13. 9. But they are also "full" ($\pi\lambda\acute{\eta}\rho\epsilon\iota\varsigma$) of the Holy Spirit—a phrase that suggests a permanent endowment of character which others can take note of, as for example in the case of those who were to be chosen for the office to which the "Seven" were appointed (6. 3).[2] And indeed the early chapters of *Acts*—to take a wider view than that of single passages—are a record of men and women developing new gifts of character through a power not their own. Here we plainly see "the fruit of the Spirit" ripening in the garden of Eden to which the Lord by his new creation had restored the human race. The joy which is so plainly manifested in the record of St. Luke is the joy of a continually growing and expanding life, not of detached moments of special illumination and power. Further, the unity of the infant Church—a unity both of heart and of outward

[1] *New Testament Teaching in the Light of St. Paul's*, 130.
[2] Cp. also 6. 5, 8; 7. 55; 11. 24.

organization—could not have been maintained by means of occasional lapses of the Spirit on certain individual members. It was an inward and organic unity, formed within the members of the Church by a never-failing Presence.

Kirsopp Lake, on the other hand, recognizes[1] that besides the presence in *Acts* of passages which suggest an intermittent gift of the Holy Spirit, there are others[2] which suggest it as something permanent and to be expected by all Christians. He, however, draws a marked distinction in this respect between the earlier part of *Acts* and the latter, in which there are much fewer references to the Holy Spirit, and these usually speak of his action as sudden and unexpected.[3] But the reason for this fact—if it be a fact—is surely to be found in the change of treatment which is to be seen in *Acts* as the book proceeds. As F. J. Foakes Jackson has put it: "In Acts the author has realized that it is his duty to relate the progress of a community although in the end he is perforce compelled to make his history revolve about two important personalities, SS. Peter and Paul, and finally to confine himself to recording the adventures of St. Paul."[4] In other words, the latter half of *Acts* is biography rather than the history of a community, and this fact affects the question before us. As the book proceeds, the subject is no longer that of a Spirit-filled society, but the career of an individual, and especially in his relations with the Jews on the one hand and the Roman authorities on the other. But even in this restricted scope, the work of the Holy Spirit is manifest, in guiding St. Paul, either directly or by means of some other Christian prophet, towards the goal which God intended him to reach. Obviously, then, it is a change of subject matter, not of doctrine or emphasis, which occasions fewer references to the Holy Spirit in the latter portion of *Acts*.

We have seen that in its earlier portion Christians are spoken of as "filled" ($\pi\lambda\eta\sigma\theta\acute{\epsilon}\nu\tau\epsilon\varsigma$) with the Holy Spirit at times of special need. This special bestowal of the Spirit is given in the latter portion by means of a vision of Christ. Thus, at Corinth, when he was hard pressed and much discouraged, "the Lord said unto Paul in the night by a vision, Be not afraid, but speak, and

---

[1] *The Beginnings of Christianity*, v. 108.
[2] He refers to chaps. 6 and 8.   [3] *Ib.*, v. 109.
[4] *A History of Church History*, 5.

hold not thy peace: for I am with thee, and no man shall set on thee to harm thee: for I have much people in this city."[1] A similar vision is granted to St. Paul after his appearance before the Sanhedrin (23. 11), and also on board the storm-tossed ship (27. 23, 24), but in this case the Visitant is described as *an angel of the God whose I am, whom also I serve*. In the Third Gospel, St. Luke records the words of Christ: "When they bring you before the synagogues, and the rulers, and the authorities, be not anxious how or what ye shall answer, or what ye shall say: for the Holy Spirit shall teach you in that very hour what ye ought to say."[2] And in the Fourth Gospel, the Holy Spirit is promised to take the place of Jesus as an Advocate[3] of the disciples when they are hard pressed or persecuted.[3] Further, in 1 *Corinthians* St. Paul refers to the Holy Spirit as the source of the help which enabled him to make good in the difficult period of his early sojourn at Corinth: "I was with you in weakness, and in fear, and in much trembling. And my speech and my preaching were not in persuasive words of wisdom, but in demonstration of the Spirit and of power."[4] This identification in function of the presence of Christ and of the Holy Spirit, in respect of this kind of help, is an additional fact of significance for the subject of this book.

But we have by no means exhausted the evidence of *Acts*. There are other indications that St. Luke did not look on the gift of the Holy Spirit as merely an *afflatus* from God upon men, but that rather he regarded it as an immanent power after the manner of, if not in the same degree as, St. Paul and St. John. "The church throughout all Judæa and Galilee and Samaria had peace, being edified; and walking in the fear of the Lord and in the comfort (τῇ παρακλήσει) of the Holy Spirit was multiplied." So the R.V. translates Acts 9. 31, and, in the view of the present writer, rightly. Others would construe *and walking in the fear of the Lord* with the preceding clause. Hort's proposal to translate παρακλήσει by "invocation" receives no support from the other passages where the word occurs, and has little to commend it.[5] Here, then, we have a phrase "walking (πορευομένη) in the comfort of the Holy Spirit" which is analogous to the

---

[1] Acts 18. 9, 10.
[2] Luke 12. 11, 12.   [3] John 14. 16; 15. 20-16. 2.   [4] 1 Cor. 2. 3, 4.
[5] H. B. Swete, *The Holy Spirit in the New Testament*, 96, 97.

Pauline "Walk by the Spirit (πνεύματι περιπατεῖτε)",[1] and suggests the presence of the Holy Spirit in the Church and its members as an inner power of life, constant and never failing. This is also true even if we were to translate "and by the comfort of the Holy Spirit was continually being multiplied (ἐπληθύνετο)". Again, in 13. 52, after St. Paul and St. Barnabas had perforce to leave Antioch in Pisidia owing to trouble created by the Jews, nevertheless "the disciples" whom the apostles had converted "were continually filled (ἐπληροῦντο) with joy and the Holy Spirit".

So far we have been commenting upon the text that underlies the Revised Version of the New Testament. The claim of the "Western" text, as represented by the Codex Bezæ and other textual authorities, to be the original text of *Acts* cannot be discussed here. It will suffice to say that recent examination, notably by A. C. Clark, has given additional force to that claim. Now, one of the features of the "Western" text of *Acts*, not commonly observed, is that it emphasizes the immanent presence and power of the Holy Spirit. Perhaps the most notable example of this is to be found at the conclusion of the synodical letter[2] conveying the decision of the Council of Jerusalem to "the brethren which are of the Gentiles in Antioch and Syria and Cilicia". It runs thus: "Fare ye well, borne on your course[3] in the Holy Spirit." There are several other examples of this, as will be seen from the following, in which the distinctive additions or wording of the "Western" text are indicated in italics. "They were not able to withstand the wisdom *that was in him* and the *Holy* Spirit by which he spake" (6. 10). "But he *in the Holy Spirit*[4] looked up stedfastly into heaven, and saw the glory of God" (7. 55). "Peter rose up *in the Spirit* and said unto them" (15. 7). "Judas and Silas being prophets also themselves *full of the Holy Spirit*[5] exhorted the brethren" (15. 32). "Paul *in the Spirit* turned, and being sore troubled, he said" (16. 18). "And when Paul had laid his hands upon them, *immediately* the Holy Spirit came on them; and they spake with tongues *and recognized them in themselves so that they also interpreted them for themselves, and*

---

[1] Gal. 5. 16.　　　　　　　　　　[2] Acts 15. 29.
[3] φερόμενοι: cp. 2 Pet. 1. 21.
[4] This is the reading of the Codex Floriacensis (sixth cent.).
[5] Read by Codex Bezæ and the minuscule 383.

some also prophesied"[1] (19. 6). "And Agrippa said unto Paul, Thou art permitted to speak for thyself. Then Paul *being of good cheer and taking courage in the Holy Spirit*[2] stretched forth his hand and made his defence" (26. 1). The corresponding phrase *in Jesus* is found in the Western text of 19. 14: "*Among whom also* the sons of one Sceva a priest *wished to do the same thing. They were accustomed to exorcize such people, and coming unto one who was possessed of a devil they began to call upon the Name, saying, We command thee, in Jesus whom Paul preacheth, to come out.* Then the evil spirit answered" etc.

Besides these, there are other passages in which the "Western" text alone has a reference to the Holy Spirit, or adds something additional to such a reference. "Having received of the Father the promise of the Holy Spirit, he hath poured forth *upon you the gift*, which ye both see and hear" (2. 33). "And when they came up out of the water, the *Holy* Spirit *fell upon the eunuch, but an angel* of the Lord caught away Philip *from him*" (8. 39). "If then God gave unto them the like gift as he did also unto us, when we believed on the Lord Jesus Christ, who was I that I could hinder God *from giving the Holy Spirit to them that believed on him?*" (11. 17). "*And when Paul according to his own counsel desired to go to Jerusalem, the Spirit told him to return to Asia.* And when he had passed through the upper country," etc. (19. 1). "And when he had spent three months there, and a plot was laid against him by the Jews, *he was minded* to sail for Syria. *But the Spirit said to him* to return through Macedonia. *Therefore when he was about to depart* there accompanied him as far as Asia Sopater" etc. (20. 3).

These additions and variations of the "Western" text do not make the book theologically different from what it is without them, or introduce any aspect of the Holy Spirit's working or presence for which there is no precedent in the non-"Western" text. As J. R. Ropes says: "The emphasis on the Holy Spirit" is "wholly in accord with the ideas and habit of the author of the book."[3] Still less can we accept the theory that they are of Montanist origin. But there seems to be a vogue among certain

---

[1] Not all the "Western" texts have these additional words.

[2] ἐν Πνεύματι Ἁγίῳ παράκλησιν λαβών.

[3] *The Beginnings of Christianity*, vol. iii, p. ccxxxiv. Ropes does not himself hold that the "Western" text is original; therefore his testimony is all the more valuable.

writers to-day of attributing "Montanism" to early writings which do not limit the Holy Spirit in his working to such channels as they think fitting.[1] Such writers do not prove their case, but rather that they are themselves out of touch with the conception of the Holy Spirit which the Church in its earliest days held in regard to his gifts and operations.

Whether, therefore, we hold that the "Western" or the non-"Western" text of *Acts* is the more primitive, while there are many passages in the book which speak only of an illapse of the Holy Spirit upon individuals or groups of individuals, there are others which suggest just as strongly an indwelling of the Holy Spirit in the Church and in individual members, or in other words an approximation to the doctrine as stated by St. Paul and St. John. And apart from particular passages the whole tenor of the book is consistent only with the belief of its author in a Spirit-filled society. The growth of the Church and the spiritual development of its members, its joyous life, its "togetherness", its conviction as to corporate and individual guidance[2] both in doctrine and practice—these are surely the clear signs of a Presence, not intermittent nor unpredictable, but permanent, abiding, inherent. True, this is more clearly seen in the earlier chapters, which speak more particularly of the corporate life of the Church. But even though in the second portion of the book the emphasis narrows upon an individual, the connecting link of the Holy Spirit binds both parts together. "Ye shall receive power, when the Holy Ghost is come upon you: and ye shall be my witnesses both in Jerusalem, and in all Judæa and Samaria, and unto the uttermost part of the earth" (1. 8). And this "witness" which is first given by the twelve Apostles and others in Palestine in face of much opposition and difficulty (chs. 1-8) is later given in the same power by Paul in more distant lands, and finally in the heart and centre of the world, in Rome itself. There could be no clearer indication than this of the author's belief in the continuous presence of Jesus in his Church through the Holy Spirit, acting, not here or there, but throughout its

---

[1] It is not irrelevant to note that there were certain persons in the second century who did not accept the Fourth Gospel, apparently on the ground that its doctrine of the Holy Spirit lent support to Montanism: Irenæus, *Hær.* iii. 11, 12 (Harvey); J. N. Sanders, *The Fourth Gospel in the Early Church*, 37.

[2] "The whole background of the book is the guidance of the Holy Spirit": K. Lake in *The Beginnings of Christianity*, v. 108.

expanding life. Further, it has been shown that the power behind this witness is more often spoken of as the presence of the Holy Spirit, but sometimes as the presence of Jesus himself[1]; even as in St. John the Holy Spirit is called "another Advocate", and as in St. Paul, for whom in his working the Holy Spirit is the equivalent of Christ.

It is the Holy Spirit who forms the fellowship, the corporateness of the Church, as it is conceived in *Acts*; and within its Spirit-filled life, and in relation to it, is placed the eucharist. We cannot, indeed, point to any phrase or title in the book and say, "This refers to the eucharist, and to it alone." But on the other hand, few if any commentators have been found to exclude all reference to it; and in particular the phrase "the breaking of bread" has been held, at any rate in some places where it occurs, to include the eucharist as part of a common meal. This fact is significant for the purpose of our enquiry. That the eucharist so formed part of a Church gathering that the sacramental and the merely social parts could be included under a common title brings it into direct relation with the operation of the Holy Spirit, who is represented in this book as clearly inspiring all activities of the Church, of whatever kind, which form part of and witness to its common life.

[1] See pp. 43, 44.

CHAPTER IV

THE PAULINE EPISTLES

THE reader of the English Bible who passes from Acts to the Pauline Epistles finds in the former an historical account of the Holy Spirit's working in the Church which adequately prepares him for the doctrinal teaching of St. Paul on this matter. This is an additional indication that Acts on the one hand and the Pauline Epistles on the other are not so different in this respect as some scholars have maintained. And when he reads St. Paul's letters in their historical order, he finds that the Apostle takes it for granted, even in the earliest of them, that the gift of the Holy Spirit is a fact forming common ground between him and his readers, which he can use as a basis of argument. "Received ye the Spirit by the works of the law, or by the hearing of faith?" he asks the Galatians.[1] "God called us not for impurity but in sanctification. Therefore he who sets at naught *this calling* sets at naught not man but God, who gives his Spirit, the Holy *Spirit, to enter* into you"[2] is the ground on which he warns the Thessalonians against sins of the flesh. The possession of the Holy Spirit and the Resurrection of Christ are equally truths which the Corinthians as well as the Apostle accepted, and from either of them as a premiss he can deduce certain consequences.[3]

As in Acts, so in St. Paul, it is the Holy Spirit who forms and maintains the unity of the Church in spite of the differences in race and social class of its members[4]; in spite of human sin and its fruits as manifested in self-seeking and factiousness[5]; and in spite of differences of opinion on matters of doctrine and practice.[6] But the source of unity, implicitly underlying the narrative of

---

[1] Gal. 3. 2.

[2] 1 Thess. 4. 7, 8: for reading and translation see H. B. Swete, *The Holy Spirit in the New Testament*, 172.   [3] Cp. 1 Cor. 12. 1 with 1 Cor. 15. 12.

[4] 1 Cor. 12. 13, Eph. 2. 18ff.; cp. Acts 2 and 4. 32-35.

[5] 1 Cor. *passim*; 2 Cor. 13. 14; cp. Acts 5 and 6. 1.

[6] Rom. 14. 17; cp. Acts 15.

Acts, is more explicitly stated in the Pauline Epistles. The question was forced upon him by the schismatical temper of the Corinthian Church, and it led him to state and develop his metaphor of the Church as a body. At Corinth he is concerned with the unity of the local Church. But later on, as he lies in his Roman prison and reflects on the diversity of races and conditions and tongues that made up the peoples of the Empire at whose centre he was, it is the unity of the Church Catholic which engages his thought. He falls back again on the metaphor of the body (although with differences in his use of it[1]), and once more by its means illustrates the theme of unity in diversity. "In one Spirit were we all baptized into one body."[2] "Giving diligence to keep the unity of the Spirit in the bond of peace. There is one body and one Spirit, even as also ye were called in one hope of your calling."[3] St. Paul also makes it clear that the unity of the Spirit persists in the life of the Church through differences of gifts and difference of function. "There are diversities of gifts, but the same Spirit", he writes to the Corinthians.[4] The same thought is to be found in the well-known passage in *Ephesians*, in which the gifts of the Ascended Christ to his Church are enumerated: "He gave some to be apostles; and some, prophets; and some, evangelists; and some, pastors and teachers."[5] Here the Holy Spirit is not mentioned by name. But the concluding words of the gigantic sentence, *in love*—"the building up of the body in love"—might have been without difference of meaning *in the Spirit*. For love is of the fruit of the Spirit. Once again, the teaching of St. Paul is present by implication in *Acts*, which associates the presence and working of the Holy Spirit with the Apostles and their special functions, with the Seven and theirs, with "helps"[6] such as St. Barnabas, and with Christian prophets such as Agabus.

I have said that, according to St. Paul, the unity of the Church persists through the variety of the gifts of its members and their several functions. This is an understatement. This very variety points to the one Spirit who distributes the gifts severally as he will[7]; and the difference in function among the members of the body of Christ is the very means by which the body grows and

---

[1] In 1 *Cor.* Christ is the whole body, in *Eph.* the head of the body.
[2] 1 Cor. 12. 13.   [3] Eph. 4. 3, 4.   [4] 1 Cor. 12. 4.
[5] 4. 7-16.   [6] 1 Cor. 12. 28.   [7] 1 Cor. 12. 11.

develops "till we all attain unto the unity of the faith, and of the knowledge of the Son of God, unto a fullgrown man, unto the measure of the stature of the fulness of Christ".[1] In our minds growth is often associated with a kind of change which leads to lack of sympathy, to misunderstanding, and even to dissension. Children and parents, taught and teachers, young and old, one generation and the next, drift apart in thought and feeling and goodwill as a result of new ideas and customs and modes of life. But the growth that comes to the Church through the presence of the Holy Spirit makes, according to St. Paul, for unity; for by its means the manifold functions of the Church are seen to be converging towards the goal when redeemed man will attain the stature for which God intended him. The same is true of the individual life, as is indicated by the use of the term "the fruit of the Spirit".[2] The Christian life, on the one hand, is a growing, developing life, through the fructifying power of the Holy Spirit; and yet on the other the person in whom this growth has taken place is a unity, for the result is *the fruit* (not "fruits", as the Anglican Litany, and not it alone, misquotes) *of the Spirit*.

In yet another way, though this time less directly, St. Paul indicates that in the Holy Spirit lies the hope of a unity which man left to himself might despair of. I refer to the relation of the individual to the society. If the Apostle is insistent that by the Holy Spirit is unity given to the body as a whole, he also no less clearly indicates that it is the Holy Spirit who gives to the individual his consciousness of his personal relationship to God. "Ye received the spirit of adoption, whereby we cry, Abba, Father. The Spirit himself beareth witness with our spirit, that we are children of God."[3] "Because ye are sons, God sent forth the Spirit of his Son into our hearts, crying, Abba, Father."[4] Thus, by the Holy Spirit there comes to a man the sense of his individual value in God's sight and his dignity as God's son. St. Paul here reiterates in another form the teaching of our Lord concerning the imperishable worth of each soul to the heavenly Father. To our human understanding the individual and the society may appear to be in opposition, and perhaps in irreconcilable opposition. But to the mind of God this cannot be so. The antinomy is resolved in the Holy Spirit, who both creates the sense of in-

[1] Eph. 4. 13.   [2] Gal. 5. 22.   [3] Rom. 8. 15, 16.   [4] Gal. 4. 6.

dividual value and also forms the fellowship of the Church. Side by side in the opening of the Anglican Church Catechism come the words: "In my Baptism . . . *I was made a member of Christ, the child of God.*" Thus, for the Christian the problem of reconciling authority with freedom cannot be regarded as ultimately insoluble. And further, since, as we have seen, the Holy Spirit is a principle of growth both in the individual and the society,[1] the Christian thinker will seek to find a solution of the problem, not in abstract thought, but in the experience of life; and in point of fact it is recognized by many who approach the matter on general grounds and apart from Christian theology that life is the only reconciler of authority with freedom.

The significance of St. Paul's teaching on the unity of the Spirit should come home to us at the present time with fresh meaning. This is an age of "problems". Perhaps we use the word "problem" as a kind of smoke-screen in order to hide from ourselves the real difficulty. By using it we externalize the difficulty and place it in the region of the impersonal. Whereas it is *we* who constitute the "problem"—we human beings, with our innate selfishness, passions and desires. To St. Paul's mind practically all the "problems" that vex us to-day were present in some form or another—the international problem, the racial (especially as between Jew and Gentile), the social, the ecclesiastical, the individual. Some of these "problems" he had wrestled with in the actual experience of his ministry, as for example in his relations with the Corinthian Christians or with the Jews; others he approached more especially from the point of view of a thinker. But St. Paul was careful not to depersonalize the "problem". He found the solution of them all in the Holy Spirit as he operates in the Church and its members. Nor would St. Paul have countenanced the attempt that many make to-day to escape personal responsibility by using loose expressions about the obligations of "the Church"—"the Church must do this or that." Even in *Ephesians*, preoccupied as it is with the doctrine of the Catholic Church, St. Paul never loses sight of the fact that a society is composed of individuals. In his view "the members which make up the One Ecclesia are not communities but individual men."[2] "As the Holy Spirit, dwelling in the heart of

---

[1] John 16. 13; Gal. 5. 22; Eph. 4. 16.
[2] F. J. A. Hort, *The Christian Ecclesia*, 168.

each member of the local community, binds all together in a corporate unity; so, by dwelling in all the faithful everywhere, it creates the worldwide unity of a Catholic Church."[1] It is unnecessary to follow out the relevance of all this to the world situation to-day, or to point out that the Pauline Epistles supply material for study by our statesmen and politicians as well as by our theologians and ecclesiastical rulers.

But the above quotation from H. B. Swete draws attention to an aspect of the teaching of St. Paul which is of essential significance for the subject of this book. I refer to the conception of the Holy Spirit as an immanent power indwelling not only in the whole body but also in each individual member of the body. The conception is indeed present in *Acts*, as we have seen, and more especially in the "Western" text of that book. But it was a fundamental conviction for St. Paul. His view of the Christian life is essentially mystical. The Christian lives in the Holy Spirit in such a way that through his presence and power the higher or "spiritual" element in his nature gains the mastery, and his virtues are themselves the "fruit" of the Spirit. Living in this divine atmosphere he breathes it, and it becomes part of himself. The Spirit does not "come" to the Christian here and now, on this or that occasion, in this or that way. He is present with him continuously, timelessly, so that the Christian is a "temple" or "sanctuary" of the Holy Spirit.[2]

The time was not ripe when St. Paul wrote for a working out of the metaphysical implications of the coming of the Holy Spirit and of his relationship to Christ. The Apostle treats the matter from an empirical point of view, and in his teaching the Spirit

[1] H. B. Swete, *op. cit.*, 310f.

[2] 1 Cor. 3. 16; 6. 19: 2 Cor. 6. 16. W. J. Phythian-Adams (*The People and the Presence*, 199) holds that when St. Paul says (1 Cor. 3. 16), "Ye are a temple (ναός) of God", he does not mean that each Christian severally is a temple, but that Christians together form the temple. See, however, Robertson and Plummer (*I.C.C.*) *ad loc*. But even if we were to accept this view for 1 Cor. 3. 16, when the Apostle has been speaking previously of divisions in the Church, it certainly does not fit 1 Cor. 6. 19, where a personal reference is demanded: "Know ye not that your body is a temple of the Holy Spirit which is in you, which ye have from God?" St. Paul is here rebuking those individual members of the Church of Corinth ("such were some of you") who had fallen into the sin of sexual impurity. Note "he that is joined" (*vv*. 16, 17) and "he that committeth fornication" (*v*. 18) for singular number.

in his working is the equivalent of Christ. Thus, he can speak indifferently of the indwelling presence of the Spirit and of that of Christ. "If any man hath not the Spirit of Christ, he is none of his. And if Christ is in you, the body is dead because of sin; but the spirit is life because of righteousness."[1] Here the inward possession of the Spirit is regarded as tantamount to the inward possession of Christ.[2] Similarly, in another passage[3] "the Lord the Spirit" and "the Spirit of the Lord" are viewed as being in practice the same. This is in accordance with our Lord's words as recorded in John 14. 18: "I will not leave you orphans: I come unto you"—where the "coming" can scarcely be other than that of the Holy Spirit. In the teaching of St. Paul and of the primitive Church, where the Spirit is, Christ is; and what the Spirit effects is in fact effected by Christ.

Accordingly, in respect of this mystical presence, St. Paul frequently uses identical phrases to describe the relation of the Christian to Christ on the one hand or to the Holy Spirit on the other. Parallel to "in Christ" or "in the Lord" is "in (the) Spirit" (Rom. 8. 9; 9. 1: 1 Cor. 12. 3: Eph. 2. 18, etc.); and parallel to "Christ in you" (Rom. 8. 10; Col. 1. 27) is "the Holy Spirit in you" (1 Cor. 6. 19). He speaks of living in Christ (Rom. 6. 2, 11; Gal. 2. 20; Phil. 1. 21) and also of living in the Spirit (Gal. 5. 25). Christians are exhorted to "walk in the Lord" (Col. 2. 6) and to "walk in the Spirit" (Gal. 5. 16, 25). The statement "in Christ ye are made full" (Col. 2. 10) becomes in Eph. 5. 18 an injunction "be filled with the Spirit". The prayer of St. Paul that "Christ may dwell in your hearts through faith" (Eph. 3. 17) in another passage of the same letter takes the form of the statement that Christians "are builded together for an habitation of God in the Spirit" (Eph. 2. 22), and is paralleled more closely in earlier letters in the phrase "the Spirit of God dwelleth in you" (1 Cor. 3. 16; Rom. 8. 9, 11). It is said of Christ in 1 Cor. 15. 45 that "the last Adam became a life-giving (ζωοποιοῦν) spirit"; in 2 Cor. 3. 6 it is the Spirit who "giveth life (ζωοποιεῖ)"; and we have seen that the phrase "the Spirit of the Lord" is used as the equivalent of "the Lord the Spirit" —i.e., as interpreted by 1 Cor. 15. 45 above, the Lord in the quickening power of his glorified life.

---

[1] Rom. 8. 9, 10.   [2] See K. E. Kirk, *Romans*, 111.   [3] 2 Cor. 3. 17.

L. S. Thornton in *The Incarnate Lord*, pp. 322-327, has an interesting discussion of this subject, in which he reaches conclusions which, if fully accepted, would modify what has been said above. He holds that, according to Pauline teaching, "both Christ and the Spirit dwell in the Christian soul, but not in the same way. Christ is the indwelling content of the Christian life. He is being 'formed' in us." He holds that the Spirit is the quickening power; and although Christ is sometimes spoken of also as such a power, St. Paul nowhere says that the Spirit is formed in us, or that we are to be conformed to the image of the Spirit, nor is he ever regarded as the *content* of the quickened life. In *Ephesians*, he says, the distinction between the indwelling of Christ and the indwelling of the Spirit is clearly marked in one sentence (3. 14-17): "I bow my knees unto the Father . . . that ye may be strengthened with power through his Spirit in the inward man; that Christ may dwell in your hearts through faith; to the end that ye, being rooted and grounded in love, may be strong to apprehend" etc. "The Spirit is the quickening cause; and the indwelling of Christ is the effect of this quickening."

On this we may remark that the passage in *Ephesians* by no means gives the "clear" distinction claimed for it by Fr. Thornton. It is not certain that the clause "that Christ may dwell in your hearts through faith" expresses the effect of the clause "that ye may be strengthened with power through his Spirit in the inward man". The grammatical construction is not self-evident. T. K. Abbott[1] holds that the "dwell" clause does not express the end or result of the "strengthened" clause, nor is it something added to it, but *a further definition of it*. (The punctuation of the R.V. would seem to suggest this.) On this construing, the passage goes over to the other side, and affirms what Fr. Thornton seeks to deny. Again, apart from the question of the interrelation of these two clauses, we must reckon with the fact that the whole passage is construed differently by Westcott, Swete, and J. A. Robinson, as follows: "that he would grant you . . . to be strengthened with power by his Spirit in the inner man, that Christ may dwell through faith in your hearts in love: ye being rooted and grounded" etc. The words "in love" are equivalent to "in the Spirit", who sheds abroad in our hearts the love of God, as stated in Rom. 5. 5. And in general theologians are

[1] *I.C.C.*, 96.

agreed that the Holy Spirit as the Love of God imparts it to the souls in whom he dwells.[1]

The natural choice of language would suggest the expression "Christ is being formed in us" rather than "the Spirit is being formed in us", since Christ was the incarnate Son of God, and we even in the flesh are sons of God, if only by adoption. But when Fr. Thornton goes on to say that "the indwelling of Christ means always the reproduction in us of the human life of Christ in its essential quality and character by a process which can be compared to impregnation and growth",[2] he uses language of a kind which St. Paul does not appropriate solely to the name of Christ. The Apostle speaks of "the fruit of the Spirit". The person who "walks by the Spirit" and is "led by the Spirit"[3]—both these terms suggest more than a quickening power—acquires a character which may be recognized as the Holy Spirit's; something is formed which bears a likeness to him that formed it. In 2 Cor. 3. 3 another metaphor is used: the Corinthian Christians are "a letter of Christ, written not with ink, but with the Spirit of the living God; not in tables of stone, but in tables that are hearts of flesh". It is not certain whether by "a letter of Christ" is meant a letter of which Christ is the Author, or a letter telling of Christ, or a letter belonging to Christ. But the *content* of the letter was written by the Holy Spirit: something was visibly formed which men could recognize as his work. Again, in Rom. 8. 14 we are told that "As many as are led by the Spirit of God, these are sons of God." When the divine sonship, "put on"[4] in baptism, is through the accepted guidance of the Holy Spirit progressively realized, when the potential is being actualized, then indeed that sonship is made manifest, it is seen to be what it is. The Holy Spirit, who first gave to the disciple his consciousness of a filial relationship to God,[5] has now led that disciple on to acquire and make his own that divine sonship. Such passages as we have referred to are sufficient to endorse the statement of H. B. Swete that the "indwelling Spirit is a constructive power which builds up a new life within, cooperating with the spirit of man in the work of restoring human life to the image of God".[6]

---

[1] H. B. Swete, *The Holy Spirit in the Ancient Church*, 330f., 405.
[2] pp. 323f.   [3] Gal. 5. 16, 18, 22.   [4] Gal. 3. 27.
[5] Rom. 8. 16; Gal. 4. 6.   [6] *The Holy Spirit in the New Testament*, 345.

The language of St. Paul concerning the indwelling Presence is
"mystical", not in the sense that it is non-sacramental (for that
Baptism is the beginning of the life of the Spirit would seem
to be a Pauline conviction), but in the sense that the presence of
Christ or of the Holy Spirit in the soul of the Christian is something which is to be regarded as constant and independent of time
or place or circumstance. We have now to consider how the
eucharistic teaching of St. Paul is to be placed in relation to it.
In the passage in 1 Cor. 11, which describes an agape followed by
a sacramental meal, we are recalled by St. Paul to the scene in the
Upper Room.[1] And as in the Gospels so in 1 *Corinthians* the
Sacrament does not inaugurate the fellowship but presupposes it
as already existing, and indeed requires it as an indispensable
background. This is most emphatically stated. St. Paul begins
(v. 17) by referring to the divisions in the Corinthian Church,
which persisted even when they met for their common religious
meals. He then goes on: "When *therefore* ye come together, it
is not possible[2] to eat a *Lord's* supper" (οὐκ ἔστι κυριακὸν
δεῖπνον φαγεῖν). The term κυριακὸν δεῖπνον refers to the whole
action, the ordinary meal followed by the eucharist, and is not
to be applied in the limited sense of the Book of Common Prayer.
St. Paul's meaning is that the schismatical and selfish behaviour
of the Corinthians made it impossible for them to eat a *Lord's*
supper[3] (the emphasis is on the adjective κυριακὸν). *A* supper
they might eat, but certainly not a *Lord's* supper; for the eating
of such a supper presupposed an already existing fellowship. And
as the passage proceeds (vv. 28-32) we leave the thought of fellowship for that of self-examination and self-discernment. "Let a
man prove (δοκιμαζέτω) himself." "If we discerned (διεκρίνομεν)
ourselves, we should not be judged." Here we are clearly in a
circle of ideas where the thought of the Holy Spirit is latent, and
in other portions of the Pauline epistles is actually expressed, as
for example in 1 Cor. 2. 11-16 with its use of similar verbs
(ἀνακρίνω, συγκρίνω); and in 12. 9, 10 "to another is given
. . . in the one Spirit . . . discernings (διακρίσεις) of spirits"
(cp. 14. 29). And we may compare 1 Thess. 5. 21, "Prove

[1] vv. 23-25.

[2] Cp. John 13. 8, where Peter is told that he can have no part in the Lord
unless he accepts the Lord's method of unselfish humility. See p. 15.

[3] Not "*the* Lord's Supper" as A.V. and R.V. There is no article.

(δοκιμάζετε) all things"; on which G. Milligan notes: "Nothing is said as to *how* this . . . is to be effected, but it can only be by a 'spiritual' standard (cf. 1 Cor. 2. 13)."[1] Thus, though 1 Cor. 11. 17-34 contains no direct reference to the Holy Spirit, St. Paul's censure of the lack of fellowship and the lack of self-discernment is a sufficient indication, especially when his teaching in other passages is remembered, that neglect to use the gift of the Holy Spirit, both corporately and individually, was at the root of the abuses which had arisen in connection with the Sacrament.

In 1 Cor. 10. 3, 4, where the spiritual meat and spiritual drink partaken of by the Israelites in the wilderness are used as types of the spiritual meat and drink of the eucharist, the previous verse speaks of the baptism which the Israelites had received at the beginning of the Exodus as a sign of their allegiance to Moses, the inference being that the Corinthians were already pledged to Christ in Christian baptism before they partook of the eucharist.

But this chapter (1 Cor. 10) calls for detailed examination. In the earlier part St. Paul's argument is as follows. *All* the Israelites (πάντες five times repeated) shared in sacramental blessings; yet the greater part of them, falling into sin, incurred the judgement of God. These examples are "typical": the same thing may happen to Corinthian Christians, who are in danger of falling into divers temptations. St. Paul has especially in mind one particular sin—namely, idolatry—as incurred through partaking in idol feasts. And so he devotes to this subject the rest of the chapter, beginning in *v.* 14 with the words, "Wherefore, my beloved, flee from idolatry." On a strictly logical method St. Paul should have first made the point that all Christians partake of the Sacraments (and nevertheless may fall into idolatry); but actually he first warns the Corinthians to flee from idolatry and then points out that they are all of them (πάντες *v.* 17, corresponding to the πάντες in *vv.* 1 (*bis*), 2, 3, 4) communicants, yet some of them sin in this respect or are in danger of so doing. Again, St. Paul might have reminded the Corinthians of their baptism as a thing incompatible with idolatry, and told them that in it they were pledged to be loyal to Christ, as the Israelites were in theirs to be loyal to Moses (*v.* 2). But instead he singles out the Holy Communion, rather than Holy Baptism, in order to support

[1] Cp. 1 John 4. 1.

his argument, because it provides him with certain pertinent points.

(a) The eucharist, being a sacrificial meal, brings the worshipper into communion with him who has ordained it, just as the Jews, when they partake of their sacrificial meals, are brought into fellowship with the altar, and therefore with him whose altar it is. This shows how impossible it is for a Christian to join in pagan idol feasts. For though the idol itself is nothing, to partake of these feasts is to have fellowship with the demonic powers which lie behind pagan worship. And so St. Paul arrives at the desired conclusion: "Ye cannot drink the cup of the Lord, and the cup of demons; ye cannot partake of the table of the Lord, and of the table of demons."

(b) The eucharist is essentially a social rite, in which *all* partake; and this fact enables St. Paul the more pointedly to draw the desired parallel between the Corinthian Christians and the Israelites. The passage following must be read and interpreted with this in mind:

> 16 The cup of blessing which we bless, is it not joint participation in (κοινωνία) the blood of Christ? The loaf which we break, is it not joint participation in the body
> 17 of Christ? seeing that we, who are many, are one loaf, one body: for we all share in the one loaf.

"The cup of blessing" means the cup over which blessing or thanksgiving has been pronounced (whether with reference to a particular *Haburah* cup or not).[1] The added words "which we bless" are not otiose, for (1) they make clear the meaning of "the cup of blessing" (e.g., that it is not intended to signify a cup which bestows a blessing); and more particularly (2) they express the fact which St. Paul was anxious to emphasize—namely, that the whole congregation took part (whether actually or through a representative) in the act of blessing. A like significance lies behind the words "which we break". Again, participation in the spiritual blessings of the eucharist is participation in common (κοινωνία). All together[2] have communion with Christ in his

[1] See pp. 21, 23.

[2] St. Paul does not intend by this to cast doubt upon the individual blessings of communion, but he is not concerned with this here. In the next chapter (11. 27-29) he lays stress upon the responsibilities (and therefore by implication the privileges) of the individual communicant.

blood and body. St. Paul then pauses to underline the significance of partaking the bread, which he mentions after the cup perhaps in order that he may go on to draw out this significance the more easily. Both the outward and visible sign (the loaf) and the inward and spiritual grace (the body of Christ) indicate the unity of the Christian assembly. The outward part or sign is one; and so is the inward part or thing signified. Therefore the whole assembly constitutes one loaf, one body. This is the first occasion in his extant writings that St. Paul speaks of the Christian community as a "body"[1]; and he has yet, in 1 Cor. 12 and Rom. 12, to develop the thought along the lines of the human organism and its several limbs or members. Hence when we read of "one body" in 1 Cor. 10. 17, we are not perhaps justified in thinking of the term in the light of his subsequent treatment of this, his most famous, metaphor of the Church. The term here is suggested by the words "the body of Christ" which immediately precede.

St. Paul's argument is cogent only on the supposition that all to whom he is writing are communicants; and it indicates that at the celebration of the Lord's Supper all partook of the sacramental elements (cp. Justin Martyr, *Apol.* i. 65. 5; 67. 5). Accordingly, it offers good evidence for the practice at Corinth at that early date of a sacramental meal as a normal and indispensable part of the Christian *cultus*. It is inconceivable that the custom was instituted and established by St. Paul on his own authority. Elsewhere in 1 Cor. he distinguishes clearly between his own injunctions and those for which he has a commandment of the Lord.[2] And in the passage under discussion,[3] and more explicitly in the eleventh chapter, the language brings us back to the scene of the Upper Room and to the words of the Lord (and this is so independently of the question whether "This do in remembrance of me" is part of the authentic tradition of those words). I have translated κοινωνία in 10. 16 as "joint participation in" the blood and the body of Christ, since the context shows that it is desirable to emphasize the full meaning of the word. It is clear that there is a connection between verses 1-13

---

n 1 Cor. 6. 15, however, he has spoken of the physical bodies of the Corinthian Christians as "members of Christ".

[2] 7. 6,10, 12, 25, 40. Cp. 2 Cor. 8. 8.

[3] I refer to the terms "body" and "blood" of Christ.

and 14-22, which commentators have not always been careful to indicate. This is found, verbally, in the πάντες of v. 17—all partake—and the πάντες five times repeated in vv. 1, 2, 3, 4; and, further, the phrase *Israel after the flesh* (v. 18), implying that the Christian Church is the new Israel, whose circumcision is not in the flesh but of the heart in the spirit,[1] looks back to *our fathers* (v. 1), which implies the same thing.[2]

We have noted that the reference to the Holy Communion in this passage is suggested by the fact that this Sacrament, being a sacrificial meal, could be pointedly used in an argument against taking part in pagan sacrificial meals. But we are not justified in taking St. Paul to mean that solely in his capacity as a communicant must a Christian shun idolatry. There is an instructive parallel in 2 Cor. 6. 16: "What agreement hath the temple of God with idols? for we are the temple of the living God; even as God said, I will dwell in them, and walk in them; and I will be their God, and they shall be my people. Wherefore, 'Come ye out from among them, and be ye separate', saith the Lord, 'and touch no unclean thing'." With this we must compare 1 Cor. 3. 16, "Know ye not that ye are the temple of God, and that the Spirit of God dwelleth in you?" Taking these two passages together we see that it is the mystical indwelling of the Holy Spirit which makes it desecration for a Christian to partake in idolatry. That is to say, "What agreement hath the temple of God with idols?" states for the Christian on more general grounds the incompatibility indicated in "Ye cannot drink the cup of the Lord, and the cup of devils: ye cannot partake of the table of the Lord, and of the table of devils." In other words, by comparing 1 Cor. 10. 21 with 2 Cor. 6. 16, 17 and 1 Cor. 3. 16, we see that the special gift of the eucharist—communion with Christ —is placed in relation to the abiding presence of the Holy Spirit.

It may be said, however, that St. Paul's solemn language in 1 Cor. 11. 27-34 about unworthy receiving of the Holy Communion and in particular about the Lord's punishment for so doing (v. 30) indicates that he held that the gift bestowed in this

---

[1] Rom. 2. 28, 29.

[2] For this reason, among others, "fellowship" is not so satisfactory a rendering of κοινωνία in this passage as "joint participation" is. In the old Israel "all ate", "all drank" (vv. 3, 4); in the new Israel all in common partake.

Sacrament is apart from and quite unrelated to any other gift of grace. But this cannot be substantiated, as we may see by a further reference to a passage quoted in part above. "Know ye not that ye are the temple of God, and that the Spirit of God dwelleth in you? If any man destroyeth the temple of God, him shall God destroy."[1] The words, "If any man destroyeth the temple of God, him shall God destroy" correspond to the words in 11. 30, "For this cause [i.e., through eating and drinking the Sacrament unworthily] many among you are weak and sickly, and not a few sleep." And further, a similar line of thought is to be found in 1 Thess. 4. 3-8, which also indicates that the kind of warning contained in 1 Cor. 11 was commonly given by St. Paul in reference to offences committed against the Holy Spirit: "This is the will of God, even your sanctification, that ye abstain from fornication . . . that no man transgress, and wrong his brother in the matter: because the Lord is an avenger in all these things, as also we forewarned you and testified. For God called us not for uncleanness but in sanctification. Therefore he that rejecteth, rejecteth not man but God, who giveth his Holy Spirit unto you." And another apostolic writer utters a like thought when he says: "Of how much sorer punishment, think ye, shall he be judged worthy, who hath trodden under foot the Son of God, and hath counted the blood of the covenant, wherewith he was sanctified, an unholy thing, and hath done despite unto the Spirit of grace?"[2] (But in this passage it is not certain that the Holy Spirit is referred to.) The significance of the passages quoted from the Pauline Epistles is increased by the fact that they come from letters written in the early period of St. Paul's literary activity within four or five years of each other and in some cases much less. It is not as if, for example, at one period of his career he spoke of life in the Holy Spirit and at another of the life of sacramental communion. In these letters he speaks of both; and for this reason the similarity of language is noteworthy.

Another passage which claims our attention is the concluding sentence of 2 Corinthians: "The grace of the Lord Jesus Christ, and the love of God, and the communion (κοινωνία) of the Holy Spirit, be with you all." Is the reference here to (a) the fellowship which comes from the Holy Spirit, or (b) the fellowship

___

[1] 1 Cor. 3. 16, 17.   [2] Heb. 10. 29.

(communion) with him which Christians enjoy? In other words, is the genitive subjective or objective? In favour of (a) it is urged (i) that as "the grace of the Lord Jesus Christ" unquestionably means the grace that comes from him, so it is natural to take the other two genitives in the same way—the love that is of God, the fellowship that is of the Holy Spirit; and (ii) that the party spirit of the Corinthians, which St. Paul rebukes so severely in the context, makes it appropriate for him to emphasize the fellowship which the Holy Spirit creates in all who accept him.

J. A. Robinson examines the use of κοινωνία in HDB i. 460-462, and comes to the conclusion that in this passage and in Phil. 2. 1 and 1 Cor. 10. 16, 17 the meaning is fellowship, sense of membership—that is to say, the fellowship that comes from God through the Holy Spirit. We have given reasons for preferring the other meaning in 1 Cor. 10. 16, 17. And the value of Robinson's investigation is impaired by the fact that though he speaks in another connection of "interpreting St. Paul by himself", he omits to refer to four passages (1 Cor. 1. 9: 2 Cor. 6. 14: Phil. 1. 5, 3. 10), in all of which κοινωνία clearly means "fellowship with" a person or thing. Further, as he allows his interpretation of 2 Cor. 13. 14 to govern that of Phil. 2. 1 (which he styles "otherwise doubtful"[1])—a precarious assumption when we consider the interval of time that separates the two epistles—it will be seen that even if he is correct about the former passage, there are on the balance a majority of Pauline passages in which κοινωνία means "fellowship with".[2]

Can it mean this in 2 Cor. 13. 14 also? The two reasons, mentioned above, for preferring "the fellowship that is of the Spirit" are not conclusive. For (a) "The grace of the Lord Jesus Christ be with you all" (or similar words) is a stock ending with St. Paul; and therefore when in this case he adds "and the love of God, and the communion of the Holy Spirit," it does not follow that the genitives "of God" and "of the Holy Spirit" are as likely to be also subjective as if the phrase as a whole had been formed in his mind at one and the same time. The *order* of the words also, the mention of Christ coming first, is an indication

---

[1] Lightfoot takes it as "communion with the Spirit".

[2] I do not take into consideration the passages in which κοινωνία means a "contribution" of alms—e.g., Rom. 15. 26, etc.

that the sentence is an amplification of the shorter and more usual formula. (b) Commentators who point out how suitable it is for St. Paul in a context of sharp rebuke to remind the factious Corinthians of the fellowship of the Church forget how difficult and complicated is the problem of the integrity of this Epistle. Is it a single letter written at one and the same time, or is it formed of fragments of two or three letters written at different times? And if the latter, we may go on to ask, of which letter was "The grace of the Lord Jesus Christ," etc., originally the conclusion? They may have been the final words of the "friendly" letter, and not of the "sorrowful" letter. In which case it was not specially needful or appropriate to emphasize the fellowship of believers.

The interpretation, therefore, of "the communion of the Holy Spirit" still remains an open question, and will probably always so remain. I am inclined to think, however, that it is more natural to pray that "communion with the Holy Spirit" may be "with you all," than it is to pray that "the fellowship of the Holy Spirit" may be "with you all".

But, whichever interpretation we may adopt, either of them is significant for the theme of this book. If St. Paul speaks of "joint participation in the Holy Spirit" as well as of "joint participation in the body and blood of Christ", the identity of phrase suggests a relationship between the two, and indeed a close relationship, since elsewhere in this group of Epistles he asserts that the last Adam, after his death and resurrection, "became a life-giving spirit".[1] On the other hand, if St. Paul speaks of a fellowship formed by the Holy Spirit and of a fellowship in the body and blood of Christ, what is this but an additional indication of what we have learned of the significance of the Last Supper, in which the fellowship of the disciples with their Lord was drawn into a closer fellowship by the sacramental meal?

Apart from the Synoptists, St. Paul is the only writer in the New Testament who quite clearly and definitely refers to the Sacrament of the Holy Communion. Moreover, he does so in language which indicates at once its general observance and also its especially solemn and sacred character. Perhaps it is his language,[2] more than anything else, which has caused readers of the New Testament to form a distinctive view of the Sacrament; and

[1] 1 Cor. 15. 45.　　　　　[2] In 1 Cor. 10, 11.

indeed for English-speaking peoples his words, or rather a mis-translation of them in the A.V.,[1] have kept simple folk from communicating through fear of unworthy receiving. Further, although the eschatological aspect is not absent from his teaching,[2] it is upon the Sacrament as a means of communion and of faith-union with Christ that his main emphasis lies. It is all the more remarkable, therefore, that when we examine his teaching as a whole, we find in it an equally strong emphasis upon the imma-nent presence of the Holy Spirit, and that he regards it as being in effect the equivalent of the immanent presence of Christ. Further, a closer examination of his letters reveals that his monitory language in reference to a profanation of Holy Com-munion is paralleled by similar language about a desecration of the human temple of the Holy Spirit. And, finally, if the Holy Communion, according to his teaching, signifies the unity of the body of believers,[3] it does not create it in the sense that the unity does not exist already; for "in one Spirit were ye all baptized into one body".[4]

The paucity of references in St. Paul's Epistles to the Holy Communion has been commented on by some as if it indicated a depreciation of the Sacrament. But this is a very precarious kind of argument, and especially so in connection with the documents in question. These are *occasional* letters—*i.e.*, they were called forth by the circumstances of the particular time in which they were written, and designed to meet and give assistance in a definite situation; and this is never so true as in the case of 1 *Corinthians*, where the references to Holy Communion occur. This being so, we should not expect to find frequent allusions to the Sacrament, if—as it is represented to be in this letter—the rite was a firmly established and commonly observed feature in the worship of the primitive Church. In our own correspondence we do not normally refer to the ordinary routine of daily life, such as meals, which we assume the recipients of our letters will take for granted. It was in fact an accidental occurrence in the Corinthian Church which caused St. Paul—to the lasting benefit of the whole Church—to speak of the Holy Communion. The argument may, indeed, be turned the other way. If the Sacra-ment was not a normal thing in the life of the Church, and if St.

[1] 1 Cor. 11. 29.   [2] 1 Cor. 11. 26.   [3] 1 Cor. 10. 17.
[4] 1 Cor. 12. 13.

Paul, as some have maintained, had under the influence of the Mystery Religions transformed a Farewell Supper of the Lord with his immediate disciples into a permanent institution, we should have expected him to refer more frequently to it. We should find him commending it to the several churches of his correspondence, and reminding them of it, if indeed he was the parent of its observance as a regular feature of Church life. The reverse is the case. He refers to his teaching concerning the Institution of the Sacrament as something he had "received of the Lord"[1]—whether by this he means a direct revelation or an account received by him through the accredited tradition of the Church. That he never again in his letters refers to the Sacrament is an indication rather that, as something generally recognized, he found no reason to speak about it unless a question of some kind should arise concerning it.

Further, in his teaching to converts upon the Christian life, St. Paul's custom was to appeal to the principle of *noblesse oblige*. "I . . . beseech you to walk worthily of the calling wherewith ye were called"[2] states in characteristic form the grounds on which he based his exhortation to Christian conduct. And more particularly he was wont, in this connection, to remind those who came from a Gentile upbringing that they had made a definite break with the past when they entered the Church. "Such were some of you," he says to the Corinthians after recounting a list of vile pagan sins, "but ye were washed, but ye were sanctified, but ye were justified in the name of the Lord Jesus Christ, and in the Spirit of our God."[3] Hence, it is not surprising to find comparatively frequent reference to Holy Baptism,[4] as indeed in any case we should expect to find in the writings of a missionary.[5] But far more frequently and constantly the appeal which St. Paul makes is not to the moment of entry upon the new life (Holy Baptism), but to the nature of the new life itself. Believers are "in Christ", or "in the Lord", or "in the Spirit"; Christ or the Spirit is "in" them. These phrases form the expression of St.

---

[1] I Cor. 11. 23.   [2] Eph. 4. 1.

[3] I Cor. 6. 11. The use of the R.V. in such passages is essential for English readers if the meaning of St. Paul is to be grasped—"ye *were* washed," etc.

[4] The noun occurs three times, the verb fourteen times.

[5] Cp., e.g., the writings of St. Patrick, in which there are several references to Holy Baptism but no direct reference to Holy Communion.

Paul's most characteristic, most intense, conviction concerning the nature of the Christian life. They occur between them more than 250 times in the genuine Paulines, "in Christ" being the most commonly found. This mystical union with Christ is not a fact, according to St. Paul, which exists only ideally or for those only who are manifestly walking worthily of their vocation. The remarkable thing is that he uses it as a ground of appeal to Christians such as the Corinthians, whom he has to rebuke severely as manifestly failing to live up to the Christian standard. "Try your own selves," he says to them, "whether ye be in the faith; prove your own selves. *Or know ye not as to your own selves, that Jesus Christ is in you? unless indeed ye be reprobate.*"[1] That is to say, unless they have rejected Christ, and abandoning faith in him are in turn by him rejected,[2] it is a fact of which they can take note for themselves that Christ dwells in them. Their union with Christ has not come to an end on account of their failings, obviously calling for rebuke though they are. Only definite apostasy can sever that union. As concerning this, the Corinthians are to "prove" (δοκιμάζετε) themselves; just as in 1 Cor. 11. 28 the Corinthian Christian is exhorted to "prove" himself before partaking of the Holy Communion.

In this connection it is to be remembered that if St. Paul may on the one hand be classed among the idealists,[3] he may on the other equally be accounted a realist.[3] To apply to him the words of Kipling, "he could dream and not make dreams his master." It is this rare combination of opposite types, scarcely ever before or since united to the same extent in any other person, that makes him one of the wonders of the world. As a consequence of this, no aspect of his theology can lightly be dismissed as "in the clouds" or purely theoretical or out of touch with actual life. Possibly in his latest epistles, when freedom of movement was denied him, and he could no longer live an active life among men, he may at times appear unduly speculative or visionary. But, be that as it may, in the epistles of the early and middle periods, when he was grappling with the problems of newly-founded churches, we must reckon him as a practical theologian, who based his teaching on no merely ideal conception of what the Christian life ought to be, but rather on affirmations concerning what he

[1] 2 Cor. 13. 5. [2] ἀδόκιμοι: cp. 1 Cor. 9. 27.
[3] I use these terms in their popular, not in their philosophical, sense.

knew the Holy Spirit to be achieving within the actual, visible Christian society. Hence it will not simply do for us on the one hand to accept St. Paul's teaching concerning the Holy Communion and what it involves to be a communicant as a serious and concrete contribution to Christian doctrine; and, on the other, to treat his constant teaching on the indwelling Spirit and what that means for Christian life as something "vague" and out of touch with reality. The fact is, as we have seen, that St. Paul bases practical appeals to his converts—surrounded and not seldom affected by a pagan environment—on the fact of this mystical union which the Holy Spirit creates between the Christian and Christ. His conviction as to the reality of this underlies the whole of his teaching; and it is in relation to this constant background that we must place his rare but precious affirmations concerning the Holy Communion.

CHAPTER V

THE JOHANNINE WRITINGS

ST. JOHN carries on to its fulfilment the teaching of St. Paul concerning the indwelling Spirit. This he does not so much by bringing forward distinctively new thoughts as by his method and manner of treating the subject. In his writings it is not the number of times that the Holy Spirit is mentioned that is significant—for actually in 1 *John* there are not many such references by name—but rather the poise and assurance with which St. John speaks of his presence. This is so for two reasons which are scarcely separable. St. John is himself the mystic *par excellence* among the writers of the New Testament. He is the master of the inner life, the great exponent of the inner light. He is himself the supreme example of the picture which he draws of the spiritual life[1]—a life in which the thought of progress from strength to strength is the law by which it is shaped.[2] He is one of those rare souls whose path the wise man described as "shining more and more unto the perfect day".[3] And now he is an old man. We can still see beneath the surface of his character the hidden fires that are ready to break out against error or wrong-doing. But his long life of communion with God in Christ has brought him a peace and calm which manifests itself throughout his writings and in particular in what he says concerning the indwelling presence of Christ and of the Holy Spirit. This is something that has become so much a part of himself in the long days of his discipleship that he speaks of it as men commonly speak of the universally accepted facts of life. "We know" is the term he frequently uses to express this inner conviction and apprehension of spiritual realities.[4] And this leads us on to the second reason why the Johannine writings speak with such assurance concerning

---

[1] 1 John 3. 2.   [2] Westcott, *The Epistles of St. John*, 122ff.
[3] Proverbs 4. 18.
[4] These remarks are perhaps truer of the Epistle than of the Gospel, which, however, we believe to be by the same author.

the Holy Spirit. Time has elapsed since the death of St. Paul. But his letters are read constantly in the local churches in some way or another connected with him or his memory. In this way their contents and doctrines have passed into the common stock of Christian ideas. Perhaps—even probably—a disciple has collected the letters and published them. And if Ephesus is the place where the Gospel and Epistles of St. John had their origin, it would be a *locus* well within the sphere of Pauline influence. So it is that in the Johannine writings we have reached a stage in which the Pauline doctrine of the Holy Spirit has been so assimilated by Church members that their teachers can assume that his immanent presence is now an accepted article of faith. St. Paul occasionally introduces this subject in a manner which suggests that he cannot quite assume it as a matter of common ground between himself and those whom he is addressing.[1] But it is otherwise with St. John, who never betrays any suspicion that those whom his words will reach can fail to acknowledge this fact as a Christian verity.

It is also in accordance with a later date of writing that St. John expresses more clearly than does St. Paul the personality of the Holy Spirit. He is the other Advocate (ἄλλος παράκλητος)[2] sent by Jesus to take his place. The masculine pronoun ἐκεῖνος is five times[3] used with reference to him, and not the neuter ἐκεῖνο as might have been more naturally expected in agreement with τὸ πνεῦμα. Finally, while St. Paul frequently uses "Spirit" or "Holy Spirit" without the article with a Godward reference, St. John seldom does this in the Gospel, and never in the Epistle.[4] Nevertheless, although the distinction between the personality of Christ and that of the Holy Spirit is sharper in the Johannine writings than it is in the Pauline Epistles, St. Paul and St. John are alike in assigning to each of the Persons similar functions in relation to the Christian disciple. The Christian abides in Christ (John 6. 56; 15. 4, 5, 6, 7: 1 John 2. 6, 24, 27, 28; 3. 6) or is in Christ (John 3. 15; 17. 21: 1 John 5. 20), and Christ abides in him (John 15. 4, 5) or is in him (John 17. 26). Similarly, the Holy Spirit abides in the disciple (1 John 2. 27; 3. 24: cp. John 7. 38) or is in the disciple (John 14. 17; cp. 2

[1] Cp. 1 Cor. 3. 16; 6. 19.
[2] John 14. 16.   [3] John 14. 26; 15. 26; 16. 8, 13, 14.
[4] πνεῦμα does not occur in 2 or 3 John.

John 2), and the disciple abides in the Spirit (1 John 2. 27).[1]
The disciple is in fellowship with (μετά) Christ (1 John 1. 3),
and the Holy Spirit is with (μετά) the disciple (John 14. 16;
cp. 2 John 2). The Holy Spirit is present with (παρά) the
disciple (John 14. 17), and so also the Father and the Son
make their abode with (παρά) the disciple (John 14. 23).
Similar to Rom. 8. 9, 10, where the "Spirit of Christ" and
"Christ" are used concurrently with identical meaning, is
John 14. 18, "I will not leave you orphans; I come unto
you"; where the "coming" can scarcely be other than that of
the Holy Spirit.

St. John's conviction as to the immanent presence of the Holy
Spirit in all believers is clearly seen when he refers to him as the
Spirit of truth. Here again St. Paul had prepared the way,
especially in 1 Cor. 2, where his discussion of the spiritual man
and his apprehension of true wisdom and true values leads him to
the conclusion "We have the mind of Christ." But St. John
develops this thought very much further. As Christ is "the
truth" (John 14. 6), so the Spirit is "the truth" (1 John 5. 7).
He is "the Spirit of truth" (John 14. 17; 15. 26; 16. 13: 1 John
4. 6) and as such guides the disciples into all truth (John 16. 13)
and teaches them all things (John 14. 26). As the truth, he
abides in the disciples (cp. 2 John 2), and gives them the power to
distinguish between falsehood and truth, between the spirit of
truth and the spirit of error. The most emphatic passage of all
is 1 John 2. 27: "And as for you, the anointing which ye received
of him abideth in you, and ye need not that anyone teach you;
but as his anointing teacheth you concerning all things, and is
true, and is no lie, and even as it taught you, ye abide in him."
When we recollect that those to whom St. John was writing
were face to face with a dangerous heresy, concerning which he
speaks in the gravest language, his statement "ye need not that
anyone teach you" is all the more remarkable. This is the language of the idealist, which we should find it difficult to apply
literally to the actual situation of the Church at any time in its
history. But that St. John can use such language is proof, if more
proof were needed, of his conviction as to the presence of the
Holy Spirit in each and every member of the Church. St. Paul

[1] μένετε ἐν αὐτῷ: but αὐτῷ may refer to Christ, not the unction of the
Spirit.

also held that a Christian does not need to go outside of himself in order to discover the truth concerning the things of the Spirit: "He that is spiritual judgeth all things."[1] But St. Paul was more of a realist than St. John, and more of an institutionalist, and he has more to say about the several functions which the members of the Church are to perform according to their several gifts. Accordingly, his antidote against heresy is not simply an appeal to the Spirit that dwells in every Christian, but "He gave some to be apostles; and some, prophets; and some, evangelists; and some, pastors and teachers . . . that we may be no longer children, tossed to and fro and carried about with every wind of doctrine, by the sleight of men, in craftiness, after the wiles of error."[2] And again, in *Colossians*, he speaks of the immanent power of Christ in those to whom he writes as something which needs to be developed within them, and that with the help of human agency: ". . . Christ in you, the hope of glory, whom we proclaim, admonishing every man and teaching every man in all wisdom, that we may present every man perfect in Christ; whereunto I labour also, striving according to his working, which worketh in me mightily."[3]

Needless to say, there is no contradiction on this matter between St. Paul and St. John in principle, but a difference only in the working out of principle, due mainly to a difference in temperament and psychology in the two men. But the point is useful to keep in mind when we proceed, as we shall now do, to examine more particularly the teaching of St. John on the theme of this book.

A difficulty of an historical kind meets us in regard to the occasion when the Holy Spirit was first given to the disciples. The Fourth Gospel places this on the evening of Easter Day, when the Risen Christ appeared to the Ten Apostles (in company, according to St. Luke, with other disciples, so that the room was thronged[4]), and breathed on them, saying, "Receive ye the Holy Spirit" (lit. "Take Holy Spirit"): "whose soever sins ye forgive, they are forgiven unto them; whose soever sins ye retain, they are retained."[5] On the other hand, St. Paul's view of the matter is congruous with the account of *Acts*, since he regards the gifts of the Spirit as the gifts of the Ascended Christ; and indeed, as

---

[1] 1 Cor. 2. 15.   [2] Eph. 4. 11, 14.
[3] Col. 1. 27-29.   [4] Luke 24. 33: ἠθροισμένους.   [5] John 20. 22, 23.

Hort acutely pointed out, the account of the Ascension is fittingly to be found at the beginning of *Acts*, not in the Gospels, since it is the preparation for the Day of Pentecost and thus for the beginning of the history of the Church.[1] Various solutions of the difficulty have been proposed: (1) that the gift of Easter Day was potential rather than actual, a sign of what was to follow; (2) that it was a foretaste only of the fuller gift that came at Pentecost; (3) that it was for a particular object only—namely, to bestow authority to remit and retain sins; (4) that it showed the double procession of the Spirit—from the Son as well as from the Father; (5) that it inaugurated the mission of the disciples, but in secret and as a preparation only for what was to follow.[2] None of these is convincing. The first is a subterfuge, as Hoskyns justly terms it; but his own explanation (the fifth) is not unlike it, and is in any case unnatural. As to the second, neither John 21 nor the Synoptic Gospels afford any evidence of quickened powers in the disciples between Easter and Pentecost; and indeed in Matt. 28. 17 some of them, when the Risen Christ appeared to them in Galilee, are said to have "doubted". The third fails to recognize that the authority conferred is not any particular gift, but is associated with the whole Gospel of salvation which the Church is commissioned to deliver. The fourth reflects the theological musings of a later age. The solution of this and of certain other difficulties in this Gospel seems to lie in the characteristic cast of mind of the author of the Fourth Gospel. "The Gospel of St. John", writes Dr. Inge, "is the charter of Christian Mysticism. Indeed, Christian Mysticism, as I understand it, might almost be called Johannine Christianity; if it were not better to say that a Johannine Christianity is the ideal which the Christian mystic sets before himself."[3] Some object to calling St. John a mystic because it seems to them to imply that it undermines or seriously disparages the historical element in the Gospel. But this by no means follows. If some mystics have shown an almost complete disregard for history or doctrine, others have not: and indeed if Dr. Inge's definition of mysticism as *the attempt to realize, in thought and feeling, the immanence of the temporal in the eternal, and of the eternal in the temporal* is at all

[1] H. B. Swete, *The Ascended Christ*, 2.
[2] E. C. Hoskyns (ed. F. N. Davey), *The Fourth Gospel*, ii. 652.
[3] *Christian Mysticism*, 44.

satisfactory, such a divorce of history from experience is contrary to its very essence. But what the mystic sets most store by is not merely exact theology or history, but rather the inner light or illumination of which they are the source. So it was with St. John. He wrote not only that "ye may believe that Jesus is the Christ, the Son of God," but also that "believing ye may have life in his name".[1] The latter clause is very significant as indicating the kind of person the Fourth Evangelist was. Another, for whom historical considerations were paramount, might "trace the course of all things accurately from the first", and write in order that he who read the Gospel "might know the certainty concerning the things wherein he was instructed".[2] But for St. John facts are significant for the spiritual truths to which they point, and especially for those truths which minister to the life in Christ. Accordingly, he is more concerned to state that the promise of the Holy Spirit was indeed fulfilled by him who promised it than to be chronologically exact as to the occasion on which it was first given. The Holy Spirit has been given, and has been given through Christ—this is enough for them to know who seek eternal life in his name. St. John, therefore, reads back the events of Pentecost into the evening of the first Easter Day when the Risen Christ, the source of spiritual power, first appeared to the disciples as a body. "He breathed on them, and saith unto them, Receive ye the Holy Spirit" answers to the descent of the Spirit as a rushing mighty wind. And, corresponding to St. Peter's proclamation of the new way of salvation, "Repent ye, and be baptized every one of you in the name of Jesus Christ unto the remission of sins",[3] is the commission "Whose soever sins ye forgive, they are forgiven unto them; whose soever sins ye retain, they are retained."[4] Thus within the pages of the Gospel is found the fulfilment of the promise of the Spirit, to which the discourse in the Upper Room had given so distinctive and prominent a place. It is hard to see why Hoskyns should pass over with a bare mention, and apparently reject, this explanation, seeing that in another connec-

[1] John 20. 31.   [2] Luke 1. 3, 4.   [3] Acts 2. 38.

[4] H. B. Swete, *The Forgiveness of Sins*, 168, says: "The evidence, so far as it goes, leads us to believe that the Church of the Apostolic age fulfilled the Lord's commission [in John 20. 23] chiefly by the preaching of the Gospel and the ministration of the two great sacraments."

tion in the Gospel—the well-known difficulty that arises from the occasion there assigned to the cleansing of the Temple—he says: "The fourth Evangelist is concerned more with the meaning of the words and actions of Jesus than with their original setting or relative order."[1]

This bestowal of the Spirit by the Son claims him as the source of power in the future, when his visible presence has been withdrawn; it also looks back to the days of the earthly ministry, as described in the Fourth Gospel, during which the words of Jesus were charged with the fulness of the Spirit that was in him. "He whom God hath sent speaketh the words of God: for he giveth not [to the Son] the Spirit by measure."[2] "The words that I have spoken unto you are spirit, and are life."[3] The latter quotation refers to the discourse on the bread of life, which must claim a prolonged attention, as it is the most substantial portion of the Johannine writings in which a eucharistic reference has been found.

This discourse in John 6. 26-63 is not infrequently referred to or quoted in popular theological writings as if its subject matter was definitely and solely eucharistic. Thus, for example, the words of *v.* 53, "Except ye eat the flesh of the Son of man and drink his blood, ye have not life in yourselves", have been used to support the statement of the Church Catechism that the Lord's Supper is, with Holy Baptism, generally necessary to salvation. Perhaps some of those who use John 6 in this way are not conscious of the logical outcome of their position. Is it really maintained that at an early stage in his ministry the Lord delivered, in the circumstances outlined in John 6, a discourse referring *solely* to a Sacrament which had not yet been instituted? If not, it would seem to follow that *either* the discourse is entirely the composition of the Evangelist, giving his views on the Sacrament, *or* a discourse of the Lord, delivered later on in the ministry, say, at the Last Supper, has been misplaced chronologically by the Evangelist,[4] as there is reason to believe he has misplaced other parts of the Gospel. With regard to the first of these alternatives, it is, I think, generally agreed that the discourses to be found in this Gospel bear the impress of the thought and spiritual experience of the Evangelist. But it does not follow that this

[1] i. 209f.   [2] John 3. 34.   [3] John 6. 63.
[4] J. H. Bernard holds that this is so of *vv.* 51^b-58.

particular discourse or any of the others does not contain the thought and mind of Jesus as expressed in the days of his ministry, however much its present form may be due to the circumstances of its transmission. That Jesus spoke of himself as the bread of life cannot be antecedently impossible for a Christian to believe; and—this being granted—that he went on to expound the meaning of this claim is wholly probable. It is a very drastic position to take up—and, if I may add, quite uncalled for—that John 6 reflects merely the mind of the Evangelist and ideas current at the end of the first century, and has no historical connection with the teaching of Jesus. It is also difficult to see why it is taken up by some who claim to have the interests of eucharistic doctrine as their main concern. Westcott is not too emphatic when he says: "To attempt to transfer the words of the discourse with their consequences to the Sacrament is . . . to involve the history in hopeless confusion."[1]

May we then hold that what we find in John 6 is really a discourse uttered at the Last Supper, but placed in its present position by the Evangelist with his customary chronological indifference? Is it a transference parallel to that of the accounts of the bestowal of the Spirit and of the cleansing of the Temple? Neither of these examples is really analogous. The occasion when the Holy Spirit was given is, as we believe, correctly stated by St. Luke, as at Pentecost; if St. John wished to include in the Gospel a mention of it, he could only do so by placing it in the position it occupies, as an incident in the post-Resurrection appearances. It is not a case of transposing an incident from one part of the ministry to another. The cleansing of the Temple is a detached episode, not necessarily connected with any particular context, and may well have circulated in primitive circles in different contexts; that it occurred at a Passover is, however, common to both traditions. Further, in both contexts, this incident is set over against the opposition of the Jews. But to suppose that the discourse in John 6 belongs properly to the Last Supper is a much more drastic assumption. This discourse has a context which suits it admirably, and out of which it naturally springs—the feeding of the five thousand. Again, it is part of a discussion in which Jesus takes part with those who adopt a

[1] *Speaker's Commentary*, 113.

critical and hostile attitude towards him, and its character is largely affected by this consideration; but at the Last Supper the audience was the most intimate group of his disciples. Thus, the transference would involve not only chronological but also spiritual issues. The same observation may be made more particularly to Bernard's suggestion[1] that at any rate *vv.* 51-58 may be a record of words spoken by our Lord at the Last Supper. St. Luke tells us that there was contention then among the disciples, as to which of them should be accounted greatest.[2] But no hint is given of an argument either among themselves or with the Lord about the meaning of the sacramental gift, or that the harmony of the gathering was affected by the mysterious words "This is my body", "This is my blood". But this is precisely what happens in John 6. The Jews and certain of the disciples are scandalized at the teaching "Except ye eat the flesh of the Son of man and drink his blood, ye have no life in yourselves"; and this contention spreads to our Lord's followers (though not to their inner circle), so that some of them definitely part company with him. "The theme of the discourse is, therefore, unbelief and faith"[3]; and by this test the Twelve are ultimately distinguished from the other disciples and the unbelieving Jews.

The Johannine context, therefore, of the discourse on the bread of life cannot be transferred to that of the Last Supper without difficulties of a kind to which the Evangelist would have been more sensitive than to merely chronological questions. But, needless to say, John 6 raises difficult questions of another kind, common to all the discourses in the Fourth Gospel; as, for example, those which arise from the general style of speech, and from the open references by our Lord at an early stage in his ministry to his sacrificial death and his pre-existence. And just because they are common problems, the critic does not eliminate them by transferring verses or chapters here and there, so as to make the Gospel into what he thinks is a more convincingly historical order. Hoskyns well says on this point: "The dislocation of the discourse on the assumption that it is possible to separate an original stratum from later interpolations is only a learned method of saying that a scholar is unable to penetrate

---

[1] p. clxx.   [2] 22. 24.   [3] Hoskyns, i. 324.

the author's meaning, and prefers to substitute two or more disjointed fragments for one homogeneous whole."[1] We cannot fully solve the problem of this or any other discourse in the Fourth Gospel, because we are unable to enter into the inner experience of the Evangelist and what a long life of Christian discipleship has meant to him. But in this particular discourse it is reasonable to suppose that what he knew of Christ through eucharistic worship would find a place in his account of the feeding of the five thousand as illustrating the general theme that Christ is the bread of life. Hoskyns indeed suggests that at the primitive eucharist there would be a reference not only to our Lord's words at the Last Supper but also to what he said at the feeding of the five thousand. But of this we have no evidence. No doubt at the eucharist primitive Christians, and especially those who had been eyewitnesses of his ministry, would be recalled in memory to more than one occasion when he had presided at a common meal and with characteristic action blessed, broken and distributed the loaf.[2] Among such occasions would stand out pre-eminently the present one. But if John intended to connect this incident definitely with eucharistic worship, his singular omission to mention that our Lord *broke* the loaves is difficult to understand. "Thus, in this particular, the Johannine narrative of the feeding of the five thousand is less suggestive of the action of Jesus at the Last Supper than are the Synoptic narratives of the same miracle."[3]

The view we take, then, is that the discourse is based on teaching originally given by our Lord on the occasion to which it is attached in the Gospel. It is presented in the characteristic style of the Evangelist, who has so received, reflected upon and assimilated the teaching of Jesus that it has become part of himself, and when given back again to the world it is given in a form of words in which it is impossible to distinguish between what the Holy Spirit has taught him concerning the inner meaning of the teaching and the original teaching itself. In the particular instance of the discourse on the bread of life this inner meaning has been deepened for the Evangelist through eucharistic worship; and if we are to pick out phrases here and there which point to this fact,

---

[1] i. 345. [2] See p. 41. [3] J. H. Bernard, i. 179.

it will be such expressions as the italicized words in "he that believeth on me *shall never thirst*",[1] and "he that eateth my flesh *and drinketh my blood* hath eternal life",[2] not because these words demand or should receive an exclusively eucharistic reference, but because they do not arise naturally from the miracle in question (in which it is not said that Jesus provided anything but food), or from the claim of Jesus to be the bread of life. In point of fact, in the fourth chapter, generally and without a sacramental reference, Jesus claims to give the water which if a man drink he will never thirst[3]; and the earliest reference to the "flesh" and "blood" of John 6—that of Ignatius, *Romans* 7— places upon the language no exclusively eucharistic significance: "I desire the bread of God, which is the flesh of Christ, who is of the seed of David; and as a draught I desire his blood, which is love incorruptible." On this Lightfoot says: "The reference here is not to the eucharist itself but to the union with Christ which is symbolized and pledged in the eucharist. Obviously any limitation to the actual reception of the eucharistic elements and the blessings attendant on such reception would be inadequate; for Ignatius is contemplating the consummation of his union with Christ through martyrdom. The indirect reference to the eucharistic elements is analogous to that which our Lord makes in John 6."[4]

The concluding words of this quotation indicate the broad lines on which serious commentators interpret this discourse— namely, of feeding on Christ in general, of which the eucharist is a special means. Thus Westcott says that the "central subject is Christ, truly man, the source and support of life".[5] What is said of "eating" and "drinking" "cannot refer primarily to the Holy Communion; nor again can it be simply prophetic of that Sacrament. The teaching has a full and consistent meaning in connection with the actual circumstances, and it treats essentially of spiritual realities with which no external act, as such, can be co-extensive. The well-known words of Augustine, *crede et manducasti*, 'believe and thou *hast* eaten,' give the sum of the thoughts in a luminous and pregnant sentence. But, on the other hand, there can be no doubt that the truth which is presented in its absolute form in these discourses is

[1] 6. 35. [2] 6. 54. [3] 4. 14.
[4] *Apostolic Fathers*, Part II, vol. ii, 226. [5] *Speaker's Commentary*, 112.

presented in a specific act and in a concrete form in the Holy Communion; and yet further that the Holy Communion is the divinely appointed means whereby men may realize the truth."[1] Bernard apparently takes a somewhat similar line to Westcott: "the discourse as a whole, and especially its third section, is couched in eucharistic language. John's doctrine of 'feeding' on Christ is, indeed, a spiritual and mystical doctrine; but it is not doubtful that he means, in *vv.* 51-58, to suggest that at any rate one mode of thus 'feeding' on Christ is through the sacrament of the Holy Communion."[2] The lines of Hoskyns's interpretation[3] are less clear. His main point is that it is a mistake to distinguish sharply between sacramental feeding and feeding upon the teaching of Christ, since primitive eucharistic worship contained both. It would thus seem that he places the entire meaning of the discourse within the ambit of the eucharist, while insisting that at the eucharist more than one means of feeding on Christ are provided. This is a less comprehensive view than that of Westcott, for example. But on the other hand Hoskyns also writes[4]: "*The living bread* or *flesh* is to the author of the Gospel a comprehensive symbolical phrase containing a whole series of suggestions"; and on the whole his language (so far as we have been able to fathom its meaning) is patient of a wider interpretation than might at first appear. C. J. Wright in *The Mission and Message of Jesus*[5] expresses in a more modern way the lines of interpretation adopted by Westcott, and like him quotes Augustine's *crede et manducasti* as expressing the meaning of the Evangelist.[6]

The bearing upon eucharistic doctrine of an adequate interpretation of John 6 is manifest. Let us endeavour, therefore, to gather together the main elements in the problem set by the discourse it contains. If we are prepared to throw history to the winds, then it is possible to regard this chapter as reflecting only ideas current at the end of the first century, and to interpret it of the eucharist alone. This seems to have been in the main the position of Renan.[7] It is strange that some writers who are

[1] *Ib.*, 113. [2] p. clxvii. [3] i. 323, 343ff.
[4] i. 345. [5] pp. 694f., 775ff.
[6] For the views of a "classical" Anglican divine, see extracts from Jeremy Taylor in NOTE at end of chapter VIII.
[7] Hoskyns, i. 23.

foremost in rejecting "liberal" theology as already outmoded and discredited, should apparently be ready to follow it on this point. But we are not furthering the interests of sacramental doctrine by an indifference to the "history" of the Gospels; and to treat chapter 6. 26-65 as revealing the mind of John only[1] is an inconsistent position for those to take up who aim at exalting the Sacrament among the ordinances of the Church. On the other hand it is impressive to note that the historical element in the Fourth Gospel has been duly recognized by all the important commentaries in English that have been written since Westcott's. The Fourth Gospel, equally with the Second, is the Gospel of Jesus Christ. It is also the Gospel according to St. John. And this author has so distinctive a personality and method that they are impressed upon everything he wrote. But the same is true, although less markedly, of the other Evangelists, from whom John differs in this respect in degree rather than in kind. Our approach, then, to the discourse on the bread of life is one that looks to find in it both "history" and "interpretation". And on both counts a broad concept of the idea of feeding on Christ is reasonable and to be expected. If we have regard to the historical occasion of the discourse, to the stage in the ministry at which it took place, and to the audience to which it was addressed, as well as to him who spoke it, the notion of limiting its application to a particular rite, not yet instituted, becomes incredible on every ground. "I am the bread of life" is co-extensive in its application with "I am the light of the world" and "I am the resurrection and the life". Again, if we have regard to him who has recorded the discourse, we shall equally be indisposed to an exclusively sacramental interpretation. The author of the Fourth Gospel was a mystic. "Persons of this temperament are, in the conduct of their spiritual life, so independent of the ordinances of religion that while they seek and find communion with God in eucharist and public worship, the fact that they know they can enjoy this blessed experience at all times and in all places necessarily puts things of the exterior senses into a subordinate place in their minds."[2] A mystic stands for direct and unmediated communion with God. He is therefore not a person who can acquiesce in any

[1] F. L. Cirlot, *The Early Eucharist*, 122-130, apparently does so.
[2] N. J. D. White, *History of the Church of Ireland* (ed. W. A. Philipps), i. 105f.

view which circumscribes the ways in which God may be found
and enjoyed. He would doubtless repudiate the notion that he
disparages the recognized means of grace; nor does he, as a rule,
do so. But what he would repudiate is the notion that a man is
shut off from communion with God unless he seeks it in some
particular way. From this point of view, therefore, a broad
interpretation of John 6 seems to be in accordance with the mind
of the writer, and a restricted and exclusively sacramental interpretation exceedingly unlikely to be so.[1]

It has indeed been argued that v. 63, "It is the spirit that
quickeneth; the flesh profiteth nothing: the words that I have
spoken unto you are spirit, and are life", indicates a point of view
depreciatory of sacramental observance, or at any rate critical of
certain materialistic views of the eucharist. In any case it is a
problem of interpretation to harmonize this verse with the
realistic language, about eating the flesh of the Son of man and
drinking his blood, which has preceded it.

A solution to this problem has been sought in different ways.
On the one hand, "eating the flesh" and "drinking the blood" of
the Son of man has been interpreted as referring solely to his
teaching, which gives meat and drink to the faithful. Thus this
passage is brought into harmony with v. 63, "the words that I
have spoken to you are spirit, and are life." On the other hand,
it is held that the realistic language of vv. 51-58 is to be read with
the eucharist in mind, but that v. 63 is to be applied to the discourse as a whole (taking also into view v. 68, "thou hast the
words of eternal life") and to its exposition of sacrificial redemption.

This diversity of interpretation indicates that the conditions
under which the Evangelist wrote were complex—I mean that
the dangers or misapprehensions to which the Christians of
St. John's circle were subject were of different and perhaps
opposite kinds. Clearly, one such danger was the presence of
"Gnostics", who denied a real Incarnation. To these persons
St. John opposes the statement that "Jesus Christ is come in the
flesh."[2] His controversy with these people appears most evi-
dently in the Epistles; but the Gospel also, with its central dogma

---

[1] See, further, the NOTE on Early Patristic Interpretations of John 6 at the
end of this chapter.

[2] 1 John 4. 2; 2 John 7.

the Word became flesh, must be read with this background in mind. Further, Ignatius says of certain docetic Christians in his day that "they abstain from eucharist and prayer because they do not acknowledge that the eucharist is the flesh of our Saviour Jesus Christ, which flesh suffered for our sins, and was raised by the Father of his goodness."[1] Hoskyns maintains[2] that St. John is dealing with such persons, and indeed suggests that the Evangelist likens them in their apostasy and unbelief to Judas (6. 70, 71). They were, in Hoskyns's view, desirous of a "more purely spiritual religion"; and the rejection of the eucharist was a logical and consistent sequel of their tenets.

But the facts must be correctly and fully stated before the matter can be seen in its true light. It would appear that the heretics in question did not altogether abstain from the Sacrament, but that they held a eucharist of their own apart from that of the Church. This Ignatius did not allow to be a "valid" (βεβαία) eucharist[3]; and accordingly he asserts that "they abstain from eucharist *and prayer*" (i.e., the prayer that accompanies the eucharist as celebrated by the Church in contradistinction to schismatical worship).[4] This fact affects the assumption that there were in St. John's day advocates of a purely "spiritual" religion who rejected sacraments or at any rate eucharist *in toto*. Further, the heresy which formed a background to St. John's writings had as a common tenet in its varying forms the belief that *matter was essentially evil*, not simply that a sacramental religion was less pure than "spiritual" religion. It is essential to keep this in mind when considering the point in question. The Fourth Evangelist was bound to attack a heresy based on this fundamentally false assumption, which ruled out the possibility of a real incarnation—namely, that Jesus Christ was come in the flesh. But it does not necessarily follow that to oppose this heresy involved the holding of "realistic" views concerning the eucharist. All orthodox folk to-day are agreed that the tenets of Christian Science are incompatible with Christian belief concerning the Incarnation and the Atonement, on account of what Christian Science holds about "matter". But a critic of Christian Science need not necessarily be a strong sacramentarian, and very often is not, without thereby incurring

---

[1] *Smyrn.* 6.   [2] i. 341.   [3] *Smyrn.* 8; cp. *Philadelph.* 4.
[4] Lightfoot, *Apostolic Fathers*, Part II, vol. ii, 306.

inconsistency. That St. John regarded the docetists as pernicious heretics does not, therefore, tell us anything about the precise nature of his sacramental beliefs.

Moreover, although united in a common theory concerning "matter", the Gnostics varied much among themselves, and indeed pursued diametrically opposite courses, when they came to put theory into practice. On the ethical side, some of them maintained a rigid asceticism (as it might seem they were logically bound to do), while others, cultivating an entire indifference to, and independence of, the world of sense, fell into the opposite extreme, and abandoned themselves to an unrestrained licentiousness.[1] Similarly, in their attitude towards sacraments, it may be true that some of them eschewed them altogether, or adopted a depreciatory view of them (although the evidence for this is not conclusive); but others appear to have encouraged a "realistic" attitude towards them. Irenæus[2] tells us, for example, of a Gnostic named Marcus, who "pretending to consecrate ($\varepsilon \dot{v} \chi \alpha \varrho \iota \sigma \tau \varepsilon \tilde{\iota} v$) cups mingled with wine, and protracting to a great length the word of invocation, makes them appear purple and red, so that it may seem that Charis[3]—one of the transcendent powers—is dropping her own blood into that cup by means of his invocation, and that those present should be filled with intense longing to taste of the draught, in order that upon them also may be showered Charis invoked by the agency of this magician". Other references to magical ideas and practices on the part of the Gnostics in connection with the eucharist are to be found in F. Legge, *Forerunners and Rivals of Christianity*, ii. 378. That these, as well as the references to Ignatius, are later than the time of the Fourth Gospel, does not preclude us from supposing with good reason that at the end of the first century there was a "magical" or "realistic", as well as a "spiritual", attitude towards the eucharist on the part of "Gnostic" Christians.

When we turn to the Fourth Gospel itself, we can detect this double tendency towards the nature of Christianity as a whole, and not simply in regard to the sacraments. St. John is fighting on a double front. Against those who would separate Christianity from history and make it merely a system of ideas, he opposes as a

---

[1] Lightfoot, *Colossians*, 77f.   [2] i. 7. 2 (ed. Harvey).
[3] A Gnostic æon—not the Christian gift of grace.

central doctrine the Incarnation, in the Gospel and even more especially in the Epistles. On the other hand there is a marked emphasis in the Gospel upon the dispensation of the Holy Spirit, which forms the climax to which the Incarnation and the Cross lead up, and provides the sphere in which the disciple attains to his high calling as a son of God. This will appear more clearly from an examination and comparison of several passages in the Gospel.

Chapters 2, 3, 4 may be looked upon as containing a group of incidents in which *water* is a prominent feature. At the marriage feast of Cana in Galilee the water spoken of belongs solely to the natural order. By means of it Jesus enriches human life on the earthly plane. The disciples, indeed, see in it a sign of his power, and "believe"[1] on him. But we do not pass, in this episode, outside the "flesh". Jesus ministers "to the fulness of human joy in one of its simplest and most natural forms".[2] In chapter 3[3] water appears under quite a different aspect. It is used in baptism both by John the Baptist and the disciples of Jesus; and in the discourse between Jesus and Nicodemus "water and spirit" are closely conjoined as the instrument of the new birth.[4] Water, therefore, has a "symbolical", perhaps we may even say a "sacramental" significance. It is a sign of something higher, to which it points by a natural and easily understood analogy. In the fourth chapter a further stage is reached. Here the water in Jacob's well is not enriched by Jesus, but is merely used to satisfy human thirst. Nor is it symbolical of inward cleansing, but is spoken of *in contrast to* what is purely spiritual. "Everyone that drinketh of this water shall thirst again: but whosoever drinketh of the water that I shall give him shall never thirst; but the water that I shall give him shall become in him a well of water springing up unto eternal life."[5] Of this water the woman of Samaria is unable to form any conception whatever, for her thoughts lie solely in the natural order: "Sir, give me this water, that I thirst not, *neither come all the way hither to draw.*" The future tense in *v.* 14, "I shall give him" ($\delta\acute{\omega}\sigma\omega$), points forward to the gift of the Spirit: and the passage is closely paralleled in 7. 37-39, where there is a similar looking forward to the coming of the Holy Spirit under the figure of living water. Thus, in

[1] 2. 11.   [2] Westcott, *ad loc.*   [3] Including 4. 1, 2.   [4] 3. 5.
[5] 4. 13, 14.

chapters 2-4 we are led, by means of the concept "water", from the purely natural, through the symbolical, to the spiritual and eternal *simpliciter*.

In chapter 5 we may discern a like progression of ideas. Jesus heals bodily infirmity of long standing (*vv.* 1-9). This healing is symbolical of the healing of the soul[1] (*v.* 14). Finally, Jesus proclaims that he raises the spiritually dead (*v.* 25).

In chapter 9 Jesus heals physical blindness (*vv.* 6, 7). The healed man receives spiritual vision also, sees in Jesus the Christ, and worships him (*vv.* 35-38). And this leads on immediately (*v.* 39) to a statement of the purpose for which the Son of God came into the world—"with a view to that ultimate decision ($\varkappa\varrho\iota\mu\alpha$) which shall distinguish man from man" according to his spiritual vision or blindness (Bernard). "The blind man, who has passed from Judaism to Christianity, passes out of the story as the typical believer, the worshipper of God in spirit and in truth. This is the climax of the narrative and the purpose for which it was told" (Hoskyns). It is clear that in this chapter and in chapter 5 the complete fulfilment of the thought can only be attained—raising the spiritually dead, in the one case, and distinguishing between good and evil, in the other—when the presence of Jesus in the flesh has given place to the presence of the Holy Spirit, the local and the temporal to the ubiquitous and the eternal.

Chapter 20. Mary Magdalene (*vv.* 11-18) recognizes the Risen Christ as her Friend and Master, but only when he addresses her by name. Her thoughts even then are on the earthly plane, and need to be directed higher: "Cling not to me; for I am not yet ascended unto my Father." Thomas also (*vv.* 26-29) recognizes the Risen Christ when he sees him, and in the end reaches a higher point than did Mary Magdalene: for he addresses Christ not as "My Master" but as "My Lord and my God". There is, however, a still higher stage which Thomas did not attain to— the spiritual vision of the unseen Christ (*v.* 29: "Jesus saith unto him, Because thou hast seen me, thou hast believed: blessed are they that have not seen, and yet have believed"). This is the conclusion of the Gospel proper, and the climax to which it leads up.

---

[1] "The healing was incomplete till its spiritual lesson was brought out clearly": Westcott, *ad loc.*

In each of these passages or groups of passages there are three clearly marked levels which rise one above the other—the natural order, the spiritual order revealed through the natural order, and the spiritual order which may be perceived only by faith. In each of these orders Jesus is Lord. In the first of them, he enriches human enjoyment, heals the infirm body, restores sight to the blind eye, and even when risen from the dead assumes the old manner of bodily intercourse with a friend. In the second stage, water is not simply water, but symbolizes a spiritual cleansing; Jesus is no longer the healer of men's bodies, but through such healing is revealed as the healer of the soul; and the Risen Christ, though seen with the bodily eye, is perceived to be more than man. In the third and final stage, we reach the region of pure spirit: water is no longer a physical substance, but the ever fresh supplies of the Holy Spirit renewing and invigorating the soul; the spiritual mission of Christ is proclaimed absolutely and in itself; and the Risen Christ is perceived for what he is by the eye of faith alone.

That this third stage is held by the Evangelist to be the highest stage is clear enough from its context in each of the passages referred to, where it forms a climax of imposing finality. But any doubt on the point is removed by those words of great moment for the understanding of the Gospel which are recorded in 16. 7: "*It is expedient* for you that I go away: for if I go not away, the Comforter will not come unto you; but if I go, I will send him unto you." The force of the words *It is expedient* cannot be made light of, and still less can it be ignored. The Lord weighs his visible presence against the invisible presence of the Spirit, and decides in favour of the latter. This is always the meaning of "it is expedient" (συμφέρει) as used in the Gospels elsewhere[1]: of two alternatives, that one is preferable which is introduced by συμφέρει. Further, the words are addressed to the Apostles who beheld the glory of the Word when he had become flesh and tabernacled among them.[2] The verb "tabernacled" (ἐσκήνω-σεν) denotes a transitory presence, soon to be replaced by the invisible but permanent[3] indwelling of the Spirit. It is not simply that the presence of Christ as revealed in the Spirit in ceasing to be local becomes universal and so adapted to the

---

[1] Matt. 5. 29, 30; 18. 6; 19. 10: John 11. 50; 18. 14.   [2] 1. 14.
[3] 14. 16: "that he may be with you for ever".

world-wide mission of the Apostles. This is no doubt a thought that lies on the circumference of the discourse. But "it is expedient *for you*". The gain is personal to the Apostles, as is made clear in *vv.* 12-33. There is, therefore, a higher blessing than that of knowing Jesus after the flesh; and this, as we have seen, is indicated also in the closing words of the Gospel proper.[1]

When we turn back again to chapter 6, we see that the discourse on the bread of life falls into line, as regards the sequence of ideas, with the other passages examined. The first stage is the feeding of the five thousand. Jesus ministers to the physical needs of the multitude. The bread that he uses for the purpose is multiplied; it is not transformed, as the water at Cana had been: for the incident of feeding is not complete in itself, but is only the first episode in a narrative in the whole of which the concept of bread is to form the main thought. But the multitude are unable to reach even the second stage in which Jesus reveals himself as the bread of the soul (*vv.* 35-51ᵃ). What they saw in the feeding lay merely on the physical plane: it was not to them a sign (σημεῖον) of spiritual truth (*v.* 26). It seems to be implied, however, in *v.* 60, that the disciples could see in the miracle a deeper meaning, although many of them were unable to understand or accept the highest teaching—the third stage—which begins at *v.* 51ᵇ.

. . . the bread which I will give is my flesh, for the life of the world.

52. The Jews therefore strove one with another, saying, How can this man give us his flesh to eat? 53. Jesus therefore said unto them, Verily, verily, I say unto you, Except ye eat the flesh of the Son of man and drink his blood, ye have not life in yourselves. 54. He that eateth my flesh and drinketh my blood hath eternal life; and I will raise him up at the last day. 55. For my flesh is meat indeed, and my blood is drink indeed. 56. He that eateth my flesh and drinketh my blood abideth in me, and I in him. 57. As the living Father sent me, and I live because of the Father; so he that eateth me, he also shall live because of me. 58. This is the bread which came down out of heaven: not as the fathers

[1] 20. 29.

did eat, and died: he that eateth this bread shall live for ever. 59. These things said he in the synagogue, as he taught in Capernaum. 60. Many therefore of his disciples, when they heard this, said, This is a hard saying; who can hear it? 61. But Jesus knowing in himself that his disciples murmured at this, said unto them, Doth this cause you to stumble? 62. If then ye should behold the Son of man ascending where he was before? 63. It is the spirit that quickeneth; the flesh profiteth nothing: the words that I have spoken unto you are spirit, and are life. 64. But there are some of you that believe not.

In 51^b, as Bernard points out,[1] a change of doctrine begins. "For Jesus speaks now, not of himself as the heavenly bread . . . but of the bread which he is, *himself*, to give them *in the future* ($\delta\omega\sigma\omega$, v. 51). This gift is described as his flesh and his blood, which he will give for the life of the world, and which when appropriated by the believer will be the source and the guarantee of eternal life." The $\delta\omega\sigma\omega$ of this verse is paralleled in the $\delta\omega\sigma\omega$ of 4. 14 of the promise by Jesus of the water of life, which, especially when compared with 7. 37-39, clearly indicates the gift of the Holy Spirit; and 6. 51 "the bread which I shall give is my flesh, for the life of the world" does not simply refer to the offering of himself on the Cross, for he goes on to speak of the appropriation by believers of his flesh and blood. We are prepared therefore for a reference to the action of the Spirit, and this we find, preceded by a reference to the Ascension, a few verses later on (vv. 62, 63). Some even of the Lord's disciples are scandalized at the saying "eating my flesh and drinking my blood", and to them he replies "Doth this cause you to stumble? If then ye should behold ($\dot{\epsilon}\grave{\alpha}\nu$ $o\tilde{\grave{\upsilon}}\nu$ $\theta\epsilon\omega\rho\tilde{\eta}\tau\epsilon$) the Son of man ascending up where he was before? It is the spirit that quickeneth; the flesh profiteth nothing: the words which I have spoken to you are spirit, and are life."

The elliptical sentence "If then ye should behold . . .?" has been variously interpreted; and its interpretation is in turn affected by the precise reference which we are to give to the words which precede it: "Doth *this* cause you to stumble?" Most commentators maintain that, while the whole discourse, and especially from v. 51 onwards, was deemed hard to receive, the particular statement which formed an occasion of stumbling was "This is the bread which came down from heaven" in v. 58. An objection to this is that previously Jesus had six times spoken of himself as the bread which came down from heaven (vv. 33, 38, 41, 42, 50, 51). The Jews had murmured at this (v. 41), and he had noted and answered their objection, only to proceed to make a much more difficult assertion (v. 51), that "the bread which I will give is my flesh, for the life of the world." This caused a dispute among the Jews themselves, some apparently dismissing the statement as impossible, others maintaining that there might be some truth in it. The main difficulty was an obvious one for all who like them took the saying in its literal meaning: "How can this man Jesus, who is standing here before us, give us his flesh to eat?" Then Jesus went on to present the statement in a form still more difficult to receive: "Except ye eat the flesh of the Son of man and drink his blood, ye have not life in yourselves." Here the words *and drink his blood*—a grave cause of stumbling to a Jew—are added; and it is now stated for the first time in the discourse that the *only* way to attain to life is by feeding on Jesus.

It is more reasonable to think that the "hard saying" at which the disciples stumbled (v. 60) is this new development in the teaching of the discourse rather than a point which has been present in it all along. No doubt the discourse as a whole was difficult to receive, but the absolute necessity for all to eat the flesh and drink the blood of the Son of man was a staggering, a "scandalizing" claim. The reason why it has been thought that the hard saying refers to the Son of man coming down from heaven is because of v. 62: "If then ye should behold the Son of man ascending where he was before?" But this verse is no mere incidental or explanatory point in the discourse; it and the following verse give the clue to the understanding of the whole, which after the Lord's manner (Matt. 13. 11; cp. 11. 25) is not imparted to the multitude but to disciples only. The Ascension is "the final spiritualizing of the Lord's Person, whereby the offence of the language as to his flesh would be removed by the apprehension of the truth as to his spiritual humanity".[1]

It is commonly supposed that the meaning of v. 62 is that the

[1] Westcott, *ad loc.*

Ascension will make the Lord's language about his flesh *more* difficult to receive, not less. In other words, that the answer to the incomplete question "If then ye should behold . . .?" is "Ye will be still more offended" *not* "Your offence will be removed". This interpretation is opposed both to the run of ideas in the passage, and, as we have seen, to the general teaching of the Gospel. Many of the disciples murmured (*vv.* 60, 61). Jesus spoke of his Ascension (*vv.* 62, 63), and then added (*v.* 64): "But (ἀλλά) there are some of you that believe not." This seems to mean: "I have given you this explanation, bidden you look to the future for the elucidation of my hard saying, but nevertheless I know there are some among you who cannot receive it." On the other hand, if the reference to the Ascension is to make understanding *more* difficult, why does he say "*But* there are some of you that believe not"? Would it not be reasonable in this case to suppose that *all* would be *confirmed* in their unbelief? Again, the general teaching of the Gospel is that the departure of the Lord's visible presence and the consequent coming of the Spirit will make things plain to the disciples which are now obscure (16. 12ff.); and frequently his language had to await this illumination before it could be understood (cp. 2. 22; 7. 38, 39; 12. 16).

The passage in question may profitably be compared with John 20. 17: "Cling not to me; for I am not yet ascended to my Father." Mary Magdalene was told to await the coming of the new order, under which Jesus would through the Holy Spirit enter into a new and vital relationship with his disciples. So here, the disciples are to wait until after he has become a life-giving Spirit, when new light will come to them concerning the meaning of his teaching and in particular of this discourse. To cling to the literal meaning of the words would be like Mary Magdalene clinging to the not yet ascended form of her Master. On the other hand, when the words (ῥήματα: the definite utterances) of this discourse are referred to their heavenly Source ("the words that *I* (ἐγώ) have spoken to you"), they will be set free from the grave-clothes of corruption and quickened into life. And when this—the third and highest—stage is reached by the disciples, when faith through sight has passed into spiritual insight (cp. 20. 29), then the meaning of the whole discourse will be plain to them.

The flesh and blood of Christ, offered on the Cross *for the life of the world* (v. 51), becomes through the Spirit a thing of spirit —that is, a quickening power. Bengel well says on "spirit" in v. 63: "non sola deitas Christi, nec solus Spiritus sanctus significatur, sed universe *Spiritus*, cui contradistinguitur *caro*." We cannot set limits to the channels through which this quickening power may enter the life of redeemed humanity. The *teaching* of Christ (v. 63) has this power when it leads men to *come to Him that they may have life*.[1] Teaching concerning Christ, when it establishes belief in him as the Son of God, will lead men on to *life in his name*.[2] The sacrifice of Christ by itself has the *immediate* power of quickening faith, hope and love in those who apprehend its message of forgiveness and reconciliation: for "I, if I be lifted up from the earth, will draw all men unto myself."[3] And in the eucharist there is, as we believe, a specially appointed means of appropriating the benefits of his passion.

The relation of the sixth chapter of the Fourth Gospel to the Holy Communion is not unlike the relation of the third to Holy Baptism. What the words "born of water and Spirit"[4] were originally intended to convey in their context has been a puzzle to which commentators have brought more learning than light. Doubtless for the Evangelist the thought of Christian Baptism was latent in them. But their *limitation* to Holy Baptism is inconsistent with the passage as a whole. Only a few verses later on the identity of the words "wind" and "spirit" in the original is used to introduce a verbal play upon them, in which Jesus refers to the incalculable and uncontrollable action of the Spirit in those who are "born anew" or "born from above": "The wind (spirit) bloweth where it listeth, and thou hearest the sound thereof, but knowest not whence it cometh, and whither it goeth: so is everyone that is born of the Spirit." "What Jesus here says is that material conditions do not limit, or prescribe, the action of the Spirit of God. The Divine Spirit is always speaking, always acting: not just *here* in this act, or *there* in that place."[5] Similarly, in chapter 6. 62, 63 reference to "Spirit" acts as a corrective of a limited interpretation that might be placed on what had previously been said concerning the bread of life. Thus, both chapters are placed harmoniously within the Gospel as a whole and the general character of its ideas.

[1] 5. 40.   [2] 20. 31.   [3] 12. 32.   [4] 3. 5.
[5] C. J. Wright in *The Mission and Message of Jesus*, 734.

Reference must also be made to 1 John 5. 6-8, although it is too obscure for any certain conclusions to be drawn from it.

> 6. This is he that came (ὁ ἐλθών) by water and blood, even Jesus Christ; not in the water only, but in the water and the blood. 7. And it is the Spirit that beareth witness, because the Spirit is the truth. 8. For there are three who bear witness (οἱ μαρτυροῦντες), the Spirit, and the water, and the blood: and these three are for the one thing (εἰς τὸ ἕν εἰσιν).

The reference in v. 6 is to the historical mission on earth of the Redeemer, marked at its beginning and end by water (his baptism) and blood (the Cross). To this the Spirit, whose function it is so to do, bears continual witness; and he can do this absolutely, because he is the truth (v. 7). Thus, there are three witnesses—an adequate number according to ancient law[1]; which in the life of the Church form an historic present (οἱ μαρτυροῦντες) and tend towards the one object, namely, the establishment of the truth concerning Christ (v. 8).[2] But some commentators, e.g. Westcott following Bede, while emphasizing the definitely historical reference of v. 6, find an extended or secondary reference in vv. 7 and 8 to the sacraments of baptism and eucharist, drawing attention (a) to the change of preposition at the end of v. 6 ("in the water and in the blood"), and (b) to the present participle (μαρτυροῦντες) in v. 8. It is doubtful if (a) can really indicate this: both prepositions "by" and "in" are referred by John to the historic mission; (b) is a more effective point: but the weakness of a sacramental interpretation is that the eucharist is denoted by the word "blood", for which there is certainly no parallel in the New Testament. Therefore, although this secondary reference would bring the Holy Spirit and his work into close connection with the eucharist, in accordance with other Johannine teaching, we cannot think it sufficiently probable to enable us to use it for the purposes of this book.

---

[1] Deut. 19. 15.

[2] See A. E. Brooke, I.C.C., 132-137, who follows mainly these lines.

G

EARLY PATRISTIC INTERPRETATIONS OF JOHN VI

Ignatius

Whether John 6 is referred to or not by Ignatius is a question which turns on (*a*) the occurrence of the phrase "bread of God" (ἄρτος τοῦ θεοῦ) in one or two places; (*b*) his use of "flesh" (σάρξ) where we might have expected "body" (σῶμα); (*c*) the combination of "flesh" and "blood" in a certain passage.

(*a*) (1) *Romans* 7: "I desire the bread of God, which is the flesh of Christ, who is of the seed of David; and as a draught I desire his blood, which is love incorruptible." On this, see Lightfoot's comment, quoted on page 79. The desire of Ignatius is for a consummated union with Christ through martyrdom. The expressions therefore cannot have an exclusively eucharistic reference.

(2) *Ephesians* 5: "If anyone be not within the altar,[1] he lacks the bread (of God)." As the words "of God" are textually somewhat doubtful the reference to John 6 is uncertain. See Lightfoot's note. He holds that eucharistic bread "is not exclusively or directly contemplated, but only taken as a type of the spiritual nourishment which is dispensed through Christ". The "bread" is "the spiritual sustenance which God provides for his people".

(*b*) (1) *Philadelphians* 4: "Be zealous therefore to use one eucharist: for there is one flesh (σάρξ) of our Lord Jesus Christ, and one cup (ποτήριον) for union with his blood." J. H. Bernard (*St. John*, vol. i, p. clxviii) argues that this is an allusion to John 6 because σάρξ is used "for the body of Christ in the eucharist, as in John 6, a phraseology not found elsewhere in the New Testament". But this begs the question. Dr. Bernard assumes that "flesh" in John 6 means the eucharistic body of Christ—the very thing he is seeking to prove. The use of σάρξ by both writers is quite insufficient to prove that Ignatius had John 6 in mind here. Lightfoot, on the contrary, thinks there is a reference to 1 Cor. 10. 16.

[1] i.e., the precinct of the altar.

(2) *Smyrnæans* 7 (see page 83): "They abstain from eucharist and prayer, because they do not acknowledge that the eucharist is the flesh of our Saviour Jesus Christ, which flesh suffered for our sins." It is gratuitous to assume that the mere use of the word "flesh" in a sacramental connection points to a reference to John 6. Further, "flesh" suits the words that follow—"suffered for our sins"—better than "body" would have done. Cp. 1 Pet. 4. 1.

(c) *Trallians* 8: "Arm yourselves with gentleness and be restored in faith, which is the flesh of the Lord, and in love, which is the blood of Jesus Christ." "The reference is only indirectly to the eucharist. The eucharistic bread and wine, while representing the flesh and blood of Christ, represent also faith and love. Faith is the flesh, the substance of the Christian life; love is the blood, the energy coursing through its veins and arteries" (Lightfoot). Whether this is a reference to John 6 is uncertain. But see a similar passage in Clem. Alex. *Paed.* I. vi. 38. 2 below, where such a reference is explicit.

Both the author of the Fourth Gospel and Ignatius were faced with the docetic heresy. Against it "flesh" would be a natural term to use as a safeguard. Certainly, the use of it by Ignatius does not necessarily involve dependence on John. On the general question of Ignatius's use of the Fourth Gospel, see *The New Testament in the Apostolic Fathers*, 81-83, and B. H. Streeter, *The Four Gospels*, 454f.

Justin Martyr

Apology i. 66: "As Jesus Christ was made flesh ($\sigma\alpha\varrho\kappa\sigma\pi\sigma\iota\eta\theta\epsilon\iota\varsigma$) and had both flesh and blood ($\sigma\alpha\varrho\kappa\alpha$ $\kappa\alpha\iota$ $\alpha\iota\mu\alpha$) for our salvation, so we are taught that of that Jesus who was made flesh ($\sigma\alpha\varrho\kappa\sigma$-$\pi\sigma\iota\eta\theta\epsilon\nu\tau\sigma\varsigma$) the eucharistic food is the flesh and blood ($\sigma\alpha\varrho\kappa\alpha$ $\kappa\alpha\iota$ $\alpha\iota\mu\alpha$)". Here the use of "flesh" rather than "body" in the eucharist is clearly determined by the context: the Word became flesh, and took "flesh and blood"—the ordinary expression for the constituents of humanity. To assume, therefore, as J. H. Bernard does, that there is a reference to John 6 is unwarranted.

Clement of Alexandria

(1) *Paed*. I. vi. 36. 4: "The expression *I gave you to drink*[1] is the symbol of perfect appropriation. For those who are full-grown are said to drink; but babes, to suck. For the Lord says, *My blood is true drink*.[2] In saying, therefore, *I gave you milk to drink* did he not intimate the perfect gladness in the Word who is milk, that is to say, the knowledge of the truth?"

(2) *Paed*. I. vi. 38. 2: "The Lord in the Gospel according to John said symbolically: 'Eat ye my flesh and drink ye my blood,' speaking in metaphor of the clearness of faith and of the eatable and drinkable properties of the promise[3]; by which the Church, compounded as a man is of many members, is refreshed and increased, is welded together and compacted of both elements, of faith, which is the body, and of hope, which is the soul, even as the Lord was composed of flesh and blood. For in very truth the blood of faith is hope, by which faith is held together as by a soul. But when hope has expired it is as if blood rushed forth and the living principle of faith is destroyed." This is a close parallel to Ignatius, *Trall*. viii, above, except that Clement takes the "blood" to indicate "hope", and Ignatius "love".

(3) *Paed*. I. vi. 42. 3: " 'Eat ye my flesh,' he says, 'and drink my blood.' Such is the suitable food which the Lord ministers, and he offers his flesh and pours forth his blood, and nothing is wanting for the children's growth. O amazing mystery! We are enjoined to cast off the old and carnal corruption, as also the old nutriment, receiving in exchange another new regimen, that of Christ, and receiving him if we can, to hide him within, and enshrine the Saviour in our bosom, so that we may do away with the affections of our flesh. But you are not inclined to understand it thus, but perchance more generally. Hear it also in the following way. The flesh figuratively represents to us the Holy Spirit; for the flesh was created by him. The blood points out to us the Word, for as rich blood the Word has been infused into life; and the union of both is the Lord, the food of the babes—the Lord who is Spirit and Word. The food—that is, the Lord Jesus—that is, the Word of God, the Spirit made flesh, the heavenly flesh sanctified."

[1] 1 Cor. 3. 2. [2] John 6. 55.
[3] I follow the text as given by Stählin.

(4) *Excerpta ex Theodoto*, 13: "He is heavenly bread and spiritual food, bestowing life by way of food and knowledge; the light of men, that is to say, of the Church. Those who ate the heavenly bread died, but he who eats the true bread of the Spirit will not die. The Son is the living bread given by the Father to those who are willing to eat: 'the bread which I give is my flesh'—either by which the flesh is nourished through the eucharist, or, which is better, the flesh is his body, which is the Church, heavenly bread, a blessed assembly."

Origen

(1) *On Prayer* xxvii. 2: "True bread is that which nourishes the true man, who is made according to God's image: he who is nourished by this becomes also according to the likeness of the Creator. But what is more nourishing to the soul than the Word or what is more precious than the wisdom of God to the mind of him who receives it; and what is more akin to the rational nature than truth?"

(2) *De Principiis* I. i. 9: "Often the names of the organs of sense are referred to the soul. . . . So we say that it makes use of teeth, when it chews and eats the bread of life which came down from heaven."

(3) *In Lev. Hom.* vii. 5: "With the flesh and blood of his word, as with pure food and drink, he gives drink to and refreshes all mankind."

(4) *In Num. Hom.* xvi. 9: "We are said to drink the blood of Christ not only in the Sacrament,[1] but also when we receive his discourses, in which is found life; as also he himself says, 'The words which I have spoken, they are spirit and life'."

(5) *In Num. Hom.* xxiii. 6: "Let the Jews eat the flesh of the lamb in the carnal sense, but let us eat the flesh of the Word of God; for he himself said, 'Unless ye eat my flesh, ye have not life in yourselves.' That which we have just been saying is the flesh of the Word of God, if only we proffer the nourishment not as 'herbs for the weak' or as 'milk for children.' If we speak the things that are perfect or solid or strong, we place before you the flesh of the Word of God to eat. For where a mystical discourse is put forward, or a dogmatic discourse

---

[1] *in sacramentorum ritu.*

solidly filled with the faith of the Trinity, where the letter of the spiritual law is drawn aside and the mysteries of the age to come are laid open, where the hope of the soul is torn away from earth and is cast heavenwards and placed in those things 'which eye hath not seen nor ear heard, neither have entered into the heart of man': all these things are the flesh of the Word of God." For the thought at the beginning of this extract, cp. Clem. Alex., *Paed*. I. vi. 36. 4, above.

(6) *In Psalm*. xxxvi (xxxvii), *Hom*. I. 2: "The wise man who hears the words of the Lord and does them, he it is who eats that bread which came down from heaven, and Jesus is his food, inasmuch as he feeds on his words and lives by his commandments."

(7) *In Psalm*. lxxvii (lxxviii), *v*. 25: *Man did eat angels' food*. "The Saviour says, 'I am the bread which came down from heaven.' Therefore this bread angels first ate, but now men also. To 'eat' in this passage means to 'know.' For the mind eats that which it also knows, and does not eat that which it does not know."

(8) *In Jer. Hom*. x. 2 (on xi. 19 (LXX)): "Let us cast wood into his bread." Origen interprets the bread (ἄρτος) as the word or teaching of Jesus by which we are nourished.

(9) *In Matt. Comm*. xii. 33: "Every rational soul is fed either on living bread or on dead bread by the opinions good or bad which it receives."

(10) *In Joh*. tom. i. 30: "A distinction must be made between 'bread' and 'vine,' since he says that he is not only the vine but also the bread of life. It may be that as bread nourishes and makes strong, and is said to strengthen man's heart, while wine pleases and gladdens and melts him, so moral lessons, affording life to him who learns them and practises them, are the bread of life; but they would not be called the fruits of the vine. On the other hand, secret and mystical speculations which gladden and inspire ecstasy, which come to those who delight in the Lord and desire not only to be nourished but also to rejoice, are called wine because they spring from the true vine."

(11) *In Joh*. tom. x. 17, 18: "Bread" is any kind of sustenance, according to Origen. To eat the flesh and drink the blood is to partake of the sacrifice of the Lamb of God and to feed upon the Scriptures, especially in their mystical sense.

Cyprian

De Dominica Oratione, 18: " 'I am the bread of life who came down from heaven: if any man eat of my bread, he shall live for ever: yea and the bread which I will give is my flesh, for the life of the world.' When therefore he says that whosoever shall eat of his bread shall live for ever, as it is clear that they live who come in contact with his body and receive the eucharist through communion, so on the other hand we must fear and pray lest any one who is debarred and separated from the body of Christ should remain apart from salvation: for he himself warns and says, 'Except ye eat the flesh of the Son of man and drink his blood, ye have not life in yourselves.' And therefore we ask that our bread, that is, Christ, may be given to us daily, that we who abide and live in Christ may not depart from his sanctification and body."

It will be seen that of these Ante-Nicene Fathers Cyprian is the only one who interprets the words of John 6 exclusively of the eucharist[1]; that in two passages an alternative to a sacramental interpretation is distinctly put forward; and that in several of them feeding on Christ's teaching is the only explanation offered. Further, few will be found to contend that Cyprian is as akin to the spirit of the Johannine writings as are Ignatius, Clement of Alexandria and Origen. A clear insight, therefore, into the general mind of the early Church concerning John 6 emerges from the Ante-Nicene exegesis of this chapter. (In compiling these references I owe much to Harold Smith, *Ante-Nicene Exegesis of the Gospels*, vol. III.)

[1] Note also the formula of the distribution of the Bread as found in the *Apostolic Tradition of Hippolytus*: "The Bread of Heaven in Christ Jesus."

CHAPTER VI

THE EPISTLE TO THE HEBREWS

THE Epistle to the Hebrews is a document which manifestly contains few if any direct references to the eucharist; and yet it is obvious that a great deal of later eucharistic teaching has been based on it. It will be necessary, therefore, to examine the Epistle afresh, not only particular passages of it, but also more especially its general characteristics, in order to discover if the use made of it in this respect has been legitimate.

The author of the Epistle (or sermon, as some have supposed) is generally reckoned as belonging to the Alexandrian school of thought. It is not within the purpose of this book to examine what merit there is in the several guesses which have from time to time been made as to his identity. The solution of the problem is now beyond our reach; and we must reckon with the possibility that its author was a person not mentioned by name in the New Testament. In early times the Western Church, and particularly the Church of Rome, appears to have had some tradition of a negative character about the person who wrote it, which survived long after other parts of the Church had accepted the view that the Epistle was Paul's or Pauline. To the facts supporting this statement, which are easily accessible in any history of the Canon of the New Testament, I add the following, which deserves to be given greater recognition than it has been in the past. Eusebius in the *Church History* iii. 3. 5 says that "it is not right to be ignorant that some have rejected the Epistle to the Hebrews, saying that it is disputed by the Church of the Romans as not being Paul's." But in his translation or paraphrase of the *Church History* made by Rufinus *c.* 400 A.D. this sentence of Eusebius appears as follows: "*I know* that among the Latins doubt is entertained concerning the Epistle to the Hebrews." Rufinus was writing after a recent stay at Rome; and the first person singular indicates the knowledge he had acquired on the spot.

I have elsewhere shown that Rufinus frequently incorporated in his version of the *Church History* materials which he had gleaned as a student or traveller during a busy life.[1] Similarly, in vi. 20. 3, where in the Greek we read that "even to this day among the Romans there are some who do not consider it [i.e., *Hebrews*] to be the Apostle's", Rufinus more emphatically says: "even now among the Latins it is not thought to be the Apostle Paul's." To these facts must be added the clear use of the Epistle by Clement of Rome, and the words in the Epistle itself (13. 24), "They of Italy[2] salute you", as suggesting that the Christians in whose name the writer speaks were a group of disciples in Rome or in Italy. As this chapter will emphasize the *differentia* between *Hebrews* and the teaching of the Pauline Epistles, the view of the early Church of Rome is significant.

Who were the Christians addressed in the Epistle, and what is the situation which it envisages? What may be described as the traditional view of the matter is as follows. The Epistle is written for Jewish Christians who are tempted to relapse into Judaism. They are living in Palestine, familiar with the *cultus* of the Temple, and fascinated by it. A date between 64 and 70 is suggested—i.e., the period of the Jewish war or just before it, culminating with the fall of Jerusalem in 70, which entailed much suffering for Jews and Christians alike. But, it is said, the Levitical service of the Temple is spoken of as still in operation (cp. 8. 4f.; 9. 6, 9; 10. 1ff.; 13. 10ff.); therefore a date prior to the actual destruction of Jerusalem is postulated, say 68, and it is further urged that if Jerusalem had already fallen, the Epistle could not fail to mention it or at least refer to it.

The objections to this view are manifold. 1. A community of Christians living in Palestine in the decade 60-70 must have contained some at least who were eyewitnesses of the Lord's earthly ministry, only some thirty years before; yet the words of 2. 3, "How shall we escape, if we neglect so great salvation? which having at the first been spoken through the Lord, was confirmed unto us by them that heard", point clearly to a second generation of Christians, and so to a later date. 2. *Hebrews* is

---

[1] *Journal of Theological Studies*, xxx, pp. 150-174.

[2] οἱ ἀπὸ τῆς Ἰταλίας. This phrase is ambiguous, meaning either residents in Italy or Italians resident for the time being outside Italy (Moffatt, *I.C.C.*, 247); but in either case connection with Italy is established.

through and through a Greek book; and the Septuagint is the Bible of its author, who is perhaps the best Greek stylist in the New Testament. 3. The tone of the Epistle has long been recognized as Alexandrian. 4. The writer never refers to the Temple at Jerusalem, and in fact neither ἱερόν nor ναός occurs in the Epistle. Throughout the writer speaks of the σκηνή or tabernacle as the *locus* of worship. 5. The employment of the present tense in reference to the Jewish *cultus* does not really demand a date before the destruction of Jerusalem. The writer is simply using the historic present of actions described in Scripture. And, as a matter of fact, Josephus and Clement at the end of the first century, and the author of the Epistle to Diognetus in the second, similarly speak of the Jewish ritual as if still in existence.[1]

We get rid of these difficulties, and reach a more satisfactory view of the matter, when we recall the philosophic standpoint of the writer, and what he is setting out to prove and for whom. His readers *were* in danger of falling away, but not to Judaism. He reminds and warns them that Christianity is the final, perfect, real, or, to use his favourite expression, *eternal* religion; and if they reject this, there is nothing further for them to fall back on. How does he do this? He starts from the presupposition that the visible world is related to the eternal world as shadow is to substance. Here we dwell among types, figures, copies only of reality. And he uses Judaism, and the Jewish worship as embodied in the tabernacle and its ordinances, to illustrate his argument. This appears ostensibly for the first time in 8. 5: "who serve that which is a copy and shadow of the heavenly things, even as Moses is warned of God when he is about to make the tabernacle: for, See, saith he, that thou make all things according to the pattern that was shewed thee in the mount." Cp. 10. 1, "the law having a shadow of the good things to come", and 9. 11, 23, 24. The sanctuary in which the Jewish *cultus* found its culminating point was a sanctuary of this world (κοσμικόν, 9. 1), and κοσμικός is a word carrying with it the idea of imperfection, inferiority, comparable to the holy place *made with hands* (9. 24)—a pattern only of the real, archetypal holy place. This is why the writer chooses the tabernacle as the

---

[1] See Moffatt's note in *I.C.C.*, p. xxii.

representative feature of Jewish worship. The σκηνή was from its very nature impermanent; it lacked foundation; it could be carried about; it was in fact comparable to the tents (σκηναῖς) which the patriarchs chose as their dwelling-place on this earth, because they looked for the city which hath the foundations, whose builder and maker is God (11. 9, 10). The Platonic point of view of the author may have perhaps derived from Philo.

As contrasted with Judaism and its typical, shadowy character, Christianity is the real, eternal, archetypal religion. And this is so because of Christ. He is the pre-existent Son of God, through whom God made the world, the effulgence of God's glory and the very image of his substance (1. 2, 3). He took our flesh and blood (2. 14), but is now returned to the heavenly sanctuary— not to a sanctuary of this world such as the Jewish priests entered, but into heaven itself, before the face of God—having offered an eternal sacrifice in virtue of his divine Being and of his perfect obedience as Man to the will of God. The writer could use Judaism to illustrate his thesis, quite independently of whether or no there were any Jewish Christians among his readers or hearers, for two reasons. First, the Old Testament was common ground on which all Christians could meet. It was the Scriptures and the only Scriptures. The Septuagint was the Bible of the new society which arose and developed in a world in which the Greek in which it was written was the common language, ἡ κοινὴ διάλεκτος. The writer or preacher could use and appeal to it, whatever type of Christian audience he was address-ing. This point has been illustrated afresh by the recently dis-covered Homily on the Passion by Melito, Bishop of Sardis (died before 190). Melito deals at length with the Passover as a pre-figurement of the Passion. He quotes freely from the Old Testament, but actually there is no direct quotation from the New. This shows that a Gentile Christian preacher, addressing a Greek audience, could take for granted in his hearers the facts of the Old Testament narrative, and assume that they would find in them an adumbration of the Gospel. The possibility, therefore, must be reckoned with that the title Πρὸς Ἑβραίους is a misnomer,[1] added at a later date by those who were impressed,

---

[1] But Ἑβραῖοι does not necessarily connote the use of Hebrew as a language; see Moulton and Milligan, *The Vocabulary of the New Testament, s.v.*

superficially, by the frequent references in the Epistle to the Old Testament sacrifices and priesthood, and consequently imagined that it must have been addressed to Christians who had been Hebrew-speaking Jews before their conversion or at any rate born in Judaism. "There may have been Christians of Jewish birth among his readers; but he addresses his circle, irrespective of their origin, as all members of the people of God, who accept the Book of God."[1]

Secondly, Judaism was, admittedly, the greatest, the truest, of the non-Christian religions. And if *it* was merely a type, a prefigurement, of Christianity, if through it God had spoken merely in divers portions and by divers manners, then Christianity to which it pointed was indeed the perfect, the absolute religion.

We cannot read the Epistle aright unless we have grasped the philosophic standpoint of the writer, that of a Platonic idealist. That is not to say that he is always consistent in applying his philosophical convictions to the verities of the Christian faith. It is true, indeed, that Christianity cannot be brought successfully under any one system of philosophy. "Christianity has always been a religion in search of a metaphysic."[2] But it is not clear how the "real thing" can appear in visible form of flesh and blood in a world of types and shadows, or how "eternal" redemption can be achieved by an act in time, *if we adopt the writer's standpoint*. Nor, again, should we expect in an idealist of his school so much emphasis on the humanity of our Lord and all that humanity implies (2. 10, 18; 4. 15; 5. 7; 12. 2). The later Alexandrians were at any rate consistent when they passed lightly over this aspect of the Christian revelation. It is worth noting, however, as I remarked above, that the "Platonism" does not appear in actual expression until chapter 8, when he is about to demonstrate the "typical" character of the Jewish *cultus*. Further, if the Christians he was addressing were not of Jewish origin, or if he was not thinking at all of their pre-Christian history, then it follows that his argument from Judaism was of an academic or theoretical kind, and not to be pressed beyond the immediate purpose for which it was introduced. Nevertheless, the writer is faithful to his philosophical

[1] J. Moffatt, *I.C.C.*, p. xvi.
[2] Quoted from Whitehead by O. C. Quick, *Doctrines of the Creed*, 125.

standpoint in the emphasis he places upon certain articles of the Creed and the brief mention he makes of others.

The Resurrection of our Lord is referred to in one passage only, and then indirectly and in phrases borrowed from the Old Testament: "the God of peace, who brought again from the dead the great shepherd of the sheep with the blood of the eternal covenant" (13. 20); and in contradistinction to the risen life of the Lord the days of his earthly ministry are spoken of as "the days of his flesh" (5. 7). This is not to say that he cast doubt upon the Resurrection as an historical event; but he is not concerned with "appearances" of the risen Christ, because his thought is centred upon the Ascension, or rather upon the fact that Jesus has ascended, that he has passed from the visible order into the invisible realities.

Another very significant fact—which is especially relevant to the subject of this book—is the absence, or almost complete absence, of reference to the Holy Spirit and his work. In 2. 4 occurs the phrase πνεύματος ἁγίου μερισμοῖς, "distributions of holy spirit". "There can be no doubt", says Westcott, "that the thought is of the divine gift (πν. ἅγ. not τὸ πν. τὸ ἅγ.) as imparted in several measures by God." Thus it is quite a different conception from that of St. Paul, who speaks (1 Cor. 12. 11) of "the one and the self-same Spirit (τὸ ἓν καὶ τὸ αὐτὸ πνεῦμα) dividing to each one severally as he will". In St. Paul it is the Holy Spirit who divides among men his several gifts; in *Hebrews* it is God who imparts to men in several measures his spirit; the passage says nothing about either the personality of the Holy Spirit or his distinctive working. In 6. 4 there is the phrase μετόχους γενηθέντας πνεύματος ἁγίου. Here again it is not the thought of the personality of the Holy Spirt but of partaking in a divine gift that is prominent. The phrase in 10. 29 τὸ πνεῦμα τῆς χάριτος ἐνυβρίσας goes back to the LXX of Zech. 12. 10, "I will pour upon the house of David . . . the spirit of grace and of compassion"; but here the "spirit of grace" denotes the characteristic quality of the Christian dispensation—namely, that of grace mediated by the Spirit of God. In 9. 14 the A.V. and R.V. are scarcely defensible when they render διὰ πνεύματος αἰωνίου "through the eternal Spirit" in the passage "How much more shall the blood of Christ, who through the eternal Spirit offered himself without blemish to God, cleanse your conscience from dead works to serve the living God?'' The meaning is rather that the offering of Christ upon the Cross, though it took place in time, *belonged to the timeless, eternal order*, because Christ belonged in his divine Personality to the realm of absolute realities (1. 3), and also because the sacrifice was offered in absolute correspondence with the holy will of God and his knowledge of men's needs (10. 9, 10).

There are three passages (3. 7; 9. 8; 10. 15) in which "the Holy Spirit" (τὸ πνεῦμα τὸ ἅγιον) occurs in connection with passages quoted from the Old Testament. In 3. 7 and 10. 15 the Holy Spirit speaks in the words of Scripture, and in 9. 8 he is said to have attached a certain meaning to the ordinance which prescribed that the high priest should enter the holy of holies but once a year. On these Swete says: "the Holy Spirit is here, as in the Old Testament, God himself in operation; God putting a word into the hearts of the legislators, psalmists, and prophets of Israel."[1]

It is thus clear that in *Hebrews* the teaching concerning the Holy Spirit falls very far short of that found in St. Paul or St. John. Why is this? Westcott points to the answer when he says, "It will be observed that the action of the Holy Spirit falls into the background in the Epistle from the characteristic view which is given of the priestly work of Christ."[2] But Westcott does not go on to indicate (what is more significant) *why* the writer lays the emphasis he does upon the work of Christ in heaven. It is apparent, however, that this is due to his idealism. In order that we should partake of the eternal results of an eternal work, we must leave this world of types and shadows for the heaven of reality. And this we can do now, at any rate to some extent, *by faith*. In a recent commentary on this Epistle the eleventh chapter has been described as a "digression".[3] But it is no more a digression than is the thirteenth chapter of 1 *Corinthians*. The eleventh chapter of *Hebrews* describes, under various examples, the life of the person who is convinced that the abiding realities—the city that hath the foundations—lie in the unseen world. Faith is "seeing him that is invisible". By faith, looking unto the ascended Christ, we stand in the heavenly Temple where Christ in his glorified humanity is the eternal

[1] *The Holy Spirit in the New Testament*, 251.　　　　[2] p. 334.
[3] By T. H. Robinson, p. xix.

pledge of the absolute efficacy of his accomplished sacrifice. The problem before the author of *Hebrews*, as before all theologians, is to show how Christ's redemptive work, accomplished once and for all in time, is to be continuously available for those whom he has redeemed. St. Paul and St. John point us to the doctrine of the Holy Spirit, who brings to men the fruits of Christ's redemptive work and by abiding in them makes it efficacious, not now and then, not here and there, but constantly, timelessly. The author of *Hebrews* does not give this answer to the problem. I think he is almost precluded from giving it by his philosophical presuppositions. At any rate, we can see that it would not fit in with his general view of things to conceive of Christ *coming to dwell in men on earth* through the Holy Spirit. His answer to the problem is to bring us up to the heavenly sanctuary, where Christ in virtue of his perpetual presence before the face of God imparts to us the efficacy of his sacrifice. The power by which we are enabled to ascend up into the holy place is faith: through it we creatures of time and sense can reach out and grasp what is invisible and eternal. This faculty existed in all the great heroes enumerated in chapter 11, but reached its highest point in Jesus, "the pioneer and perfecter of faith",[1] on whom our gaze is to be fixed as he sits at the right hand of the throne of God: indeed Christians themselves are now come to (προσεληλύθατε), are even now standing in, the heavenly Presence.[2]

It is in virtue of the eternal redemption wrought by the sacrifice of Christ that Christians are enabled with boldness "to enter into the holy place" (10. 19). But *Hebrews* is singularly silent concerning the means, other than faith, through which the fruits of this sacrifice are made available for those on whose behalf it was offered. The sacrifice is spoken of as having a direct, immediate operation and efficacy: the blood of Christ cleanses the conscience (9. 14), sprinkles the heart from an evil conscience (10. 22). The offering of Christ has "perfected for ever them that are sanctified" (10. 14); and in particular its efficacy is due to the fact that it was offered in absolute correspondence with the will of God (10. 10). The only mediator is Jesus, who ever liveth in heaven to make intercession for us

---

[1] 12. 2: *not* "our faith", as A.V. and R.V.　　　[2] 12. 22-24.

(7. 25). This he does in virtue of his appearance as both priest and victim before the face of God (9. 24). Angels are "sent forth to do service for the sake of them that shall inherit salvation" (1. 14); but how they further men's salvation is in no way suggested: and the context definitely assigns to them a position of inferiority—they are but "ministering spirits" in contrast to the place of honour assigned to the Son. In one passage, however, Holy Baptism appears to be associated with the work of the Atonement (10. 22): "Let us draw near with a true heart in fulness of faith, having our hearts sprinkled from an evil conscience, *and our body washed with pure water.*" There is nothing as definite here as the Pauline doctrine of being "baptized into the death of Christ" (Rom. 6. 4), but the reference to Holy Baptism, if indeed it be such, suggests a connection, or at any rate a parallelism, between the cleansing power of Christ's sacrifice on the one hand and the Sacrament on the other. It is not indicated what efficacy the writer attributed to "laying on of hands" (6. 2), or indeed in what connection the rite was used. "Faith" —with all the wealth of meaning and illustration that the writer attaches to the term—"faith" is the means, above all others, by which the Christian appropriates to himself the finished work of Christ, and by which he is raised to the heavenly place, where Jesus, the object of his faith, is. The Epistle seems to reach a decisive point at the close of the tenth chapter, when the "two ways" of death and life are sharply distinguished: "We are not of them that shrink back unto perdition; but of them that have faith unto the saving of the soul (πίστεως εἰς περιποίησιν ψυχῆς)."

Besides "faith", the need of human effort and co-operation is frequently emphasized in this Epistle. We are to "give diligence" (4. 11; 6. 11, 12); to "draw near" to God (7. 25; 10. 22); "to hold fast the confession of our hope that it waver not" (10. 23); "to lay aside every weight, and the sin which doth so easily beset us" (12. 1). And, on the other hand, with a solemnity and severity perhaps unequalled in the New Testament, the deadly results of wilful sin and of apostasy are described (4. 11; 6. 4-8; 10. 26-31; 12. 15-17, 25).

But there is nothing in *Hebrews* to correspond with the Pauline doctrine of the indwelling of Christ through the Spirit, or of faith-union with Christ. Christians are indeed sharers (μέτοχοι) in Christ (3. 14), and in Holy Spirit (6. 4, see above), as they are in a heavenly calling (3. 1)—i.e., participators in a common blessing; but this is quite a different conception from that of the Pauline "in Christ" or "in the Spirit". Again, in *Hebrews* Christians "bear the reproach" of Christ (13. 13; cp. 11. 26); whereas St. Paul speaks of "the fellowship (κοινωνίαν) of his sufferings" (Phil. 3. 10). We can clearly see, therefore, that there is only a superficial resemblance between the ascent by faith into the heavenly realities, of which *Hebrews* speaks, and the translation into "the heavenlies" referred to in Ephesians 1. 20, 21; 2. 6 (cp. Col. 3. 1, 2). A different theology and method lies behind the two conceptions. In the Pauline we die and are raised together with Christ, and have been made to sit with him in "the heavenlies" by the process of mystical union through the power of the Holy Spirit. *Hebrews*, as we have seen, is silent on the vital point, by what means the redeeming power of Christ is communicated to and made effective for the soul.

In one or two places, however, in the Epistle some commentators have found a reference to the eucharist. Of 10. 22, "having our hearts sprinkled (ἐρραντισμένοι) from an evil conscience, and our body washed with pure water", Westcott says: "The two phrases appear to contain allusions to the Christian sacraments. That to the eucharist is veiled: that to baptism is unquestionable."[1] It is doubtful if even this guarded language is justified. The reference to "sprinkling with blood", which by itself would not naturally suggest the eucharist in any case, is much more applicable to the Atonement itself, in view of 9. 13, 14, where "the blood of Christ" cleanses the conscience, even as under the old dispensation the sprinkling (ῥαντίζουσα) of the sacrificial blood availed to the purifying of the flesh. And we may compare also 12. 24: "the blood of sprinkling (ῥαντισμοῦ) that speaketh better things than that of Abel." Westcott has not been followed on this point by more recent commentators. A more important passage,[2] and much more difficult to interpret,

---

[1] See p. 108 above for baptismal reference.

[2] The following discussion of this passage is taken from an article of mine in *The Expository Times*, vol. LV, no. 11, the publishers and editors of which have kindly given permission for its reproduction here.

is Hebrews 13. 10-16; which must be transcribed in full,
together with the preceding verse.

> 9. Be not carried away by divers and strange teachings: for
> it is good that the heart be stablished by grace; not by meats,
> wherein they that occupied themselves were not profited.
> 10. We have an altar, whereof they have no right to
> eat which serve the tabernacle (ἔχομεν θυσιαστήριον, ἐξ
> οὗ φαγεῖν οὐκ ἔχουσιν ἐξουσίαν οἱ τῇ σκηνῇ λατρεύοντες).
> 11. For the bodies of those beasts, whose blood is brought
> into the holy place by the high priest as an offering for sin,
> are burned without the camp. 12. Wherefore Jesus also,
> that he might sanctify the people through his own blood,
> suffered without the gate. 13. Let us therefore go forth
> unto him without the camp, bearing his reproach. 14. For
> we have not here an abiding city, but we seek after the city
> which is to come. 15. Through him then let us offer up a
> sacrifice of praise to God continually, that is, the fruit of
> lips which make confession to his name. 16. But to do good
> and to communicate forget not: for with such sacrifices God
> is well pleased.

The paragraph vv. 10-16 is the longest in the thirteenth
chapter, which otherwise consists of short counsels and messages
and a benediction. A connection in thought may be detected
running through several of the paragraphs; but the absence of a
connecting particle in the Greek clearly shows where each new
paragraph begins. Thus, for example, all commentators point out
that the subject matter of v. 9 is not unconnected with the
subject matter of vv. 10-16. What they have failed to note is that
the writer regarded v. 10 as beginning a new paragraph—a fact
not without significance.

The case of those who interpret v. 10 of the eucharist is best
presented in the words of Westcott: "Briefly the argument is
this: We Christians have an altar, from which we draw the
material for our feast. In respect of this, our privilege is greater
than that of priest or high-priest under the Levitical system.
Our great sin-offering, consumed in one sense outside the gate,
is given to us as our food. The Christian therefore who can
partake of Christ, offered for his sins, is admitted to a privilege
unknown under the old covenant."

Among the objections which may be offered to this interpretation of the passage are the following. (1) Verse 9 gives the mind of the writer on the subject of religious practices connected with food, the observance of which he strongly disparages; and it is strange that almost in the same breath he should go on to speak of the great privilege the Christian enjoys in partaking of his sacrificial meal. True, verse 10 begins a new paragraph: but we do not expect the writer to say in *v.* 10 the opposite of what he has said in *v.* 9 without giving us some warning. (2) No indication is given in *vv.* 11, 12 that Jesus is to Christians *more* than the perfect sin-offering. If Westcott is right, the writer has failed to mention in these verses what is the chief point in the argument. (3) At the close of the paragraph (*v.* 16), the writer indicates the kind of sacrificial offering he approves—namely, praise to God and service to men; it is *with such sacrifices* that God is well pleased. This is surely quite inconsistent with the view that in *v.* 10 the writer is speaking of a Christian sacrificial meal which he regards as "a privilege unknown under the old covenant".

Those who dissent from the view presented by Westcott usually interpret *v.* 10 as follows: οἱ τῇ σκηνῇ λατρεύοντες simply means "worshippers"—i.e., *Christian* worshippers, referring to the same persons as the subject of ἔχομεν: "the altar of Christian worship is not an altar from which the worshippers of the sanctuary have a right to eat."[1] It follows then that "in real Christian worship there is no sacrificial meal; the Christian sacrifice is not one of which the worshippers partake by eating."[2] This point they find reinforced in *vv.* 11, 12, which speak of the sin-offering—an offering that was *not* eaten by the priest or worshipper—and compare it with the offering of Christ. Finally, the language of *v.* 16 is brought in to reinforce further the argument that the kind of sacrifice which in the mind of the writer God approved was not a sacrificial meal but rather praise and good works. Some even go farther and maintain that the passage is polemical and directed against a realistic view of the Lord's Supper which the author of *Hebrews* noted and was impelled to protest against.

[1] J. M. Creed in *The Expository Times*, L. 13.
[2] J. Moffatt in *I.C.C.*, 234. So also, more or less emphatically, Dods, T. H. Robinson.

While I am prepared to endorse the view that *v.* 10 does not bear the meaning which Westcott and others have read into it, there are several points in the arguments of Westcott's opponents which seem to me to call for criticism. (1) οἱ τῇ σκηνῇ λατρεύοντες is a strange phrase for Christian worshippers. There is no apparent reason why the writer should express himself in this way, or so obscurely. J. M. Creed, in his admirable summary of views on this passage,[1] confesses to "some hesitation" in accepting this interpretation of the phrase, although in the main he approves the point of view of Moffatt and the others. (2) That the author of *Hebrews* should be taken to imply that "in real Christian worship there is no sacrificial meal" is startling and difficult to accept. We may indeed infer with comparative certainty that he was not the kind of person who would set great store by sacramental observances. He was, as Moffatt observes, "a spiritual idealist"[2]. But he might well be this, and yet not prepared to repudiate the Christian eucharist altogether or openly to disparage it. It may be that if he had followed his Platonic idealism to its logical conclusion, he might have been led to this position. But few men, if any, are absolutely logical in applying their philosophical or religious convictions to their actual practices; and, as we see from 6. 1, 2, the author of *Hebrews* had a place for sacramental acts, although he was eager that his readers should not simply rest upon them, but rather go forward in the Christian life to "perfection". Further, we are not justified in assuming too close and intimate connection between *v.* 9, with its disparagement of "meats", and the following verse. In any case, what those "meats" exactly were—whether Jewish food taboos or pagan cult feasts—we do not know. And St. Paul at any rate was able to combine a healthy contempt for "meats" with a deep reverence for and appreciation of the Lord's Supper. These considerations, as it seems to me, should make us pause before we accept an interpretation of 13. 10 which makes the writer assert that no place for the eucharist can be found in Christian worship. (3) It is true that the Jewish sin-offering was not eaten, according to the Law: but it is rather strange, if the object of *vv.* 11, 12 is to emphasize this point and to use it as a parallel with the Christian sin-offering, that the author does not

---

[1] In *The Expository Times*, as above.   [2] *I.C.C.*, 234.

say so in so many words. No doubt it is implied in the statement that the bodies of the victims "are burned without the camp". But he does *not say* "the sacrifice is not for eating."

I venture, therefore, to put forward a modified interpretation of the passage with a view to removing the difficulties I have mentioned. The true meaning of οἱ τῇ σκηνῇ λατρεύοντες is to be seen by a comparison of 8. 4, 5: "Now if he were on earth, he would not be a priest at all, seeing there are those who offer the gifts according to the law; who serve (λατρεύουσι) that which is a copy and shadow of the heavenly things, even as Moses was warned of God when he was about to make the tabers nacle (τὴν σκηνήν): for, See, saith he, that thou make all thing- according to the pattern that was shewed thee in the mount." "They which serve the tabernacle" primarily refers to the Jewish priests, who, by a use of the historic present, could be spoken of in writings long subsequent to 70 A.D. as if they were still functioning[1]; but also in a wider sense to all whose worship is of a sensuous character. This wider, figurative use of σκηνή is compatible with either view concerning the recipients of the Epistle, whether they were Jewish or Gentile Christians, but is perhaps more natural if they were Gentiles and the writer's argument from Judaism was merely academic. σκηνή as used in *Hebrews* always refers to an earthly tabernacle or, as in 11. 9, to the earthly, transitory habitation of the patriarchal heroes of faith. It never means the higher, heavenly tabernacle, unless as defined by ἀληθινή in 8. 2, or μείζων καὶ τελειοτέρα as in 9. 11. To take σκηνή as the *locus* of *Christian* worship, as Moffatt and others do, is to run counter to the ideas which the Epistle associates with the word. The meaning of *v.* 10 is that Christians have an altar whereof they have no right to eat whose worship is sensuous and earth-bound. The writer does not specify exactly what the Christian altar is: but his general meaning cannot be in doubt. Jesus is not "on earth" (8. 4), but at the right hand of the throne of God (12. 2); and the altar is in the sphere of invisible realities, whether it be Jesus himself or Jesus conceived of as high priest and victim. The writer is concerned merely to state the incompatibility between the two kinds of worship, the earthly and the heavenly. His object is negative—to point out

---

[1] See above, p. 102.

that the one kind of worshipper cannot share in the other's worship.[1] He does not tell us whether or no Christians eat of *their* altar. In any case, the metaphor of eating, under the term γεύεσθαι is applied in 6. 4, 5 to partaking generally of spiritual realities; cp. also "taste of death" (γεύσηται θανάτου) in 2. 9.

The object of the two following verses, 11 and 12, is not to show that the Jewish sin-offering and the Christian sin-offering are, neither of them, eaten; still less is it to suggest, as Westcott and also Hicks[2] do, that as contrasted with the Jewish sin-offering the Christian sin-offering *is* eaten; but rather to seize on a detail in the prescribed Levitical ritual[3] which to the mind of the writer was significantly paralleled in the Passion narrative. The bodies of the beasts slain as a sin-offering were burned *without the camp*; Jesus suffered *without the gate*. (It is obvious that there is no parallel in the death of Jesus corresponding to the fact that the bodies of the beasts were burned; and it is not clear what Westcott means by saying that our great sin-offering was "consumed in one sense" outside the gate.) The writer attaches deep spiritual significance to the situation of Calvary in its relation to Jerusalem. It calls us not so much to unworldliness (Moffatt) as to *other-worldliness*. Jesus had left the city, the earthly Jerusalem, behind him when he offered the perfect, eternal sacrifice upon the Cross. We must follow him in this as in all else. "Let us therefore go forth unto him *without the camp*, bearing his reproach. For we have not here an abiding city, but we seek after the city which is to come." The words "bearing his reproach" turn our thoughts back to the example of Moses (11. 23-28), who "accounted the reproach of Christ greater riches than the treasures of Egypt", and remind us that we too are to "endure as seeing him who is invisible". Other-worldliness must govern the spirit of our worship as of all else. Christians also have left behind them the earthly Jerusalem and "are come unto . . . the heavenly Jerusalem . . . and to Jesus the mediator of a new covenant, and to the blood of sprinkling that speaketh better than that of Abel" (12. 22, 24: words from which can be under-

---

[1] Therefore it is unnecessary to ask who precisely, other than Jewish priests, are included in those whose worship is sensuous. It is as if we were to say nowadays that such and such a thing was incompatible with "true religion".

[2] *The Fullness of Sacrifice*, 236. [3] Lev. 16. 27.

stood what and where, in the mind of the writer, the "altar" is). "Through him, then," as he ministers in a tabernacle not of this world, "let us offer up a sacrifice of praise to God continually." And then, as if to indicate that true other-worldliness does not neglect the duties that fall to the Christian in this life, the writer adds: "*But* to do good and to communicate forget not: for with such sacrifices God is well pleased."

The several paragraphs in chapter 13 are concerned, as is fitting in a final chapter (cp. St. Paul, *passim*), with practical exhortations: e.g., in regard to hospitality, care for prisoners, marriage, and so forth. *Vv.* 10-16 are no exception to this; their object is to set out the duty of Christian worship and service. They are not primarily doctrinal; rather, they presuppose the philosophical and theological position taken up in the main body of the Epistle, and especially in its latter portion. Any interpretation, therefore, of *v.* 10 which fails to take this into account must be unsatisfactory.

It is unfortunate that so much eucharistic teaching of a later age should be based upon an Epistle which contributes little or nothing to the subject in question. In view of the great emphasis it lays upon the sacrificial offering of Christ, the writer's silence concerning the eucharist is all the more significant. Again and again he speaks of the blood of Christ or of the covenant, and here would be the place to bring the eucharist in, if he wished to speak of it as a sacrificial meal. But this he does not do; and we must draw the appropriate conclusion. His teaching cannot be brought in to support the view—which, if maintained, must be maintained on other grounds—that sacrificial actions performed at a tabernacle of this world and with material objects have their efficacy because of the concomitant sacrificial action of Christ in heaven. And, further, "the idea of a continuous offering in heaven, which some have read into the Epistle, rests upon mistranslation and misconception of the writer's teachings."[1] "The modern conception of Christ pleading in heaven his Passion, 'offering his blood,' on behalf of men, has no foundation in the Epistle. His glorified humanity is the eternal pledge of the absolute efficacy of his accomplished work. He pleads, as older writers truly expressed the thought, by his Presence on the Father's Throne. Meanwhile men on earth in

[1] J. M. Creed, *op. cit.*

union with him enjoy continually through his blood what was before the privilege of one man on one day in the year."[1]

If in this quotation from Westcott we substitute the words "by faith" for the words "in union with him", we reach a truer account of the matter. The argument of the writer is that we must leave the material, visible world behind and ascend to the heavenly sanctuary, if we are to feed on that sacrifice which was offered once for all, and is eternal because Jesus is in the sphere of invisible realities. Perhaps the most significant and crucial passage is 9. 24: "For Christ entered not into a holy place made with hands, like in pattern to the true [Moffatt: 'a mere type of the reality!']; but into heaven itself, now to appear (νῦν ἐμφανισθῆναι) before the face of God for us (ὑπὲρ ἡμῶν)." The combination of νῦν with the aorist infinitive is unusual, and claims our attention. Moffatt takes νῦν as "now at last", and compares it with "at the end of these days" in 1. 2. Westcott, on the other hand, says: "This combination appears to affirm two complementary truths and to exclude two opposite errors. The manifestation of Christ, in whom humanity is shewn in its perfect ideal before the face of God, is 'one act at once' (ἐμφανισθῆναι); and still for us who work in time it is in the case of each believer a present act (νῦν). There is, to look at the subject from the opposite side, no succession in the fulfilment of his work; and, on the other hand, it cannot in any sense grow old."[2] If we take this passage as Moffatt does, it obviously has no bearing on the matter, but refers simply to the eternal fact of Christ's appearance before God in heaven. If, on the other hand, with Westcott, the νῦν refers to us who live "in time", then the verse assures us, what we are told in other passages in the Epistle, that by faith we may be even now translated into the heavenly sphere and so make new for ourselves the eternal work of Christ and through him have access to the Father. 10. 19: "Having therefore, brethren, boldness to enter into the holy place by the blood of Jesus . . . let us draw near (προσερχώμεθα) with a true heart in fulness of faith." Westcott translates the verb "let us come to God", thus indicating the use of the same word as in 12. 22: "Ye are come to (προσεληλύθατε) the mount Sion . . . and to Jesus the mediator of the new covenant, and to the blood of sprinkling." Cp. also 4. 14-16: "Having then a

[1] B. F. Westcott, *Hebrews*, 232.　　　　[2] *Hebrews*, 275.

great high priest who hath passed through the heavens . . . let us therefore come unto (προσερχώμεθα) the throne of grace with boldness.'' Clearly, in all this the writer's idealism is manifest. "We are no longer in the lower world of matter, but in the higher one of spiritual realities and values."[1]

The Epistle, therefore, is deficient in its teaching both in regard to the Holy Spirit and also to sacramental grace. But it is to be noted that there is one passage in it which contains *in effect* the doctrine of the Holy Spirit as it is set forth in St. Paul and St. John. I refer to the long quotation from Jeremiah[2] concerning the new covenant, which the writer uses in order to indicate the supersession of the old covenant by one based on better promises:

> Behold the days come, saith the Lord,
> That I will make a new covenant with the house of Israel and
>   with the house of Judah;
> Not according to the covenant that I made with their fathers
> In the day that I took them by the hand to lead them forth
>   out of the land of Egypt;
> For they continued not in my covenant,
> And I regarded them not, saith the Lord.
> For this is the covenant that I will make with the house of
>   Israel
> After those days, saith the Lord;
> I will put my laws into their mind,
> And on their heart also will I write them:
> And I will be to them a God,
> And they shall be to me a people:
> And they shall not teach every man his fellow-citizen,
> And every man his brother, saying, Know the Lord:
> For all shall know me,
> From the least to the greatest of them.
> For I will be merciful to their iniquities,
> And their sins will I remember no more.

We can see from 10. 16, 17, where part of the passage is quoted again, that the two points in it which the author of *Hebrews* deemed specially significant were the statement that henceforth the law of God would be written on the heart and

---

[1] T. H. Robinson, *Hebrews*, 189.   [2] 31. 31-34, *ap*. Heb. 8. 8-12.

mind, and the concluding promise concerning the remission of
sins. The first of these, we may not doubt, he related to the fact
that the sacrifice of Jesus cleansed *the conscience* (9. 14; 10. 22);
the latter is the great theme of the Epistle as a whole. Now,
this "new covenant" passage of Jeremiah, to which *Hebrews* gives
such prominence, has been rightly looked upon by many as the
point at which the Old Testament most nearly touches the New.
"Whereas other prophets did much to interpret religion and to
enforce its demands, [Jeremiah] transformed the very conception
of religion itself." "His doctrine was an anticipation of the
Gospel in that it asserted the worth of the individual to God and
the personal character of religion, in its assurance of forgiveness,
its transcendence of legalism, and the inwardness of its ethic."[1]
In other words, it is prophetical of the dispensation of the Holy
Spirit, as might be illustrated from St. Paul's Epistles *passim*;
e.g., 2 Cor. 3. 3, "Ye are an epistle of Christ . . . written not
with ink, but with the Spirit of the living God; not in tables of
stone, but in tables that are hearts of flesh"; and 1 Cor. 2. 9-16
with the concluding words "we have the mind of Christ":
for the "heart" of which Jeremiah spoke is not only the emotional and ethical but also the intellectual life. In particular, the
words "they shall not teach every man his fellow-citizen, and
every man his brother, saying, Know the Lord: for all shall know
me, from the least to the greatest of them" are paralleled in
1 John 2. 20, 27, "Ye have an anointing from the Holy One,
and ye know all things . . . ye need not that any one teach you"—
language which, as we have noted,[2] asserts in the most unqualified
way the fact of the indwelling Spirit.

But the writer is so dominated by his conviction as to the
eternal worth of the sacrifice of Christ, and its power to cleanse
the heart and conscience, that he is silent about the vehicles or
channels by which this grace is communicated to men. The
forgiveness and peace and illumination, which St. Paul and St.
John trace to the indwelling presence of the Holy Spirit, these
for the author of *Hebrews* stream unmediated to the soul from the
heavenly altar, where our great High Priest stands in the very
presence of God. Nevertheless, the general effect of the picture
that the Epistle gives of the Christian in respect of his unrestricted
access to God through Jesus Christ is not very different from that

[1] A. S. Peake, *Century Bible*, vol. i, 46, 47.   [2] p. 71.

of the other apostolic writers; so much so that for long it was regarded in many parts of the Church as Paul's or Pauline: for it is only when we examine it in detail that the differences become apparent. Neither in *Hebrews* on the one hand, nor in St. Paul and St. John on the other, is there any suggestion which limits the approach of the Christian to God to certain times or occasions: the way stands free and open, always and at all times, for the children of God.

CHAPTER VII

IMPLICATIONS OF THE NEW TESTAMENT EVIDENCE

IN his summing up of the New Testament evidence on the subject, Yngve Brilioth[1] distinguishes "three chief ways in which the element of mystery in the eucharist is apprehended. The first is that of the personal presence of the Lord. . . . This is the 'Synoptic mystery-type,' or, *the presence of our Lord as priest.* The second is the 'Johannine mystery-type,' or *the presence of our Lord in the Sacrament* . . . And third, we have noted the mystery of communion-fellowship, whereby those who are united with Christ in the Sacrament are united also with one another and share in the communion of saints, being made one bread, one body, through partaking of the one bread. This might be called the 'Pauline type,' or, *the presence of Christ in his mystical body.* But these three modes of the eucharistic mystery are in no way exclusive of one another: rather they are complementary and necessary to one another."

We are not concerned here to defend the adequacy of this summing up—although it seems reasonable enough if the concluding sentence of the quotation is given its due emphasis—but rather to use it as a starting-point as we consider the significance of the evidence of chapters I to VI of this book. In each of the "types" distinguished by Brilioth, we have seen that the eucharistic doctrine, and in particular the doctrine of the "presence", is placed against a much wider background, of which it forms an integral part. If, in the Synoptic tradition, the Lord feeds his own with the sacred gifts—to use Brilioth's own phrase—he does so in the middle of a meal, the whole of which was eloquent of a host and his guests, or of a family sacrifice at which the head of the house acted as priest. And the union of Christ with his disciples was a union of which the bestowal of the sacred gifts formed the culminating point in a transaction which from

---

[1] *Eucharistic Faith and Practice, Evangelical and Catholic,* 286.

beginning to end testified to a union of heart and will between the Master and his disciples. Again, the Johannine teaching about eating the Lord's flesh and drinking his blood cannot—so we have argued—be interpreted exclusively of sacramental feeding. In this we have the mind of the early Church as expressed through its theologians; and, moreover, apart from the exegesis of the one particular chapter in which the question arises acutely, it is difficult to see how such a restricted interpretation can be maintained when the Gospel as a whole and the general character of its teaching are kept in view. With regard to the third—the Pauline—type, it is the argument of this book that the eucharistic doctrine of the "presence" must be considered in relation to the indwelling of Christ in the members of his mystical body, the Church. We cannot, however, accept the view, which the words of Brilioth might seem to suggest, that in Pauline thought the eucharist makes us members of that body, and therefore partakers of the "presence", in the sense that we are not members of the body and indwelt by Christ independently of reception of the elements at Holy Communion. This would be to run counter to the general Pauline teaching that from the beginning of their entry into the Church all its members are partakers of the Holy Spirit, not on certain occasions only, but for so long as they do not banish him by continuance in wilful sin. And the moment when the divine indwelling begins for each member is not left doubtful: "In one Spirit were we all baptized into one body."[1] All the baptized partake of the indwelling presence of Christ or of the Holy Spirit (for no distinction is made in this respect between the one Person and the Other), as members of the body. The language of 1 Cor. 10. 16, 17 "The cup of blessing which we bless, is it not joint participation in the blood of Christ? The loaf which we break, is it not joint participation in the body of Christ? seeing that we, who are many, are one loaf, one body: for we all share in the one loaf" suggests that the eucharist is a means of renewing our fellowship with Christ and with one another, but it certainly does not teach that it effects this *de novo*. The whole action takes place in "the fellowship of the Holy Spirit"[2]—however we precisely interpret this phrase—in virtue of which the Christian is "in Christ" and Christ is "in

---

[1] 1 Cor. 12. 13.   [2] 2 Cor. 13. 14: see pp. 62-64.

him", as a man is in the atmosphere he breathes, and the atmosphere is in him as enabling him to breathe.[1]

It may be, as some would hold, that we are to distinguish a fourth, eschatological, type of eucharistic teaching in the New Testament—that presented by St. Luke in the shorter text of the account of the Last Supper, and in *Acts*. The difficulties, textual and exegetical, in the Lucan account of what corresponds to the Institution of the Sacrament in *Matthew* and *Mark* are notorious; and it is unlikely that with our present knowledge they can be resolved. We must, however, amplify here what was said in an earlier chapter.[2]

Luke 22. 14-20

14. And when the hour was come, he sat down, and the apostles with him. 15. And he said unto them, With desire I have desired to eat this passover with you before I suffer: 16. For I say unto you, I will not eat it, until it be fulfilled in the kingdom of God. 17. And he received a cup, and when he had given thanks, he said, Take this, and divide it among yourselves: 18. for I say unto you, I will not drink from henceforth of the fruit of the vine, until the kingdom of God shall come. 19. And he took bread, and when he had given thanks, he brake it, and gave to them, saying, This is my body which is given for you: this do in remembrance of me. 20. And the cup in like manner after supper, saying, This cup is the new covenant in my blood, even that which is poured out for you.

Codex D and certain Old Latin MSS. omit 19b (the words after "body") and 20; and two of these O.L. MSS. place 19a after 16. The Peshitto reads 19 and 20 in full, but omits 17, 18. The Old Syriac texts present a complicated problem, differing among themselves.

---

[1] G. Dix, *The Shape of the Liturgy*, 250, states that the Anglican Liturgy "has one remarkable expression" of the doctrine as expressed by S. Thomas Aquinas that the "spiritual benefit" or *res* of the sacrament is "that we are very members incorporate in the mystical Body of thy Son which is the blessed company of all faithful people". The statement is inaccurate. What the prayer asserts is: "thou . . . *dost assure us thereby* . . . that we are very members incorporate", etc. The eucharist supplies to the communicants an assurance, a confirmation of the fact that they are members of the Body.   [2] See p. 22f.

It has been supposed[1] that this passage consists of three separate *strata* of tradition: (1) *vv.* 14-18, the tradition of a primitive community, say at Cæsarea, for whom the breaking of bread was little more than a fellowship-meal pointing to the Parousia; (2) *v.* 19a, an addition by St. Luke himself, taken from St. Mark, containing the words "This is my body"; (3) *vv.* 19b, 20, a further addition, or scribal interpolation, containing the words "This do in remembrance of me" and a reference to the eucharistic cup. While no solution of this *crux* is wholly satisfying, this one seems open to question from more than one point of view. (*a*) There is no textual evidence that *v.* 19a was ever absent from the passage. (*b*) If it was, St. Luke must at an earlier stage in the composition of the Gospel have been satisfied to record an account of the Last Supper which included no reference to the eucharist. This is strange for at least two reasons. His intimacy with St. Paul must surely have made him familiar with the Pauline tradition of the Last Supper recorded about the year 55 or 56, and before the first draft of the Gospel—Proto-Luke—containing the matter L+Q was made, *c.* 60. Even if some of the matter L had been compiled, *c.* 52, before the date of the composition of 1 *Corinthians*, nevertheless the Pauline tradition was delivered to the Church of Corinth by the Apostle when he was among them (*c.* 49-52), and it was not new then. The hypothesis, therefore, that Luke inserted in his Gospel the words "This is my body" only when he became acquainted with *Mark* is unsatisfactory. It may be, however, that with *Mark* before him Luke made some alterations in *v.* 19a (as he did in other parts of the Passion narrative), though retaining the Pauline "gave thanks" in preference to the Marcan "blessed". And, secondly, we would also call in question the sharp distinction made by some modern writers between the eschatological view of the Last Supper, as indicated, e.g., in *vv.* 14-18 and in the action spoken of in *Acts* as "the breaking of bread", on the one hand, and the sacramental, faith-union, conception, of which the words "This is my body", "This is my blood" supply the focal point, on the other. We shall return to consider this later on when we deal with larger issues.[2] But it will suffice here to indicate that the eschatological and the sacramental are by no means mutually

[1] E.g., by V. Taylor, *Jesus and His Sacrifice*, 175ff.; *The Atonement in New Testament Teaching*, 238.   [2] See pp. 171ff.

exclusive, and were in fact combined by St. Paul, who speaks of the eucharist both as a means of communion (1 Cor. 10. 16), and also as pointing forward to the Parousia: "As often as ye eat this bread, and drink the cup, ye proclaim the Lord's death till he come" (1 Cor. 11. 26). Similarly, it is unsafe to interpret the phrase "the breaking of bread" or "to break bread" as used in *Acts* in the sense only of a fellowship-meal and as necessarily excluding the idea of sacramental feeding. No doubt, the phrase does not always bear the same significance: sometimes its connotation is wider, sometimes narrower; but it is difficult, especially in view of the evidence of 1 Cor. 11. 17-34, to suppose that a sacramental observance is not included in the term as used, for example, in Acts 20. 7. In fact, we see in "the breaking of bread" another indication of the truth for which we are contending—namely, that the eucharist is to be placed in the life of the early Church, not in isolation, but in intimate relation with the fellowship which Christians enjoyed in the Spirit with the Lord and with one another. And even if we are to distinguish in the Lucan writings a fourth type of eucharistic teaching, we are not inclined, for the reasons just mentioned, to differentiate it from the Pauline type so sharply as some would have us do; even as we hold that the facts do not justify us in distinguishing sharply the teaching of St. Paul and St. John on the Holy Spirit, on the one hand, from the teaching of the Lucan writings, on the other. It may be that in the early Church Christians were not different in their attitude towards the Sacrament from what they are to-day—I mean, that even with the whole of the evangelical tradition concerning it behind them they singled out one or another feature of it for special emphasis; just as in the modern Church some will give prominence to one of its manifold aspects —Sacrifice, Communion, Memorial, Fellowship—others will lay stress upon another. For example, possibly to the author of *Hebrews*[1] the eschatological aspect was the one that appealed most: "Not forsaking the assembling of ourselves together, as the custom of some is, but exhorting one another; *and so much the more, as ye see the day approaching*" (10. 25). But it is one thing to suggest this, another to suppose that *in a community* one aspect only of the eucharist was recognized, or that there certain parts

[1] In this Epistle occurs the only reference in the New Testament to a "Second" Coming (see 9. 28).

only of the tradition of the Last Supper were known. And—to revert to the passage Luke 22. 14-20—we think, as already stated,[1] that the least unsatisfactory view is to accept the whole of it, including 19b, 20, as Lucan, representing the Pauline tradition (19, 20), together with some other tradition (15-17) of an incident which was not preserved generally, as being insignificant; and that the omission in some texts of 19b, 20 was due to the action of scribes who left out the reference to the eucharistic cup, supposing, wrongly, that it had been referred to in v. 17.

The connection between the eucharistic presence and the indwelling presence of Christ through the Holy Spirit is further indicated when another fact of New Testament teaching is taken into consideration. Vincent Taylor in his *The Atonement in New Testament Teaching* has made it clear that in the teaching of St. Paul and St. John faith-union with Christ and eucharistic union with him are associated; and that, conversely, in *Hebrews* the ideas of faith-union and of eucharistic union are both absent.[2] He goes on to point out that both are also absent in other writings of the New Testament—e.g., 1 *Peter* and *Revelation* (and in his view *Acts* also). This association, or non-association, he holds to be not merely synchronous but also causal; in other words that when faith-union with Christ was a deep and dominating experience the significance of the eucharist as a means of communion with the living Christ was recognized also; and that, conversely, when the idea of faith-union was absent, eucharistic observance fell into the background. This is an important observation and full of suggestion. We would, however, enter one *caveat*. It is dangerous to infer, when we are dealing with occasional writings such as the Epistles of the New Testament, that absence of reference to Christian rites is necessarily an indication of their non-observance or of their inferiority in the mind of the writer. The Epistles were not written in order to give future generations a *conspectus* of the life of the Church at that time. Even in the case of the Epistle to the Hebrews, although we believe that the writer's philosophical outlook would lead logically to a non-sacramental religion, we cannot thereby infer that in practice he was logical; and actually he does refer

[1] See p. 23.   [2] Pp. 98-102, 187, 203, 204.

to sacramental rites other than the eucharist.[1] As regards 1 *Peter*, which Dr. Taylor mentions, if we consider that St. Peter is in any way behind this Epistle, and if further we accept the tradition connecting him with the Second Gospel, we shall not be disposed to believe that the Epistle envisages communities in whose life sacramental communion was absent. But we hold it to be a significant thing that in the Epistles faith-union with Christ and sacramental union with him do *in fact* go together.[2] In pointing out this, Dr. Taylor has made an important observation; and also when he goes on to show that with St. Paul the dominant note of Christian experience is faith-union with the living Christ, and that in this deep and full experience sacramental communion finds its appropriate context and significance. We believe the same is true of St. John. But St. John is more "mystical" than St. Paul and—as we should hold—less "institutional", and accordingly less inclined to give prominence to human or material *media*. In both, the abiding presence of the Holy Spirit is axiomatic.

In any case, whatever differences of emphasis in doctrine or use there may have been in the several parts of the primitive Church concerning the eucharist, when we reach the second century we hear of it as the normal act of worship on the Lord's Day, if indeed Acts 20. 7 does not already indicate this for an earlier date, at any rate in "Pauline" churches. But if we place the eucharist in the position it soon came to occupy in the apostolic and sub-apostolic Church, we must also place it against the doctrinal background of the early Church, and in particular the conviction that Christ through the Holy Spirit is present in the members of the Church, not here and there, not now and then, but constantly, timelessly. The Church has rightly held the fact of the presence of Christ in the Holy Communion to be a matter of great importance, since indeed it is a conviction held in common by Christians of widely different schools of thought, however much they may disagree about the *mode* of his presence. But as a matter of history the truth which all confess has led to errors both of a theological and a practical kind. And we can understand without much difficulty how easily erroneous opinions and consequences might emerge in this connection.

[1] See pp. 110ff. [2] *Id.* p. 241f.

Indeed, some scholars are of the opinion that they can find eucharistic controversy latent in the Fourth Gospel and in the Epistle to the Hebrews.[1] We may believe, however, that the early Church was delivered from many errors on this subject, because for it the sacramental presence was not a thing apart, isolated, or wholly other from the indwelling presence of the Holy Spirit in the Church and its individual members.

The great Christian doctrines are as a rule related one to another. The doctrine of the Trinity would have been misleading, even dangerous, had it not been formulated in a community where there was already a firm conviction as to the unity of God. First came Judaism, then Christianity. The monotheism which the Jews in the process of their religious and theological development were enabled to reach formed an essential foundation for the building thereon of the richer, Christian doctrine of God. When this foundation was neglected, and a Hellenistic conception of God substituted, as it was in later times, by the Arians, a false doctrine resulted, which was only a veiled paganism with its plurality of gods and demi-gods. Again, the doctrine of the Atonement cannot be rightly considered apart from the doctrine of the Trinity and of the unity of the Person of Christ. And as a matter of history certain theories of the Atonement have been false or misleading or defective simply because they have not been based on the foundation of the one God in Three Persons and it has been forgotten that the Persons of the Trinity are one in will and in purpose of love; or, as happened in medieval times, because exclusive attention was paid in such theories to the manhood of Christ upon the Cross. Similarly, the doctrine of the eucharist has often gone astray because it was not placed in the context of the doctrine of the Holy Spirit, and all the more so because this is a fundamental and universally relevant doctrine, and because the Church now lives under the dispensation of the Holy Spirit. And this means, further, that we must place the two doctrines in their proper order, the wider before the more restricted: first, that of the indwelling presence of the Holy Spirit; then, that of the presence of Christ as imparted to recipients of the Holy Communion. This is the New Testament order, and it must not be reversed.

[1] See pp. 82ff., 111ff.

Brilioth has pointed out[1] that this was not forgotten by Anglican theologians of the last century who were connected with the revival of a sacramental religion.[2] And—to come to more recent times—at the Conference on Reservation held at Farnham Castle in 1925, the fact of Christ's presence in his Church was frequently mentioned as of importance in relation to the fact of his presence in the eucharist.[3] But it was only touched upon, and never seriously discussed by the distinguished theologians who took part. Some of them, however, expressed the view that the fact of Christ's continual presence in the Church and in the heart and life of the individual disciple was fundamental to their discussion.

In the unhappy controversy that has from time to time raged around the nature of Christ's presence in the Holy Communion, both parties have been contending for certain things that are true. On the one hand, there are those who are convinced that they must affirm that the grace of the eucharist is something *given*, received indeed by faith, but not created by faith. This truth seems to be safeguarded by the twenty-eighth of the Anglican Articles: "The body of Christ is given, taken, and eaten, in the Supper, only after a heavenly and spiritual manner. And the mean whereby the body of Christ is received and eaten in the Supper is Faith." On the other hand, there are those who are convinced that they must at all costs maintain the truth that God is spirit, and that anything which tends to localize the divine presence leads in the long run to idolatry—that is, to a false conception of God, which must inevitably lower both religion and worship. Both of these contentions are in their main object evangelical.

The criticism I would make of Zwinglianism, or (if Zwingli did not actually hold it) of the view that the Sacrament is a bare memorial, is that it is merely self-edification: it offers no grace, it contains no Gospel. And the criticism I would make of certain kinds of eucharistic teaching of an opposite

[1] *Eucharistic Faith and Practice, Evangelical and Catholic*, 215.

[2] He quotes (p. 215), e.g., R. M. Benson, *Spiritual Letters*, p. 10: "Reservation after the Roman manner is objectionable to my mind not because it expresses the Real Presence in the Sacrament too strongly, but because it implies a denial of the Real Presence in the baptized."

[3] See Report (S.P.C.K.), pp. 5, 17, 31, 40, 80, 89, 96, 103, 104, 114, 149.

tendency is that I cannot reconcile them with the New Testament teaching concerning the Holy Spirit and his presence in the Church.

The great saying of the Lord contained in the Fourth Gospel, *God is spirit: and they that worship him must worship in spirit and truth*,[1] is relevant here, although not in the way that it is sometimes applied. It does not refer directly to absence or presence of externals in worship or to the use or disuse of sacraments. To "worship in spirit and truth" is not necessarily a worship from which material *media* are absent. The context shows that the saying has reference to the conception of God as localized. The Samaritans supposed that Mount Gerizim was the place where God should be worshipped; the Jews, Jerusalem. Both suppositions postulated that God's presence was attached to a particular place in such a way that other places less sacred were inferior for the purpose of worship. To such notions the Lord opposes the truth *God is spirit*. "God is absolutely free from all limitations of space and time" (Westcott). We cannot say that he is here in such a way that he is not also there, or that he "comes to" us at a particular moment in such a way as to exclude his presence with us always. Moreover, *Christian* worship is essentially a worship in spirit and in truth: *in truth*, because the Son has perfectly revealed the Father, and *in spirit* because all the worshippers have immediate access to God through the Son. Judaism and Samaritanism could not provide men with the means of such worship, for Judaism had a partial, and Samaritanism in addition a partly erroneous, revelation of God; and each of them had its particular "holy" place, the existence of which tended to prevent worship "in spirit".

We see, therefore, that the saying has a relevance to eucharistic worship, not as depreciating outward and visible signs *per se*, but rather in regard to the place we give them in the whole scheme of grace. If, for example, we were to limit the grace of God in Christ to those occasions when we receive the Holy Communion or participate in sacramental rites, we should be in danger of narrowing the field of God's grace and of forming a defective conception of it, and thus of falling short of that worship which is "in spirit and truth". The danger of this is one that the practice of Reservation is likely to lead to. "Not long ago I

[1] John 4. 24.

was in a church in which there was displayed on the closed doors of a chapel, where the sacred elements were kept, a card, with the written words, 'God is here. Let no one enter except for prayer'."[1] But the danger is also present whenever we allow ourselves to fall into a limited conception of the ways in which God and the human soul meet in communion. And even when this limitation is expressly rejected, the form of rejecting it may betray a way of looking at the matter which is not the New Testament's. It is not uncommon, for example, to hear from the pulpit some such expressions as these: "It is no part of the Christian faith to deny that God in Christ is present everywhere in his Church; but we hold that he is specially present to a greater degree in the Holy Communion." Very true: but this is scarcely the Scriptural way of putting it. We should begin with the truth of the general presence, not speak of it merely as something which we do not deny, and then go on to speak of the sacramental presence, as on this wise: "God in Christ is always present with the members of his Church; but we believe that normally he is specially present with them to a greater degree in sacramental communion." (I say "normally", for even those who would by no means describe themselves as mystics can reckon up in their lives blessed moments or times when without the aid of any external *media* or of sacred associations God was with them with an intensity and intimacy above that experienced when engaged in worship in church.) When we admit in a rather patronizing way the truth of the perpetual presence of Christ in the members of the Church, we are but displaying our own failure to grasp the New Testament conception of the life of the Church. On the other hand, when we begin with the New Testament conception, we are then able to integrate into the perpetual presence of Christ in the whole body and its members his presence in the Holy Communion as its most significant and culminating point. To understand this is to worship "in spirit and truth". To forget it is to miss the fulness of the message that the doctrines of the Incarnation and the Holy Spirit have brought concerning human life and its relationship to God in Christ. And it is to be feared that in some popular teaching and language concerning the eucharist the presence of Christ in the Sacrament is affirmed in such a way that the larger, wider pres-

[1] Quoted from Dr. A. J. Tait in *Reservation*, p. 11.

ence is lost to sight. For example, in a post-communion hymn familiar to many, the words occur

> Jesu, gentlest Saviour,
> Thou art in us now.

But what would St. Paul or St. John have made of that "now"?

A pupil, so the story goes, brought to Michelangelo a half-finished drawing, and asked for criticism of detail. The great artist glanced at it, and taking up a piece of chalk wrote across the canvas the single word *amplius*, "broader". The work may have been good enough in its way; but the design and the treatment were narrow. A larger conception and bolder hand were needed, if justice was to be done to the subject.[1] A similar criticism may be made of much that is written on the subject of the eucharist. The aim is often narrow and limited. The main emphasis is upon details and upon single points of doctrine. Many of the things that are said are true and just. But the treatment as a whole is defective because it is not placed in the larger setting of the life of the Church.

In a previous chapter[2] we referred to Acts 9. 31: "The church throughout all Judæa and Galilee and Samaria had peace, being edified; and walking in the fear of the Lord and in the comfort of the Holy Spirit (τῇ παρακλήσει τοῦ ἁγίου πνεύματος) was multiplied." The translation is not certain, and on Hort's suggestion to render τῇ παρακλήσει by "invocation" H. B. Swete has a very suggestive note. Pointing out that the meaning given by Hort to παράκλησις appears to be without example in LXX or New Testament, he adds: "Moreover the attitude of the primitive Church towards the Spirit was rather one of joyful welcome than of invocation; the cry *Veni, Creator Spiritus* belongs to a later age, when the Spirit was sought and perhaps expected, but not regarded as a guest who had already come, and come to abide."[3]

Obviously, this opens up a line of thought which is particularly relevant to our subject. And, first of all, the word "invocation", or in its proper Greek equivalent ἐπίκλησις, at once suggests

[1] Quoted from J. H. Bernard, *Via Domini*, 183.
[2] See p. 44.
[3] *The Holy Spirit in the New Testament*, 96, 97.

a reference to the use of the term in connection with the liturgy. When we compare the Roman and Greek views of the consecration of the elements, it would seem that generally speaking the Greek view is theologically more satisfactory, and devotionally more "spiritual", as we say. "The consecration of the holy gifts attributed by Western theology to the moment when the priest pronounces the words of Christ, 'this is my body . . . this is my blood,' this consecration is effected—according to Orthodox thought—during the *whole* liturgy, beginning with the 'preparation.' It is completed at the moment when the words of our Lord are pronounced and when the Holy Spirit is invoked ('epiclesis') . . . For Communion of the sick and dying in their homes, the holy gifts are preserved in a casket on the altar, but they are never exposed for adoration outside the liturgy, as in Catholicism."[1]

This description of Orthodox eucharistic worship brings before the imagination a liturgical action in which the power and presence of the Holy Spirit is active from beginning to end, even in the introductory portion, when the holy gifts are being prepared through the ministry of the priest and the deacon—a portion of the service sometimes printed in smaller type in Orthodox manuals, and not part of the liturgy proper. Clearly, as compared with a consecration supposedly effected merely by the pronouncing of certain words—and these *not* the words used by our Lord in blessing or giving thanks—it is a conception much more in accordance with the kind of worship that is "in spirit and truth". The *epiclesis* is not a bare formula, effecting at a certain moment, and apart from everything else, the consecration of the elements; but it is rather a climax, a more intense and solemn invoking of him in whom the entire action is carried on. And this *theologumenon* is given practical effect to in the refusal to admit reservation for purposes other than those stated in the words of Bulgakov, as given above.

On the other hand, we must distinguish, in the liturgies which contain an *epiclesis*, (*a*) those in which the Invocation is upon the elements alone, and (*b*) those in which the Holy Spirit is invoked upon both the communicants and the elements.

The prayer of Invocation of the Holy Spirit upon the eucharistic elements had been prepared for, and perhaps adapted from,

[1] S. Bulgakov, *The Orthodox Church*, 155.

similar prayers in the rite of Holy Baptism. In the evangelical accounts of the Baptism of our Lord the work of the Holy Spirit is manifest, and "it was in baptism that the Holy Spirit's work was from the first recognized and emphasized as the most prominent feature."[1] This included from early times a prayer to God that through the coming upon it of the Holy Spirit the water might be sanctified. In the eucharist some form of consecration of the elements had to be devised by those who recognized that the Evangelical accounts had left them no record of the words spoken by our Lord when blessing the bread and wine. In Eastern liturgies to the account of the Institution of the Sacrament is added the Invocation of the Holy Spirit, and the latter is regarded, as we have seen, as the completion of the consecration. Many of those who do not consider the Invocation as a perfectly satisfactory solution of the difficulty nevertheless prefer it to the Western theory which has turned the Lord's words of administration into words of consecration. In any case, so far as the subject of this book is concerned, the invoking of the Holy Spirit upon the *elements*, as is done in liturgies (*a*), is not a matter which need be further discussed.

It is otherwise with the prayer as found in liturgies (*b*), that the Holy Spirit will descend upon communicants as well as elements, "that they that partake thereof may obtain forgiveness of sins and eternal life". Why should the congregation of the people of God, the body of Christ, assembled before God in the most solemn and "religious" act of worship, pray for the descent of the Holy Spirit upon them, as if he were not already with them and abiding in them? Have we not moved away from the doctrine of the New Testament to that of "a later age when the Spirit was sought and perhaps expected, but not regarded as a guest who had already come, and come to abide"? It is to be noted that the Eastern liturgies which *omit* the petition that the Holy Spirit may descend upon the *congregation* are among the most primitive: the Liturgy of the Eighth Book of the Apostolic Constitutions and the Ethiopic and Nestorian Liturgies.[2] These would seem to go back to a time when the Scriptural conception of the abiding presence of the Holy Spirit obtained. Further, there is a very

[1] W. H. Frere, *The Anaphora*, 72.

[2] J. Norman, *Handbook to the Christian Liturgy*, 263. See, further, NOTE at the end of this chapter.

significant passage in the last of five Catechetical Lectures of Cyril of Jerusalem which he delivered to the newly baptized in the year 348.[1] "We call upon God who loveth man to send forth the Holy Spirit upon the things that are set before him (τὰ προκείμενα), that he may make the bread to be the body of Christ, the wine to be the blood of Christ: for in very truth whatsoever the Holy Spirit shall touch, the same is sanctified and changed." Then later on Cyril says: "After this" (the Lord's Prayer) "the priest says, 'Holy things for the holy.' The things set before God (τὰ προκείμενα) are holy, having received the coming upon them (ἐπιφοίτησιν) of the Holy Spirit. Holy also are ye, having been accounted worthy of the Holy Spirit. Holy things, therefore, correspond to (κατάλληλα) holy persons. Then ye say, 'One is holy, One is Lord, even Jesus Christ'; for truly there is One who is holy, holy by nature: we too are holy, not however by nature, but by participation[2] (in Christ) and by means of spiritual discipline and prayer." This passage of Cyril, exhibiting no doubt not only his own convictions but also those of the Church of Jerusalem of his day, clearly demonstrates the *correspondence* (as he terms it) between baptized persons, by virtue of their gift of the Holy Spirit, and the gift which they receive in Holy Communion. And indeed those liturgies which invoke the Holy Spirit upon the communicants as well as upon the elements witness also to the same conviction, although they display a defective grasp of the Holy Spirit as *abiding in* the members of the Church.

We cannot now trace the steps or stages through which the early Church passed until the thought of the Holy Spirit as a visitor replaced that of a guest. Nor indeed would it be safe to make generalizations upon so wide and far-reaching a subject. The faith of the early Church concerning the Holy Spirit is most clearly seen, so far as sacramental rites are concerned, in the conviction of the early Fathers as to his special attachment to Holy Baptism, or else to Holy Baptism together with the complementary rite of Confirmation. When the normal recipient of baptism was an adult who consciously renounced paganism, the Sacrament was clearly indicated as the means whereby a complete break was made with the past and new life

---

[1] *Catech.* xxiii (*Mystag.* v). 7. 19 (Migne, *P.G.* xxxiii, 1113f., 1124).

[2] μετοχῇ, cp. Hebrews 3. 14—i.e., through the Incarnation.

was given for the future. The new society entered through baptism was governed by an entirely different ethical code from that of paganism, and to a certain extent also from that of Judaism; and it held out for the neophyte potentialities of grace whereby a life of progressive sanctification was possible. Thus the reality of the Holy Spirit's presence in the Church was manifest in the early centuries of Christianity, as a destructive and a constructive power in each Christian, to a greater degree than in later ages, when nominal membership of the Church became more common. Possibly the early decades of the fourth century, when Christianity became the religion of the State, and the Church grew in numbers at the expense of quality, saw the beginning of a change in this respect—the change to regarding the Holy Spirit as a visitor rather than guest. And indeed it is not unlikely that Montanism with all its extravagances was a not altogether unhealthy reaction against a loss of living belief in the Holy Spirit which had already manifested itself in the Catholic Church by the end of the second century. In the earlier period the prayer of the Christian disciple was not so much that he might receive the Holy Spirit, but rather that he might not lose him through apostasy or other wilful or deadly sin. It was such fear which caused the early Church to dwell in almost an unhealthy manner on such grave passages in the New Testament as Hebrews 6. 4-6; 10. 26-31: 1 John 5. 16, 17: 2 Peter 2. 20-22. The background against which these passages stand out in dark relief is that of a divine society in which the members are ever advancing towards the heavenly vision,[1] are becoming partakers of the divine nature,[2] and—in the thought of *Hebrews*—have access to, and are present with, the High Priest in the heavenly sanctuary.

Among the writings of the early Fathers there is perhaps none more relevant to our subject than the treatise *De Spiritu Sancto* of St. Basil of Cæsarea (c. 329-379), from which we may quote a few passages. The Holy Spirit is "the supplier of life . . . omnipresent, the origin of sanctification, intellectual light, supplying through himself illumination so to speak to every faculty of the mind for the discovery of truth . . . filling all things with his power, yet capable of being partaken of by the worthy alone, not shared in a single measure, but distributing energy

[1] 1 John 3. 2.   [2] 2 Peter 1. 4.

according to the proportion of faith, simple in essence yet various in powers, wholly present in each person and wholly present everywhere, impassively divided and partaken of entire, after the manner of the rays of the sun, whose gracious beams are present to him who enjoys them as if he were the only one, yet they shine upon land and sea and are mingled with the air. So, too, the Holy Spirit is present with every one who receives him as if with him alone, yet he emits grace sufficient and in full measure for all, to be enjoyed by all who partake of him according to the capacity, not of his power, but of their nature" (chapter 22). And again: "Strange to tell, yet none the less true, that the Spirit is frequently spoken of as the *place* of them that are being sanctified; and this manner of speech, so far from belittling the Spirit, rather glorifies him. . . . Concerning the Spirit when he says, 'Behold there is a place by me, and stand thou upon the rock,'[1] what can he mean by the place but the contemplation in the Spirit, from which when he had come to it Moses was able to see clearly God as he appeared to him? This is the special place of true worship. For 'Take heed,' he says, 'that thou offer not thy burnt offerings in every place, but in the place which the Lord thy God shall choose.'[2] Of what kind, then, is a spiritual burnt offering? It is 'the sacrifice of praise.'[3] And in what kind of place do we offer it? In the Holy Spirit. Where do we learn this? From the Lord himself when he says: 'The true worshippers in spirit and truth shall worship the Father.'[4] This place Jacob saw when he said, 'The Lord is in this place.'[5] So the Spirit is verily the place of the saints, and the saint is the proper place for the Spirit, and styled his temple"[6] (chapter 62). This is all the more significant since St. Basil attaches the importance that we should expect an Eastern Churchman to do to the Invocation of the Holy Spirit at the consecration of the elements (chapter 66). It might be urged, however, that St. Basil is referring in these passages to persons of exceptional holiness (τῶν ἁγίων or τῶν ἀξίων are the terms employed) when he speaks of them as the dwelling-place of the Holy Spirit. In view of his adherence throughout the treatise to Scriptural language, and the actual reference to 1 Cor. 6. 19 above, this is unlikely. But if it should be so, he is then reflecting the conditions and using the terminology of an age later than that

[1] Exod. 33. 21.   [2] Deut. 12. 13, 14.   [3] Ps. 50. 14.
[4] John 4. 23.   [5] Gen. 28. 16.   [6] 1 Cor. 6. 19.

of the Apostles, when, as indeed he mentions at the end of his treatise (chapters 76-79), the Church presented a sorry spectacle to itself and to the world; and like Augustine for a similar reason he visualizes an inner circle of Christians who manifestly and in contrast to their fellows display the fruit of the indwelling Spirit. In this case, St. Basil prepares us for the transition to less Scriptural ideas concerning the Holy Spirit in the Church, when he was regarded as a visitor rather than as a guest. But even supposing that this is so, the significance of his statement concerning the soul as the "place" of the Holy Spirit, and his interpretation of John 4. 23, 24, are of real importance in the theology of the eucharist, and particularly when we are endeavouring to return to the thought of the primitive Church.

If it be true, however, that the truth of the indwelling Spirit of Christ was in danger of being lost by the end of the fourth century, the danger certainly became greater subsequently when Church discipline became slack as a result of internal dissensions, and when the barbarian invasions of the fifth century led to a political and moral disintegration which we of the twentieth do not find it difficult to imagine. And further, when the recipients of Holy Baptism came normally to be infants, as the case would be when Christianity became the recognized, settled religion of a country, the meaning of the Christian profession, and conception of the Church as a divine Society called out of the world to live a life of its own, tended to become obscured. But this book is not a treatise on historical theology, and we are not concerned to trace, if it were possible to do so, how and when these changes came about. Certainly, to-day we must reckon as one of the chief causes which have contributed to loss of conviction concerning the Holy Spirit the degradation—it is scarcely too strong a word—which has been allowed to overtake the practice of Holy Baptism. When we consider that the sacrament of Christian initiation is looked upon by many members of the Church as a harmless social custom or as a badge of conventional respectability, and that it can be engaged in by people who do not hold the Christian faith or ethic and have no intention of bringing the child up in a Christian manner, we need not wonder that a Church which acquiesces in this kind of beginning for its members feels the result in the whole character of its life. Added to this is the hole-and-corner method generally followed in the administration of the "Publick" Baptism of Infants. All this has resulted in a loss of moral power in the Church, and of the sense of a dedicated Church life in which the members partake of the Holy Spirit and are consecrated by his presence. This has become all the more evident in a century which before it is halfway over has witnessed two world catastrophes with their disastrous effects upon religion and morality.

There are welcome signs that the first Sacrament of the Gospel is about to receive greater attention from those who are concerned about a renewal of the life of the Church. This will involve not only a consideration of methods of administration and questions of discipline, but also a review of the theology of the Sacrament. For too long in the modern Church the sacramental outlook has been unhealthily concentrated on the eucharist, so that on many lips sacramental life and grace means simply eucharistic life and grace. The outward and visible sign of this ecclesiastical and theological[1] emphasis is to be found in our churches, when we compare the attention paid to the decoration and furnishing of the west end as compared with that of the east. We hope that no one will for a moment imagine that the writer of these pages is seeking to depreciate in the eyes of any the place of the eucharist in the life of the Church. On the contrary his object is rather to indicate that laudable efforts to give the eucharist its fitting place in the life of Church folk generally have failed because too exclusive attention has been focused upon it, to the exclusion of other truths with which it is indissolubly connected. The result has been, practically, that while the devotion of a few has been notably quickened in and around eucharistic worship, the main stream of Church life has not been so quickened; and that indeed "sacramental" emphasis has been accompanied by a general falling off in attendance at public worship in any of its aspects, sacramental or non-sacramental. Further, lack of emphasis upon Holy Baptism and the indwelling life of the Holy Spirit, of which Baptism is the beginning and to which it looks forward, has resulted in eucharistic doctrine becoming more and more isolated.[2] This, we believe, has led,

[1] In *Doctrine in the Church of England* (1938) three pages are devoted to Holy Baptism, forty-seven to Holy Communion.

[2] "One of the worst fruits of the Eucharistic controversies which have vexed the Western Church in recent centuries has been their tendency to distract

not in our own generation alone, to false and inadequate theology, and to errors both in theory and practice. We must, therefore, in the next chapter pass on to consider the two Sacraments of the Gospel in their mutual relationships.

NOTE ON CHAPTER VII
On the Invocation of the Holy Spirit upon the Communicants

Evidence for holding that the earlier form of Invocation was upon the elements only may be cited from recent works on Liturgiology.

Cyprian held that as regards the lapsed, and profane persons, and heretics, who have put themselves without the Church, "the Holy Spirit has departed from them," and the brethren must be separated from such: "since neither can the oblation be hallowed where the Holy Spirit is not, nor does the Lord benefit anyone by the orisons and prayers of one who himself has done violence to the Lord."[1] On this E. G. C. F. Atchley remarks[2]: "Anyone who held these views could not have had a prayer for the Holy Ghost to come on the celebrant and the communicants as in the later forms of the epiclesis: for in their opinion, obviously, unless he were already present in them the whole service was null, and a sham."

Two quotations from the *Didascalia Apostolorum*, as edited by R. H. Connolly,[3] are relevant. This work in its original Greek form is to be placed in the second (or perhaps the first) half of the third century.

> A believer is filled with the Holy Spirit, and an unbeliever with an unclean spirit: and his nature does not receive an alien spirit. He therefore who has withdrawn and separated himself and departed from the unclean spirit by baptism, is filled with the Holy Spirit; and if he do good works, the Holy Spirit continues with him, and he remains fulfilled; and the unclean spirit finds no place with him, for he who is filled with the Holy Spirit does not receive him.[4]

---

men's minds from the theology of baptism": E. G. Selwyn, *The First Epistle of St Peter*, 361f.   [1] *Ep.* lxv. 4.

[2] *On the Epiclesis of the Eucharistic Liturgy and in the Consecration of the Font*, 46.
[3] Oxford, 1929.   [4] p. 246.

If the Holy Spirit is always in thee, without (just) impediment dost thou keep thyself from prayer and from the Scriptures and from the eucharist. For consider and see, that prayer also is heard through the Holy Spirit, and the eucharist through the Holy Spirit is accepted and sanctified, and the Scriptures are the words of the Holy Spirit, and are holy. For if the Holy Spirit is in thee, why dost thou keep thyself from approaching the works of the Holy Spirit?[1]

As with Cyprian, so also with the author of the *Didascalia*, Atchley points out that there is no room in his theological beliefs "for a petition for the Holy Spirit to come on the priest and the congregation; for he was already in them".[2]

Atchley holds that Narsai (second half of the fifth century) "is the earliest witness to the petition that the Holy Spirit may come upon the congregation, as in the later Greek and other oriental liturgies".[3]

It will be observed that the petition[4] in the early *Apostolic Tradition of Hippolytus* is that the communicants may be *fulfilled* with the Holy Spirit for the *confirmation* of their faith.

Gregory Dix in *The Shape of the Liturgy*[5] says: "It is true that the liturgies of *S. Basil* and *S. Chrysostom* as they now stand pray that God will send down the Holy Ghost *upon us* as well as upon the elements. But it is also noteworthy that no such addition to the petition is to be found in the fourth century sources. And the Greek theological tradition (rightly, as I think) makes nothing of this clause in its explanations of the invocation; indeed, I remember only one modern Greek manual which so much as mentions it. The authentic 'Eastern' formulation of doctrine is that the invocation consecrates the eucharist. By the action of the Holy Spirit upon the elements the communicants receive the body and blood of Christ."

[1] p. 244.
[2] *Op. cit.* 39; W. H. Frere, *The Anaphora*, 45, says of the *Didascalia*: "We seem, in a sense, to be back in the atmosphere of the early chapters of the 'Acts of the Apostles' when the sense of his [i.e., the Holy Spirit's] working was keenest." [3] *Ib.* 124. [4] 4. 12. [5] p. 296.

CHAPTER VIII

HOLY BAPTISM AND HOLY COMMUNION

HOLY BAPTISM is the means of entry into the divine life of the Church, or into the life of the Holy Spirit. Holy Communion is the means of renewing that life, or, more exactly, of renewing our union and fellowship with Christ. Seeing that the New Testament does not distinguish in its working the indwelling of Christ from the indwelling of the Spirit, it is not a needless question to ask, what are the *differentiæ* of the grace of Holy Baptism and that of Holy Communion; in what sense, if any, is the presence of Christ as imparted in Holy Communion distinct or different from his presence in other sacramental rites and in the spiritual life by which the Christian lives all the time?

As a starting-point we may take two differing points of view, one from a "classical", the other from a modern, Anglican divine. The words of Hooker[1] are remarkable, and worthy of more attention than has been given to them: "The grace which we have by the holy eucharist doth not begin but continue life. No man therefore receiveth this sacrament before Baptism, because no dead thing is capable of nourishment. That which groweth must of necessity first live. If our bodies did not daily waste, food to restore them were a thing superfluous. And it may be that the grace of Baptism would serve to eternal life, were it not that the state of our spiritual being is daily so much hindered and impaired after Baptism. In that life therefore where neither body nor soul can decay, our souls shall as little require this Sacrament as our bodies corporal nourishment, but as long as the days of our warfare last, during the time that we are both subject to diminution and capable of augmentation in grace, the words of our Lord and Saviour Christ will remain forcible, 'Except ye eat the flesh of the Son of Man and drink his blood ye have no life in you.' "

[1] *Ecclesiastical Polity*, v. 67.

It will be noticed that Hooker here not only emphasizes the kinship of the grace of Baptism with that of Holy Communion, in that the latter renews what was first given by the former, but also suggests, in a somewhat speculative manner, that the necessity of Holy Communion lies, not in the distinctiveness of its gift, but in the practical conditions under which the life of the Christian is carried on, and that he even hints at an ideal state of the Church on earth in which the Sacrament of Holy Communion would not be required for the sustenance of the soul. On this we may remark that Hooker is not untrue to the New Testament in emphasizing the grace of Holy Baptism, but that he seems to isolate the act of Baptism unduly from the whole life of the Church into which Baptism admits. It is true, as he notes, that the Christian finds much to "hinder" and to "impair", as he pursues his journey; but it is also true that in the life of the Church there is much—apart from Holy Communion—to nourish and quicken the life which began at Baptism. In addition, his language reflects a period in the life of the Church when the partaking of the Holy Communion had come to occupy a less normal place for the faithful Christian than it did in the early Church. But, theologically, Hooker's language is important. It is in fact as if one were to interpret the longer text of John 13. 10, "He that is bathed needeth not save to wash his feet, but is clean every whit", in this way: that the baptized person is "bathed" (i.e., has taken a complete bath), and needs only to be cleansed in the eucharist from such sins as he incurs as a wayfarer on the dusty road of life. And it will scarcely be maintained that the act of bathing the whole body and the act of washing part of it are acts different *in kind*.

On the other hand, from a different point of view, O. C. Quick has an interesting discussion in *The Christian Sacraments*[1] of the *differentiæ* of the two Sacraments. We hope that a necessarily abbreviated quotation from the whole passage does not do the author an injustice. "Here"—i.e., in the eucharist—"the Christian believes that he takes into himself the very life which makes him one with God. We do not deny—nay, we are eager to affirm—that he does indeed receive that same life in Baptism also. But not according to the same manner of divine operation; else he would have to be baptized as often as he made his com-

[1] Pp. 185-187.

munion, unless one of the sacraments were to be made altogether superfluous. But Christian experience seems to show that what the Christian actually receives in Baptism, beyond the symbolical seal of membership with Christ, is but the initial impulse of the divine power to start him upon his heavenward way. The habitual and ever more profound renewal of that contact with God which he requires, takes place, so far as sacramental media are concerned, in the communion of the eucharist. Here, then, is the empirical basis of the Church's constant belief that the presence of Christ in the eucharist is to be accounted something different from his presence in Baptism, something more intimately close, more vitally apprehensible, than even his coming to accept and endow a new member of the Father's family."

This seems to us to do less than justice to the doctrine of Holy Baptism as taught in the New Testament, in the early Fathers, and in the Anglican formularies. Indeed we think that Quick himself would have admitted this.[1] And it is to be remembered that he had just been making a courageous attempt to grapple with the difficulties which arise concerning the effects of Holy Baptism on "original sin", and the use of language with reference to infants which had formerly been intended to describe the pre-Christian state of adult catechumens.[2] It is not essential, however, for our present purpose to consider the question of "original sin" and the relation of Baptism to it. A better starting-point of the discussion is to be found in the statement of the Church Catechism that in Baptism the infant is made "a member of Christ, the child of God, and an inheritor of the kingdom of heaven". The first of these is a gift bestowed upon the baptized person in common with others. He is admitted into a society, *incorporated* into Christ's holy Church. It also carries with it the fact and promise of union with Christ, to whose body the new member belongs. The second is an individual gift, and is nothing less than the being born into the redeemed family of Christ, brought into a filial relation to God in Christ.[3]

[1] "The main difference in this method of interpretation [of Holy Baptism] is the fact that in some measure it changes the emphasis of New Testament theology." *Ib.* 179.   [2] Pp. 172ff.

[3] All men are in one sense children of God (cp. Acts 17. 28); but there is no more difficulty in postulating a special sonship of Christian believers than there is in holding that, though God has given a revelation of sorts to all men, he has given a special revelation to those who believe in his Son.

But these gifts, in the case of an infant especially, are potential, and at first depend—humanly speaking—for their development on the child's environment. If the portion of the family of God who bring up a child have themselves forgotten their relationship to God, and act as if in ignorance of it, and if their membership in the body of Christ is little more than a name, the gift of Holy Baptism may well remain undeveloped. Similarly, natural birth carries with it great potentialities. But if the child belongs to a family who live in the fetid atmosphere of the slums, or if its parents treat it in defiance or ignorance of the plain laws of health, the child cannot grow up to be physically what it otherwise would have been. Or it may be that in the family into which it is born there is a tendency towards disease which if not guarded against in the case of the child in question will almost certainly manifest itself in him also. It is true that in the world outside this human family there are those who understand and act upon the laws of health and skilled physicians to give advice. But for practical purposes these do not exist for the unhappy child we are thinking of, since he cannot or does not get in touch with them. And likewise, for the newly-born member of Christ whom we have in mind, the living Church does not exist as a practical proposition—as that whereby, through Christian nurture and education, what is potential in him might become actual and the divine likeness imprinted upon him at the font might become apparent.

Hooker may not have had in mind just such a case as this when he refers to the fact that "the state of our spiritual being is daily so much hindered and impaired after Baptism." But he puts his finger on the difficulty that must arise in forming an empirical conception of the grace of Holy Baptism, especially when the subject of it is an infant for whom early environment makes all the difference. If in comparing the grace of Holy Baptism with that of Holy Communion we have recourse to the test of experience, as O. C. Quick would have us do, we must first be careful to see that in each case the conditions under which the experiment is made are similar. For example, we might compare the observed spiritual life of young children of the Orthodox Church, who receive as infants the eucharist immediately after Baptism, with that of young children of the Anglican Communion, who do not. It might be difficult to observe that the addition of

Communion in the case of the Orthodox child made such a difference that we could take note of it. But under the conditions which obtain, for example, in the Anglican Communion, it is scarcely possible to deduce from observed "results" anything which would enable us to "compare" the grace of the two Sacraments. The fact is that the person who is a regular communicant is a person, come to years of discretion, who takes seriously his position as a member of the Church. He is one who has been brought up to realize "what a solemn vow, promise, and profession" he has made in Baptism; or else he has been converted, perhaps in later life, and has come to understand what life in the redeemed family of God involves. In other words, the spiritual life imparted at Baptism is developing as it was meant to do in the life and worship of the Church, and what was potential is becoming actual, not by means of sacramental feeding alone, we may be sure, but also through those other spiritual helps which the Church and its fellowship, and especially the fellowship of the Christian family, afford. The gifts of the two Sacraments are, in any case, seen, not in isolation, but in conjunction and in co-operation. To revert once more to the physical analogy, a young man with finely developed bodily powers does not owe it alone to his following the rules of health and exercise when he was in his "teens", but just as much, if not more, to the possession of healthy parents, to medical skill and attention when he was being born, and to a proper environment and upbringing in infancy and in early childhood. It is impossible to say, when presented with the young man's physical condition as a completed thing, where what he unconsciously received ends and what he consciously went on to develop begins. Similarly, the grace of Holy Baptism and the grace of Holy Communion commingle in one who "has led the rest of his life according to this beginning". We cannot say that baptismal grace ends at a certain point, and that then another kind of sacramental grace begins—indeed, that Baptism is administered but once might suggest that its effects were permanent. In any case it is difficult to follow O. C. Quick when he says, "*Christian experience seems to show* that what the Christian actually receives in Baptism, beyond the symbolical seal of membership in Christ, is but the initial impulse of the divine power to start him upon his heavenward way." In the case of an infant, by what empirical evidence are we, or can we be, assured that Holy Baptism confers, and confers only, an initial impulse? On the other hand, experience has often shown that adult Baptism has been to him who has received it a great deal more than just a start upon the Christian career. Under such a limited description could not be brought the experience of Cyprian, for example, who testifies that "as soon as by the help of the water of birth the stains of my former life were wiped away, and calm, pure light from on high was shed upon my heart, now cleansed; as soon as I had drunk in the Spirit from heaven, and a second birth had restored me and made me a new man: forthwith, in marvellous wise, what had been doubtful received assurance, what had been shut from me was laid open, what had been dark was illumined; a way was opened out for what before seemed difficult, what was thought impossible could be done; what had been born of the flesh and lived before in bondage to its pleasures confessed that it was of the earth, and what the Holy Spirit now quickened in me began to be God's own."[1] But this is by no means all. "If you keep the way of innocence," he tells Donatus,[2] "the way of righteousness, if you walk with a firm and steady step, if, depending on God with your whole strength and with your whole heart, you only *be* what you have begun to be, liberty and power to do is given you in proportion to the increase of your spiritual grace. For there is not, as is the case with earthly benefits, any measure or stint in the dispensing of the heavenly gift. The Spirit freely flowing forth is restrained by no limits, is checked by no closed barriers within certain bounded spaces; it flows perpetually, it is exuberant in its affluence. Let our heart only be athirst, and be ready to receive: in the degree in which we bring to it a capacious faith, in that measure we draw from it an overflowing grace." It would be a curious exegesis of this eloquent passage which found in it Holy Baptism as an initial impulse only to good living. It is rather "a well of water springing up unto eternal life",[3] choked only by those daily hindrances and impediments of which Hooker speaks. Similarly, Augustine was not untrue to the faith of the early Church when he reflects in the *Confessions*[4] that it had been better

---

[1] *Ad Donatum*, 4: quoted from J. F. Bethune-Baker, *An Introduction to the Early History of Christian Doctrine*, 382.

[2] Translated in *The Ante-Nicene Fathers*, v. 276.

[3] John 4. 14.   [4] i. 11.

with him had he been baptized in boyhood (as he almost was, on the occasion of an illness), for then the grace given would have saved him from much sinning. And no doubt also, in modern times, the test of experience in the mission field would demonstrate the grace of Holy Baptism to be much more than a bare impulse along the way of Christ.

We cannot point to any recorded instance in the New Testament of an infant being baptized; but it is a sound exegesis that finds in the words "Children, obey your parents in the Lord"[1] an indication that the children in question had been baptized, since for St. Paul an unbaptized Christian would have been a contradiction in terms. "In one Spirit", he says, for example, to the Corinthians, "were we all baptized into one body."[2] Of this life "in the Lord", or, as St. Paul more commonly expresses it, "in Christ", the grace of Baptism formed for these children more than a merely initial part. Perhaps they were communicants also. They had, in any case, been taught to pray and to worship and to read the Scriptures. Their parents, presumably Christian, had brought them up in the nurture and fear of the Lord. There was also the influence of the Christian society, under which they came. All this contributed to form the supernatural life, the indwelling life of the Spirit, the life "in Christ". It is not possible in their case, or in ours to-day, to separate the different elements or to say where one begins or another ends. That does not mean that each kind of grace is the same, or of equal importance, or of equal intensity. But we must be careful not to separate, as absolutely distinctive and different, one kind of grace from another. That all coalesce in producing this "mystical" life in the Spirit indicates that ultimately they have a common source and are formed of a common stuff. At any rate, they are not like oil and water, incapable of mixing. And this is indicated in the case of the eucharist when we say that we are "strengthened and refreshed" by it, and indeed also by the term "bread of life", and by the whole symbolism of feeding which is involved in this Sacrament.

This life "in the Spirit" must be taken as a whole when we are asked to consider difficult questions which arise in individual cases. It is sometimes asked, for example, how we are to justify the traditional place and honour given by the Church to

[1] Eph. 6. 1.   [2] 1 Cor. 12. 13.

Holy Baptism, when persons have been known to live lives of loyal and sincere discipleship who have never been baptized.[1] The answer to this is not simply—though it is very relevant— that the Sacraments are ordinances of the Church's corporate life, and that we must estimate their value by reference to the life of the Christian society rather than to any individual. There is the further consideration that the river of grace is made up of many tributaries. Involuntary absence of Holy Baptism in an individual may be compensated for from other sources, but a refusal to receive Baptism, if the discovery was made that it had never been administered, would indicate not merely a technical but also an actual defect in the person in question, as evincing self-will in the face of what the New Testament prescribes and Christians have from the first practised.

An interesting example of this kind of difficulty, coming from the early Church, is preserved for us in a fragment from the pen of Dionysius, Bishop of Alexandria c.247-c.264. He writes thus[2] to Xystus, Bishop of Rome: "Of a truth, brother, I have need of counsel, and I ask an opinion of thee. The following matter has come before me, and I am fearful lest after all I be mistaken. Of the brethren who meet together for worship there is one, reckoned faithful, of long standing, a member of the congregation before my ordination, and, I think, before the appointment of the blessed Heraclas.[3] Having been present with those who were recently being baptized, and having heard the questions and answers, he came to me in tears, bewailing himself and falling before my feet, confessing and swearing that the baptism with which he had been baptized by the heretics was not such as this and had nothing in common with it, inasmuch as it had been full of impieties and blasphemies. He said that he was now altogether pricked in heart, and had not courage so much as to lift up his eyes to God, after beginning with those unholy words and deeds; and therefore he begged that he might receive this most pure cleansing and reception and grace. This I for my part did not dare to do, saying that his long-standing communion with us had been sufficient for this purpose. For since he had heard the Thanksgiving and joined in saying the Amen, and had stood beside the Table and stretched forth his hands to receive

[1] See *Doctrine in the Church of England*, 138f.
[2] Eusebius, *H.E.*, vii. 9. 1-5. [3] Bishop of Alexandria c.233-c.247.

the holy food, and had received it and partaken of the body and blood of our Lord for a long time, I should not dare to build him up again from the beginning. But I kept exhorting him to be of good courage, and to approach for the participation of the holy things with firm faith and good hope. Yet he never ceases his lament, and he shudders to approach the Table, and scarcely, though invited, does he dare to take his stand with the 'consistentes' at the prayers.''

This very interesting passage raises more than one important question; but we quote it only so far as it concerns the subject of the present chapter. Dionysius of Alexandria, it would appear, took a middle course between those on the one hand who with Cyprian disallowed altogether the validity of Baptism by heretics, and those who on the other, like Stephen, recognized Baptism by whomsoever performed, provided it was in the name of the Trinity or, it may be, even of Christ alone.[1] Actually Dionysius accepted the Baptism of Montanists and, apparently, of Novatianists. So it may be that, notwithstanding the man's recollection of what took place at his Baptism, Dionysius was not altogether certain that Baptism in the name of the Trinity had not been administered—the man's testimony being especially concerned with "the questions and answers" and with "impieties and blasphemies", neither of which involves, necessarily, an invalid *formula*. But the significant point for our purpose is that Dionysius was reluctant "to build him up again from the beginning"[2] because this aged disciple had been a communicant of long standing. This stood in place of Baptism.[3] This cannot fairly be pressed to mean that Dionysius held that the grace of the Eucharist was identical with that of Baptism, but rather that one who had for many years been a faithful communicant partook of that corporate spiritual life into which Holy Baptism admits us as members of Christ. It at least indicates the view—for which we are contending—that the grace of Baptism and the grace of the Eucharist are "of like substance", and that in this exceptional

---

[1] See C. R. Feltoe, *Dionysius of Alexandria*, 40ff.; H. J. Lawlor in *Eusebius, Ecclesiastical History*, vol. ii, 240ff.; E. W. Benson, *Cyprian, His Life, His Times, His Work*, 354ff.   [2] ἐξ ὑπαρχῆς ἀνασκευάζειν.

[3] εἰς τοῦτο γεγονέναι: cp. Lam. 4. 10 (LXX): "The hands of the pitiful women have sodden their children. They were for meat (ἐγενήθησαν εἰς βρῶσιν) to them in the destruction of the daughter of my people.''

and doubtful case Eucharist might be taken to include Baptism. The Sacraments are, in other words, *in pari materia*. Normally, both are joined together in that full κοινωνία which is nothing less than the fellowship of the Spirit.

In that κοινωνία many other spiritual forces enter than those of the two great Sacraments of the Gospel. The life of the member of Christ's body is nourished by prayer, his own and others', by worship other than sacramental, by spiritual teaching and education, by devotional reading and study of the Bible, by the influence of a Christian home, by contact with other souls which are also partakers of the grace of Christ. And so we might go on—to enumerate only those normal and obvious sources of spiritual edification and refreshment through which the indwelling Spirit manifests his presence and bestows an increase of himself. To individual members there come at times moments—alas, too rare and brief—of spiritual elevation and joy and refreshment, the value of which cannot be measured by duration of time or by predictability of occurrence: stored in the memory they form an object of recollection which enables the soul to look back on these times of refreshing during long periods "in a barren and dry land where no water is".[1] Formal theology cannot tabulate all the unmediated ways of contact with Christ which even a feeble member of his may enjoy; and ecclesiastical writers are over prone, perhaps anxious, to ignore them. But no theologian who aims at a complete or balanced account of the sources of the "communion of the Spirit" will fail to take them into calculation or to give them their due place in the spiritual experience. "It is possible that the broken prayers of an illiterate believer may place him on a higher level than many reach with the help of the most uplifting of eucharistic celebrations. And we know that 'if by any just impediment a man is hindered from receiving the Sacrament of Christ's body and blood,'[2] he may be assured that spiritual communion will suffice. The essential thing is not the external act of communion, important as that is, but the union and fellowship with himself which the Lord is pleased ordinarily to give through the Sacrament. When these are attained, the purpose of the Sacrament, as far as regards the individual Christian, has been fulfilled, even if for reasons beyond

[1] Psalm 63. 2.
[2] See rubric after the Communion of the Sick.

human control the Sacrament itself cannot be administered or cannot be received."[1]

In the post-baptismal life, apart from the gifts bestowed by him in the rite of Confirmation, the presence of the Holy Spirit, at any rate in Western minds, is chiefly associated with the individual needs of daily life, where his presence and help and guidance may be counted on to direct the Christian's thoughts, words and ways in accordance with the will of God. Both liturgical and popular language speak of this aspect of his work. "Grant us by the same Spirit *to have a right judgement in all things.*"[2] "Defend, O Lord, this thy Child with thy heavenly grace, that he may . . . *daily increase in thy Holy Spirit more and more.*"[3] "Mercifully grant that thy Holy Spirit *may in all things direct and rule our hearts.*"[4] "We humbly pray thee so to guide and govern us by thy Holy Spirit, *that in all the cares and occupations of our daily life we may never forget thee, but remember that we are ever walking in thy sight.*"[5]

Or, to turn to the language of hymns:

> And his that gentle voice we hear,
>   Soft as the breath of even,
> *That checks each thought, that calms each fear,*
>   And speaks of heaven.

> Come, gracious Spirit, heavenly Dove,
> With light and comfort from above:
> Be thou our Guardian, thou our Guide,
> *O'er every thought and step preside.*

This belief concerning the presence of the Holy Spirit in everyday matters has a sound theological basis. He it is who teaches us that "God is spirit", that is, free from all limitations of space and time. We are not to say "Lo, here!" or "Lo, there!" for the kingdom of God is within us.[6] The Holy Spirit is a timeless possession, and therefore has not to be waited for. He is at hand in every circumstance and in all thinking, because

---

[1] H. B. Swete, *The Holy Catholic Church*, 180 f.
[2] Collect of Whit-Sunday.   [3] In the Order for Confirmation.
[4] Collect of the Nineteenth Sunday after Trinity.
[5] From a prayer For Recollection of the Presence of God in the Prayer Book of the Church of Ireland.   [6] Cp. Luke 17. 21.

the promise concerning him, in accordance with his nature, is that he will be with the disciple for ever.[1] Again, St. Paul's phrase "the fruit of the Spirit"[2] indicates that his action in the formation of the Christian character is a *seminal* force; and we cannot conceive of such a force as being now present, now absent. It is rather an integral part of the personality in whom appear those graces which St. Paul enumerates as forming that character. And, indeed, the use of the singular *"fruit* of the Spirit"* indicates this more clearly than if the Apostle had claimed the Spirit as the root of certain qualities severally distributed.

On the other hand, the divine presence at Holy Communion,[3] of which every communicant is conscious, is associated in the mind with the historical element in our faith. Aptly, indeed, when St. Paul refers to the eucharist does he recall us to "the night in which he was being betrayed".[4] The action of the liturgy brings us back to the Upper Room of nineteen hundred years ago, in which, as we believe, an historical Figure did *then* what he is doing now. We identify him who is with us in the sacrament with the Spirit of *Jesus*—to use the phrase restored to us by the Revised Version.[5] Our experience of communion is intensified and defined, not only by the use of outward and visible signs, but also by signs which are themselves of an historical character, having been chosen (as we believe) for this purpose by Jesus himself, and so used by his disciples ever since. Again, the definite character of the presence is indicated by being associated with a corporate rite—which must needs be held at a certain time and place, and of which definite notice must be given —celebrated, unlike Holy Baptism, by a person who has been definitely set apart to minister on behalf of the congregation. And, before we partake of the elements, we find opportunity in the earlier part of the liturgy to make a definite act of repentance.

All these facts suggest—on psychological grounds[6]—reasons

---

[1] John 14. 16.   [2] Gal. 5. 22.

[3] By this I mean the presence in the whole service and action. I am not considering the relation of the presence to the elements.

[4] 1 Cor. 11. 23.

[5] Acts 16. 7.

[6] I need not say that I do not suggest that the intenser experience rests on *purely* psychological grounds.

why it is that Christians for the most part have had an intenser experience of the divine presence at the Holy Communion than when engaged in other devotional exercises. By nature most men are conscious of being creatures of time, and what they plan to do with a definite object and at a definite time means more to them than what they do casually and "as the spirit moves them". And it is generally acknowledged that the *historical* element in Christianity has given it a superiority over other religions in its appeal to the ordinary man.[1] "In the eucharist," says Hooker[2] with his usual insight, "we so receive the gift of God, that we know by grace what the grace is which God giveth us, the degrees of our own increase in holiness and virtue we see and can judge of them, we understand that the strength of our life begun in Christ is Christ, that his flesh is meat and his blood drink, not by surmised imagination but truly, even so truly that through faith we perceive in the body and blood sacramentally presented the very taste of eternal life, the grace of the Sacrament is here as the food which we eat and drink." These words in which Hooker contrasts the grace of the Eucharist with that of Baptism are applicable in a wider sense as a contrast between spiritual influences which come to us from a definite, known source, and those which come to us we know not how or when.

But, further, the Holy Communion is visibly associated not only with the scene of the Institution, but also with the Cross, the shadow of which overhung and dominated that scene. I refer here not so much to the Cross under its redemptive, theological aspect as to its significance as an inevitable element in life, the Saviour's and also the disciples'. Form-criticism has in this respect done us a service by pointing out that the story of the Passion was the earliest piece of narrative of considerable size to be put together in the earliest stages of Gospel-making. Thus, from almost the first, Christians found the supreme act of their redemption placed in the setting of one of the greatest stories of the world. This unsurpassed narrative makes its appeal by reason not only of its unconscious art, but also of its human interest.

---

[1] In this connection the words of St. Augustine (*Conf.* vii. 14) are significant: "I read there [i.e., in the Platonists] that God the Word was born not of flesh nor of blood, nor of the will of man, nor of the will of the flesh, but of God. But that the Word was made flesh and dwelt among us, I read not there."

[2] *E.P.* v. 67.

Christians discover themselves in that story. It is only too easy to understand why the several actors in the Passion acted as they did. They are, alas! human figures, in whom are mirrored the weakness, the blindness, the treachery which every Christian finds without much difficulty in himself. The communicant, therefore, has his gaze focused not simply on an historical incident, but, even more, on an incident which is ever alive and ever full of fresh significance for himself. As one who is conscious that he is daily hindered and impaired—to recall again Hooker's words—in his way of life as a Christian, he finds in the Sacrament that which meets exactly the circumstances of his pilgrimage. Crosses there are not of his own making, arising from the changes and chances of this mortal life, and inherent also in a faithful Christian profession, and crosses there are of his own making, arising from human infirmity. Both are comprehended in the historical setting of the Passion in which the Institution of the Sacrament is placed.

Moreover, the humanity of our Lord is associated in Christian thinking with the grace of the Sacrament; and this glorified humanity which is offered to men in the Sacrament is the pledge of their victory over the difficulties of life which spring both from within and without. But it is a humanity glorified and quickened through suffering and death. And therefore we may hold with good reason that the Western Church is both theologically and practically justified in making the Cross the central point around which the eucharist is to be placed, rather than the Incarnation as the Easterns do. It is true that as early as Justin Martyr a parallel—albeit expressed in somewhat confused language—is to be found between the becoming flesh of the Son of God and the grace of the eucharist. But the Scriptural emphasis is in another direction—that of Calvary; and for the sake of wayfaring men in the circumstances of actual life we cannot but rejoice that this is so. Whatever may be the defects of the Communion Office as found generally in the Book of Common Prayer as severally authorized in the churches of the Anglican Communion, it is no inconsiderable merit that it never loses touch with reality. The Prayer for Purity, the Ten Commandments, the Confession, Absolution and Comfortable Words, the Prayer of Humble Access and the character of the Consecration Prayer itself—if these taken together have on the one hand unduly crowded out the eucharistic element in the Office, they have on the other brought the worshipper and his needs in contact with the pardon and peace of the Cross to a degree unequalled in any other liturgy.

And, once again, the bread and wine, which are the outward and visible sign of the grace received in the eucharist, are themselves intimately related to the life and work of the communicant. They represent, at any rate indirectly, the fruits of his labour and toil. This is not made so apparent as it might be in the Office of the Book of Common Prayer, but is still indicated, if obscurely, in the Offertory, when the order of the actions— the placing of the bread and wine upon the Holy Table after the offering of the alms—suggests that the elements afterwards to be consecrated represent or are procured by the gifts of the congregation. But those who have read the vivid description,[1] based on the *Ordo Romanus Primus*,[2] by Bishop Gore of the Offertory and Communion in early days in the West, will realize how significantly this representation could be made by the action of the liturgy then.

"You would have seen the Pope and his attendant ministers going down among the congregation and making a very elaborate collection of loaves and wine, in bags and immense flagons, from the whole congregation. That was their corporate oblation, and it was elaborately carried out, the Pope himself offering his loaf, the clergy their loaves, the chief officers of the city their loaves, and the men and women of the congregation their loaves and offerings of wine." Then follows the account of the offering of this oblation, and its consecration; after which: "The oblation of the people, offered, accepted, consecrated, is now again, by a process which is very elaborately described, prepared for the great corporate communion, the bread broken and put into bags held by acolytes, and the wine in the chalice which had been consecrated poured into bowls or flagons of still unconsecrated wine which were thereby apparently held to be consecrated, and then the great communion of the people."

Such a visual connection between the fruits of men's labours and the sacramental gifts is no longer apparent to-day. But the

---

[1] Quoted by J. A. Robinson, *Giving and Receiving*, 86, 87; cp. G. Dix, *The Shape of the Liturgy*, 110ff., for an earlier period.

[2] An eighth-century document, but going back in substance to the fifth.

relationship itself remains, however obscured or ignored in later liturgies. "The strengthening and refreshing of our souls, as our bodies are" strengthened and refreshed "by the bread and wine"—these words relate the inward to the outward by the symbol of food: and this in turn relates the eucharist to the labour and toil which has gone to provide the communicant's daily bread. For many this provision involves all kinds of difficulties, not only physical hardship but also anxiety and mental distress. With a truly prophetic note the Book of Genesis speaks of the "thorns and thistles",[1] as well as the sweat of the face, which are to thwart and hinder man's toilsome efforts in this world to provide his daily bread. The eucharist, therefore, by means of its divinely appointed symbols, is placed in intimate relation to the actual life of man, who in his present "fallen" condition must expect to find the ground "cursed for his sake" —that is, to find nature difficult or even hostile as he endeavours to extract from it a livelihood.

And here again, by reason of its historical and personal reference as well as by the symbols employed, the eucharist brings to the worshipper its own peculiar message of grace adapted to his needs. For the Cross was the end of the earthly life of One who could in his last moments upon it utter the words "It is finished"[2]; and in that triumphant expression of work perfectly fulfilled may be gathered up the partial achievements and never completed endeavours of his brothers and sisters who at the end of their lives will be able to say, not "It is finished", but only "It is ended". Nevertheless, in virtue of his glorified humanity made available for partakers in the Sacrament, they can pray that their work in life may be accepted not on its own merits and achievements, but only "as found in him" who alone brought human life to its perfection. Also, this grace bears in addition an eschatological significance, for it is but a foretaste of that blessedness which shall be theirs who have re-entered the Garden of Eden, and "in the Lord" rest from their labours[3]—from the toilsome conditions when the "curse" prevailed upon them—and find in work nothing but the joy of service.

And so we may find many reasons, arising from the sacramental

---

[1] 3. 18. [2] John 19. 30.
[3] Rev. 14. 13.

symbolism of the eucharist, its historical associations with our redemption, and its significance for the actual condition of the Christian in the world, which combine to constitute the Holy Communion as the most intense and significant point in his devotional life. It goes without saying that above them all is the fact of its divinely appointed Institution. Some might prefer to give no other reason than this. But it is to be remembered that he who instituted the Sacrament and, as we may believe, enjoined its observance upon his disciples, also promised to them the abiding presence of the Holy Spirit within them, and told them that his departure from their midst was their gain, since it was the necessary prelude to the coming of the Spirit. Therefore, the blessings of sacramental communion and of communion in the Spirit are, both of them, of Dominical dispensation; although the latter is less exclusively connected in respect of its source with the Son.[1]

But the words of the Lord, "This is *my* body", "This is *my* blood", suggest—what spiritual experience confirms—that the Holy Communion stands out from all other means of communion in respect of the *intimacy* of the gift. Here is something which is attached to, and attaches us to, the Person of the Redeemer in a special degree. In it, to repeat the words of Hooker quoted above,[2] "we know by grace what the grace is which God giveth us . . . we understand that the strength of our life begun in Christ is Christ." Or, as Gore expresses it,[3] "it is the completest degree of participation in Christ's manhood which . . . is identified with Holy Communion." Nevertheless, though a difference in degree may sometimes become a difference in kind, it would be hazardous for a writer on Christian doctrine, however much he may recognize the intenser experience of the divine presence in Holy Communion, to affirm that it is wholly other than that presence of the Holy Spirit which is associated with prayer and other non-sacramental ways in which he makes his grace known to us. We have, we think, shown in previous chapters, that so far from asserting this "other-ness", the several writings in the New Testament suggest the contrary. And it is further relevant to note that as the sacramental gift brings to us

[1] "The Comforter . . . whom the Father will send in my name . . . whom I will send unto you from the Father": John 14. 26; 15. 26.
[2] p. 153.   [3] *The Body of Christ*, 70.

the grace that flows from the Cross and Resurrection, so does also the gift of the Holy Spirit, through whatever channels that gift may be bestowed. The Holy Spirit comes to the members of the Church from him who through death and resurrection became a life-giving spirit.[1] The Holy Spirit brings to them the fruits of the redemptive work of Christ. "It is by the imparted gift . . . of literal membership in him; by the indwelling presence, the gradually disciplining and dominating influence, of his Spirit —which is his very Self within, and as, the inmost breath of our most secret being; that the power of his atoning life and death, which is the power of divinely victorious holiness, can grow to be the very deepest reality of ourselves."[2] The connection between the operations of the Holy Spirit and the Atonement is most clearly seen in what may be described as his *destructive* power, whereby the evil passions, resulting in the "works of the flesh", are gradually subdued and eliminated. But every achievement of the Holy Spirit within us, constructive as well as destructive, every advance in holiness or in truth no less than every conquest over sin, is ultimately the result of Christ's atoning work. The experience of the Holy Spirit, therefore, no less than the experience of Christ in the sacrament, should turn our thoughts, if we think deeply on the matter, to the *historical* facts of our redemption. Quite obviously, however, it does not do this so readily. The Cross and its meaning is brought before the communicant more directly than it is, for example, before him who proves the power of the Holy Spirit through private prayer. And, as we have suggested, it is this felt relation between grace given now and grace achieved for us in the earthly work of Christ, that is a principal moving factor in the experience of the sacramental presence.

Perhaps we may use an analogy taken from physical things and modern life. The person who is injected with a serum as a preventive against infection, or who is treated with a newly discovered drug such as penicillin, does not ordinarily, unless he is of a thoughtful disposition, connect this safeguard or this healing with all that has gone before to achieve it—I refer to the prolonged researches, the sweat of body and of mind, the disappointments and failures, the sacrifice of time and money, it

---

[1] 1 Cor. 15. 45.   [2] R. C. Moberly, *Atonement and Personality*, 284.

may be even of life itself, which were involved in reaching at long last success and so providing for humanity in the future freedom from disease and conquest over disease. But if such a person at the time of his receiving the remedy were to read an historical account of these researches, or, better still, to listen to a play on the radio in which the actors in this scientific achievement were portrayed, his imagination would surely be notably quickened with a sense of what had been done, and done for *him*.

In the Holy Spirit is to be found the healing power of the soul —that which wards off its disease and keeps it in health. That we associate this power, as we have noted, mainly with its operation in daily life and the unmediated channels of grace tends to divert our thoughts from the historical sources of this healing in the redemptive acts of Christ. Nevertheless, the connection between the power and its ultimate source is intimate; and the New Testament, and especially St. Paul's Epistles, do not allow us to forget it. It is well, for example, to meditate on such passages as these: "Ye are not in the flesh, but in the spirit, if so be that the Spirit of God dwelleth in you. But if any man hath not the Spirit of Christ, he is none of his. And if Christ is in you, the body is dead because of sin; but the spirit is life because of righteousness. But if the Spirit of him that raised up Jesus from the dead dwelleth in you, he that raised up Christ Jesus from the dead shall quicken also your mortal bodies through his Spirit that dwelleth in you." "The fruit of the Spirit is love, joy, peace, longsuffering, kindness, goodness, faithfulness, meekness, temperance: against such there is no law. And they that are of Christ Jesus have crucified the flesh with the passions and the lusts thereof."[1] The alternation between "Spirit" and "Christ" in these passages, as in others that might be quoted, may cause difficulty to the commentator or to the theologian with the "one-track" mind, but is eloquent of the connection referred to above.

Conversely, if in the eucharist the historical acts of redemption in Christ are prominent in the liturgy and in our minds, it is all the more needful to remember that the eucharist is of vital meaning to us because we are in the Spirit, in whom indeed the

[1] Rom. 8. 9-11; Gal. 5. 22-24.

whole action is performed. Speaking of the gifts given in the bread and wine of the Sacrament, R. C. Moberly well says[1]: "What they were at the moment of Calvary they have not been again since the Resurrection, and are not, anyhow or anywhere, now. What is given in the eucharist is what is, and not what is not. Calvary indeed is an inalienable element in what they are. The thought of Calvary is expressly recalled and emphasized in the terms in which they are given. But they are themselves not a material but a spiritual gift. The value of the material is not its material but its spiritual value. It is the body and blood not as slain in death; but as, through the fact of death, victoriously alive. It is the humanity triumphant, perfect, consummated in Spirit. It is no exception to the universal principle, that the Pentecostal Church is $\Pi\nu\epsilon\hat{v}\mu\alpha$; and therefore that everything in the Church is what it is only within the region, and informing principle, of Spirit."

"Where the Church is, there is also the Spirit of God; and where the Spirit of God is, there is the Church, and all grace." These words of Irenæus[2] justify the above quotation from Moberly, and are applicable to the general subject of this book. It is in accordance with this principle that certain passages from writings and liturgies in the early Church speak of the content of the eucharist as "Spirit"; and, bearing this in mind, we need not regard such statements as aberrations from the main tradition. They may be so in actual terminology, but in inner meaning they are not. Some of the passages quoted by E. G. C. F. Atchley[3] do not seem to me to be relevant; but reference must be made to a remarkable passage which occurs in a sermon of Ephrem Syrus[4]: "He called the bread his living body, and filled it with himself and the Spirit. . . . Take, eat in faith, nothing doubting that this is my body,[5] and he who eats it in faith eats in it fire and Spirit; but if anyone eats it doubting, to him it is nothing but bread. . . . Take of it, eat ye all of it, and in it eat Holy Spirit, for it is truly my body." Other references of similar import are given to the liturgy of St. James[6] and to Theodore of Mop-

---

[1] *Atonement and Personality*, 274f.   [2] *Hær*. iii. 38. 1 (Harvey).

[3] *On the Epiclesis of the Eucharistic Liturgy and in the Consecration of the Font*, pp. 41, 44, 93.   [4] Sermo iv, *In Hebdomadam Sanctam* (Lamy, i. 416).

[5] Or, less probably, ". . . nothing doubting; for this is my body".

[6] See F. E. Brightman, *Liturgies Eastern and Western*, 52.

suestia[1] by Gregory Dix,[2] who also cites, for early Western usage, the petition from the *Apostolic Tradition of Hippolytus*, "that thou wouldest grant to all who partake to be made one, that they may be fulfilled with Holy Spirit".

It is natural enough that liturgiologists who are wedded to the Western tradition concerning the effective formula of consecration should be "puzzled"[3] by such statements. But when it is maintained that the difficulty of assimilating the idea of consecration by the Holy Spirit with that of consecration by the Son has never been met quite convincingly by anyone from the fourth century to the present day,[4] it may not be out of place to suggest that a return to Biblical theology would be a help. In the light of this the varied language to be found in early liturgical references is to be interpreted, and in particular the language of Ephrem Syrus quoted above. On the other hand, if we fail to view the doctrine of the eucharist in relation to the conviction of the early Church concerning the presence of the Holy Spirit in all the members and all the functions of the Church, we shall also fail to appreciate the fact that what appear to be two divergent traditions concerning the eucharist had a common origin in a theology which, because it still retained its Biblical character, had not lost the capacity of comprehending both.

This chapter began with a question concerning the relationship between the grace of Holy Baptism and that of Holy Communion, and two differing points of view on this subject. The writer, while deprecating dogmatism on this mystery of divine grace, believes that he has produced evidence which goes to show that Hooker is nearer the truth than Quick is, especially when we read into the concept "Holy Baptism" the multiform divine life into which members of the Church are admitted by that Sacrament. This evidence would seem to call in question the assertion that "the Church's constant belief" is "that the presence of Christ in the eucharist is to be accounted something different from his presence in Baptism".[5] It may be that what is meant is that the presence of Christ in relation to the water of Baptism, on the one hand, and to the elements of bread and wine, on the other, has for the most part been differently conceived. But that is quite another matter, into which we cannot

[1] *Catecheses*, vi.   [2] *The Shape of the Liturgy*, 266.
[3] G. Dix, *ibid.*   [4] *Id.*, p. 282.   [5] *The Christian Sacraments*, 187.

enter now. To assert that the grace of Baptism and the grace of Eucharist are different in kind, and to do this on the ground of "the Church's constant belief", is perilous. And indeed, when Quick speaks of the "renewal"[1] in the eucharist of the contact with God made first at Holy Baptism, the very word "renewal" which he uses to describe the effect of the eucharist suggests a kinship between the grace of the one Sacrament and that of the other.[2]

The life of the Christian is life in the Spirit, a life of grace. And if the grace of the Gospel has often been likened in Holy Scripture and Christian poetry to a river, so also the life of the disciple may be compared to the course of a river in all its vicissitudes from source to sea, which is continually being fed by tributary or by rain from heaven with that which is akin to itself: so that, however changed its circumstances or its aspect at one time or another, it is still the same river, whether in the freshness of its early springs, or in the toiling sluggishness of its middle course, or in its final sweep towards the ocean which is to receive it. The river also, like the Christian, has a name, which for the mind of man preserves its identity and maintains its continuity through change. If, then, we are enabled to view the course of a river, or the life of a Christian, as a whole, and note its unity, how much clearer must that unity appear to God, who feeds the one and the other from his manifold sources of renewal! And how slow should we be to distinguish one such source from another, or to attempt to say where one begins or another leaves off! If the river, like the Christian, is—in the words of Hooker—much hindered and impaired in its course, God gives it, not something different in kind, but the increase of that which it already possesses. And so both the river and the Christian move by the grace of God to the determined end.

Those who have forgotten it will be glad to be reminded of the magnificent passage which forms the conclusion of *Sohrab and Rustum*, and may find in it thoughts not irrelevant to the subject we have been pursuing.

> But the majestic river floated on,
>   Out of the mist and hum of that low land,
>   Into the frosty starlight, and there moved,

[1] *Ib.*, 186.   [2] See, further, NOTE at the end of this chapter.

Rejoicing, through the hush'd Chorasmian waste,
Under the solitary moon;—he flow'd
Right for the polar star, past Orgunjè,
Brimming, and bright, and large; then sands begin
To hem his watery march, and dam his streams,
And split his currents; that for many a league
The shorn and parcell'd Oxus strains along
Through beds of sand and matted rushy isles—
Oxus, forgetting the bright speed he had
In his high mountain-cradle in Pamere,
A foil'd circuitous wanderer—till at last
The long'd for dash of waves is heard, and wide
His luminous home of waters opens, bright
And tranquil, from whose floor the new-bathed stars
Emerge, and shine upon the Aral Sea.

NOTE

The following extracts from Jeremy Taylor, *The Worthy Communicant*, may serve to illustrate matters that have been treated in the preceding chapters, and in particular the relationship between Holy Baptism and Holy Communion on the one hand, and between sacramental and non-sacramental (what Jeremy Taylor calls "out of the Sacrament") grace on the other.

Section II, 4. St. John[1] having thus explicated this mystery in general, of our eating the flesh and drinking the blood of Christ, added nothing in particular concerning the Sacraments, these being but particular instances of the general mystery and communion with Christ. But what is the advantage we receive by the Sacraments, beside that which we get by the other and distinct ministries of faith, I thus account in general.

The *word* and the *spirit* are the *flesh* and the *blood* of Christ; that is, the ground of all. Now because there are two great Sermons of the Gospel which are the sum total and abbreviature of the whole word of God, the great messages of the word incarnate, Christ was pleased to invest these two words with two Sacraments, and assist those two Sacraments, as he did the whole word of God, with the presence of his Spirit,

[1] Chap. 6.

that in them we might do more signally and solemnly what was in the ordinary ministrations done plainly and without extraordinary regards.

Believe and repent, is the word in baptism, and there solemnly consigned; and here it is that *by faith* we feed on Christ: for *faith* as it is opposed to *works*, that is, the *new covenant of faith* as it is opposed to the *old covenant of works*, is the covenant of repentance; repentance is expressly included in the new covenant, but was not in the old; but by faith in Christ we are admitted to the pardon of our sins if we repent and forsake them utterly. Now this is the word of faith; and this is what is called the flesh or body of Christ; for this is that which the soul feeds on, this is that by which the just do live; and when by the operation of the Holy Spirit the waters are reformed to a Divine Nature or efficacy, the baptized are made clean, they are sanctified and presented pure and spotless unto God. This mystery St. Austin[1] rightly understood when he affirmed that *we are made partakers of the body and blood of Christ when we are in baptism incorporated into his body; we are baptized in the passion of our Lord*, so Tertullian,[2] to the same sense with that of St. Paul, *we are buried with him by baptism into his death*[3]; that is, by baptism are conveyed in it a *visible word*, the word in symbol and visibility, and special manifestation. Consonant to which doctrine, the Fathers by an elegant expression called the blessed Sacrament "the extension of the incarnation."

So that there are two things highly to be remarked:

1. That by whatsoever way Christ is taken *out of the Sacrament*, by the same he is taken *in the Sacrament*, and by some ways here, more than there.

2. That the eating and drinking the consecrated symbols is but the body and lesser part of the Sacrament: the life and the spirit is believing greatly, and doing all the actions of that believing, direct and consequent. So that there are in this two manducations, the *Sacramental* and the *Spiritual*. That

---

[1] "*ad infantes apud Bedam.*"

[2] *De Baptismo*, 19: *passio domini in qua tinguimur*; Cyril, *Catech.* xx. 6 (*P.G.* xxxiii. 1081): Baptism is ἀντίτυπον τῶν τοῦ χριστοῦ παθημάτων.

[3] Rom. 6. 4.

does but declare and exercise this: and of the sacramental manducation as it is alone, as it is a ceremony, as it does only consign and express the internal; it is true to affirm that it is only an act of obedience: but all the blessings and conjugations of joy which come to a worthy communicant proceed from that spiritual eating of Christ, which as it is done out of the Sacrament very well, so in it and with it, much better. For here being (as in baptism) a double significatory of the spirit, a word, and a sign of his appointment, it is certain he will join in this ministration. Here we have bread and drink, flesh and blood, the word and the spirit, Christ in all his effects and most gracious communications.

. . . For greater things than these we can neither receive nor expect: but these things are not consequent to the reception of the natural body of Christ which is now in heaven, but of his word and of his spirit, which are therefore indeed his body and his blood, because by these we feed on him to life eternal. Now these are indeed conveyed to us by the several ministries of the Gospel, but especially in the Sacraments, where the word is preached and consigned, and the spirit is the teacher and the feeder, and makes the Table full, and the Cup to overflow with blessing.

Section III. . . . For the mystery is this; by immersion in baptism and emersion we are configured to Christ's burial and to his resurrection: that's the outward part: to which if we add the inward, which is there intended, and is expressed by the Apostle in the following words, *knowing that our old man is crucified with him, that the body of sin might be destroyed, that henceforth we should not serve sin*,[1] that's our spiritual death, to us all the effects of Christ's death; the flesh and blood of Christ crucified are in baptism reached to us by the hand of God, by his holy Spirit, and received by the hand of man, the ministry of a holy faith. So that it can without difficulty be understood that as in receiving the word and the spirit illuminating us in our first conversion, we do truly feed on the flesh and drink the Blood of Christ, who is the bread that came down from heaven; so we do it also, and do it much more in baptism, because in this,

[1] Rom. 6. 6.

besides all that was before, there was superadded a rite of God's appointment. The difference is only this; that out of the Sacrament the spirit operates with the word in the ministry of man; in baptism the spirit operates with the word in the ministry of God. For here God is the preacher, the Sacrament is God's sign, and by it he ministers life to us by the flesh and blood of his Son, that is, by the death of Christ into which we are baptized.

And in the same divine method the word and the spirit are ministered to us in the Sacrament of the Lord's Supper. For as in baptism so here also there is a word proper to the ministry. *So often as ye eat this bread and drink this cup, ye declare the Lord's death till he come.*[1] This indeed is a word of comfort. *Christ died for our sins*[2]; that is, our repentance which was consigned in baptism shall be to purpose; we shall be washed white and clean in the blood of the sacrificed Lamb. This is *verbum visibile*,[3] the same word read to the eye and the ear. Here the word of God is made our food in a manner so near to our understanding, that our tongues and palates feel the metaphor and the sacramental signification; here faith is in triumph and exultation: but as in all the other ministries evangelical, we eat Christ by faith; here we have faith also by eating Christ: Thus eating and drinking is faith; it is faith in mystery, and faith in ceremony; it is faith in act and faith in habit; it is exercised and it is advanced; and therefore it is certain that here we eat the flesh and drink the blood of Christ with much eminency and advantage.

The sum is this. Christ's body, his flesh and his blood, are therefore called our meat and our drink, because by his incarnation and manifestation in the flesh he became life unto us: so that it is mysterious indeed in the expression, but very proper and intelligible in the event, to say that we eat his flesh and drink his blood, since by these it is that we have and preserve life. But because what Christ began in his incarnation he finished in his body on the cross, and all the whole progression of mysteries in his body was still an operatory of life and spiritual being to us; the Sacrament of

---

[1] 1 Cor. 11. 26.   [2] 1 Cor. 15. 3.

[3] Augustine, *contra Faustum* xix. 16 (*P.L.* xlii. 357); *In Evang. Joh.* tract. lxxx (*P.L.* xxxv. 1840).

the Lord's Supper being a commemoration and exhibition of this death which was the consummation of our redemption by his body and blood, does contain which answers to our configuration with the death of Christ in baptism; *that like as Christ was raised up from the dead by the glory of the Father, even so we also should walk in newness of life*[1]; there's the correspondent of our configuration to the resurrection of Christ: that is, if we do that duty of baptism, we shall receive that grace; God offers us the mercy at that time, when we promise the duty, and do our present portion. This St. Peter calls the *stipulation of a good conscience*[2]; the *postulate* and *bargain* which man then makes with God; who promises us pardon and immortality, resurrection from the dead, and life eternal, if we repent toward God and have faith in the Lord Jesus, and if we promise we have and will so abide.

The same[3] is the case in the other most glorious Sacrament; it is the same thing in nearer presentation: only what is begun in baptism proceeds on to perfection in the holy communion. Baptism is *the antitype of the passion of Christ*[4]; and the Lord's Supper σημαντικὸς τῶν παθημάτων, that also represents Christ's passion; baptism is the union of the members of Christ and the admission of them under one head into one body: as the apostle affirms, *we are all baptized into one body*[5]; and so it is in the communion; *the bread which we break, it is the communion of the body of Christ; for we being many, are one body and one bread*[6]: in baptism we partake of the death of Christ; and in the Lord's Supper we do the same, in *that* as babes, in *this* as men in Christ: so that what effects are affirmed of one, the same are in greater measure true of the other; they are but several rounds of Jacob's ladder reaching up to heaven, upon which the angels ascend and descend; and the Lord sits upon the top.

---

[1] Rom. 6. 4.   [2] 1 Peter 3. 16.

[3] "Et institutio paria, et significatio similia, et finis facit aequalia. S. August. apud Bedam in 1 Cor. 10."   [4] Cyril, *Catech*. xx. 6 (as above).

[5] 1 Cor. 12. 13.   [6] 1 Cor. 10. 16, 17.

CHAPTER IX

IN THY LIGHT SHALL WE SEE LIGHT

WHEN we relate the gift of the eucharist to the life of the Church, of which the Sacrament forms only a part, we see that the problem of the nature of the sacramental gift is not an isolated problem, but that it is akin to a much larger one —namely, how we are to relate God's apartness from the Christian to his indwellingness in him, how he can be said to "come" to those in whom he is already present.

Ultimately, I suppose, the problem is one of philosophy rather than of theology—that is to say, the relation of time to eternity. One who is not a philosopher, but who has only read what others more competent than he have said on this subject, may at any rate take refuge in the observed fact that there appears to be no kind of agreement among philosophers of different schools as touching this profound and, it would seem, baffling question. That being so, the theologian need not hesitate to proceed at once to the material that lies before him in the record of God's revelation in Christ, not in order to discover an answer to the abstract question (for none is given there either), but rather to see how that revelation holds together, when it speaks of God's relation to the Christian, these two facts at first sight opposed and even contradictory.

The problem comes into view at once as a theological problem when we consider the relation between the doctrine of the Holy Spirit and the eschatological hope of a "Second" Coming. The tendency in much modern theology has been to regard these two things as incompatible. To illustrate this, we have only to refer to the history of theology during the last fifty or sixty years in regard to the conception of the "Kingdom of God" as found in the Gospels. It was a shattering blow—or so it seemed—to much of the "liberal" theology which had preceded it, when Schweitzer declared that the dominant thought of Jesus consisted in the belief that a supernatural, transcendent, kingdom or rule of God would

168

come in the immediate future. This conception left no room for the picture of a gradually developing and progressing kingdom, as men accept more and more of the ethics of Jesus, which had been prevalent. It is a fair question whether the views of Schweitzer were and still are hailed with delight by some persons, less because they presented a picture of Jesus which the Church can whole-heartedly accept than because they seemed to bring about the discomfiture of the hated "liberals". W. F. Howard very pertinently says, with reference to Schweitzer's work, that it was carried out "with a thoroughness that was logical rather than convincing".[1] That was it. Truth there was in his contention, and—at the time—needful truth. But was it the whole truth? Did it fit every situation? Was it the solution of every problem? The answer of subsequent theology would seem to be "no". The views of Schweitzer have really proved too violent in their relentless consistency for Christians to stomach. And we are now in a phase of thought in which what is called "realized eschatology" is the dominant opinion in the interpretation of the Gospels. According to this view, "the kingdom of God is and remains for Christ the future kingdom of the final age, thought of in strictly eschatological terms, following on the 'Messianic woes,' following on the divine judgement. But what distinguishes his eschatology from that which had preceded it is, on the one side, that he already lives in the present active miracle of the final age, that with clear vision he sees this as something which is already coming into being and growing up around him, he knows himself to be supported by his powers already pressing on as an advance guard, and by their support and inspiration he works and preaches. On the other side, by his works, speech, parables, charismatic conferring of power, he mediates to a circle of disciples following in his steps a contact with this miracle of the transcendent as a personal possession."[2]

One advantage of this view is that, whereas in Schweitzer's interpretation of the Gospels the teaching of Jesus on human conduct was merely an "interim-ethic", to serve for the brief period that lay between his ministry and the imminent coming of

---

[1] *Christianity according to St. John*, 106. Already the eschatological school of interpretation of the Gospels has received trenchant criticism in *The Second Advent* by T. F. Glasson.

[2] R. Otto, *Reich Gottes und Menschensohn*, E.T., p. 155.

the kingdom, according to "realized eschatology" the teaching of Jesus, as well as he himself and his marvellous acts, brings men into touch with the transcendent realities which have been manifested on earth. Thus there is an attempt to include the whole of the material in the Gospels as pointing to the present fact of the supreme crisis inaugurated by the advent of the Son of God among men. But an exponent of this view, such as C. H. Dodd, will make no room in the teaching of Jesus for the idea of the kingdom as an immanent process, a divine principle, working in society; and he interprets those parables which seem to speak of growth—such as the Seed Growing Secretly, the Mustard Seed and the Leaven—as applicable only to the actual situation during the ministry of Jesus.[1] The coming of Jesus, the *eschaton*, the climax of history, was a harvest prepared for by a long period of growth *in the past*: for according to this view any idea of a lapse of time between the Ministry and the Second Advent must be ruled out from the teaching of Jesus.

On this we may remark that this interpretation, no less than Schweitzer's, is carried out "with a thoroughness that is logical rather than convincing". C. H. Dodd would, we think, himself admit that the interpretation he gives of the parables of growth *appears* (although no doubt he would not allow that it actually is) strained and artificial, and that it is opposed to their general interpretation by the Church.[2] But apart from this particular point we must confess that we are fundamentally distrustful of any attempt to bring our Lord's conception of the kingdom under any single view. That the kingdom was indeed the dominant note and theme of his teaching, that he could bring it to bear upon every department of life, human and divine, is *a priori* a reason for hesitating to circumscribe it. As has been often remarked, Jesus Christ was above the heads of his reporters. He may also be equally above the heads of his interpreters, and especially when they endeavour, in a matter concerning which he spoke so constantly and his words are so variously recorded, to weave it all into a neat, consistent pattern. This is not to say that modern study of this subject has not brought valuable results. Far from it. Schweitzer has made a contribution; so have Rudolph Otto and C. H. Dodd; and, we may add—if the

[1] *The Parables of the Kingdom*, 193.   [2] *Id.*, 176, 193.

word can be tolerated—so did the "liberals" in their day. Time will assess the contributions of these writers and schools more accurately than we can at present; but time will also note that they were all of them unduly influenced by the circumstances and tendencies of their own day; and what they have said will be reckoned as contributions, not as solutions, to the study of a theme which is of eternal significance. The practical outcome of this for us at present is that we will refuse to be dominated in our general outlook by any one of them.

Similarly, in regard to the other writings of the New Testament, we note a like tendency in much theological study to-day to place in absolute contrast present possession of the Spirit and eschatological hope. It has been pointed out, for example, that when in later life St. Paul became more "Church-conscious", and developed his conception of the Church as the body of Christ, the thought of a "Return" of Christ—and more especially of an imminent "Return"—grew fainter and fainter. Similarly, it has been maintained that because for St. John judgement and eternal life are *now*, those passages therefore in the Johannine writings which speak of a future judgement or future manifestation of Christ[1] are either interpolations or else incongruous relics, inconsistently retained, of a traditional hope which the writer had himself discarded as a personal belief. But I believe that from a religious no less than from a theological standpoint it is unsound and misleading to draw this sharp distinction. It would be right, however, to distinguish, in the first place, between the hope of a future consummation and that of an *immediate* Return. As the latter hope died out, there was no doubt greater emphasis laid upon the "present possession" of Christ—that is to say, his presence through the Spirit in the life of the Church. But this Spirit-possessed life was not regarded, either by St. Paul or St. John, as *a substitute for* a future consummation. There was still a looking forward to that Appearance or Manifestation which was to fulfil and give its significance to the present life in the Spirit. Again, we must distinguish between this future hope and the imagery in which it was at first clothed. If in some of the later books of the New Testament (but not *Revelation* or 2 *Peter*), the visible accompaniments with which the

[1] E.g., John 5. 29; 6. 39, 40, 44, 54; 21. 22: I John 2. 17, 18, 28; 3. 2.

Jewish Apocalyptists and their Christian successors or imitators had associated the last things tend to disappear, it does not follow by any means that the hope itself, to which the imagery was only as a husk to its kernel, disappeared also. We may on the contrary affirm that both St. Paul and St. John were impelled by their present possession of the Spirit to find in eschatology that which gives its appropriate fulfilment to their religious experience.

St. Paul expresses, for example, at all stages of his literary activity his conviction concerning the indwelling presence of Christ through the Spirit. In *Galatians*, which is perhaps the earliest in point of time of his extant letters, he says, "I live; and yet no longer I, but Christ liveth in me"[1]; and he speaks of "the fruit of the Spirit"[2]—a phrase which indicates in a different manner the same fact. Very striking is the expression of this conviction concerning all the Galatians in the opening verses of chapter 3, especially as read in Moffatt's translation:

> O senseless Galatians, who has bewitched you—you who had Jesus Christ the crucified placarded before your very eyes? I simply want to ask you one thing: did you receive the Spirit by doing what the Law commands or by believing the gospel message? Are you such fools? Did you begin with the Spirit only to end now with the flesh? Have you had all that experience for nothing (if it has really gone for nothing)? When He supplies you with the Spirit and works miracles among you, is it because you do what the Law commands or because you believe the gospel message?

On the other hand, if the Epistles to the Thessalonians are the earliest of the Pauline letters, they sufficiently (if not so strikingly as *Galatians*) indicate his belief concerning the Holy Spirit.[3]

The epistles of the middle period—1 and 2 *Corinthians* and *Romans*—contain more fully than any other group of his writings teaching on the Holy Spirit and his work in the individual Christian. In *Philippians*, one of his later epistles, he recalls *Galatians* when he says, "To me to live is Christ."[4] The same

---

[1] 2. 20.   [2] 5. 22.
[3] 1 Thess. 1. 5, 6; 4. 8; 5. 19: 2 Thess. 2. 13.   [4] 1. 21.

conviction is indicated in all his epistles,[1] whether later or earlier, by the phrase "in Christ" or "in the Lord", which expresses most characteristically St. Paul's mystical view of the Christian life.

Nevertheless, at the same time, this conviction concerning an indwelling presence is to be found side by side with the hope of a "future" or "nearer" presence, without any indication on the part of St. Paul that there was any inconsistency or antinomy which needed explanation or resolution. Thus, it has been said that "eschatology does not come prominently to expression in Galatians; but it is presupposed, as it is in all the New Testament writings; and no interpretation of Galatians can afford to neglect it."[2] Gal. 1. 4, 5. 21 and 6. 7-9 sufficiently indicate eschatological beliefs in a letter which is occupied with topics of a very different character. The Epistles to the Corinthians make a large contribution to our knowledge of St. Paul's teaching on the "last things", and indicate very clearly, 1 *Corinthians* especially, the belief that he at that time held concerning an imminent coming of Christ. In *Philippians*, side by side with the statement that "to me to live is Christ"[3] is another that he has "the desire to depart and to be with Christ, which is very far better"[4]; and side by side with the mystical injunction "Rejoice in the Lord" comes the eschatological warning "The Lord is at hand."[5] But perhaps the most illuminating passage on this subject is Romans 8. 22, 23: "For we know that the whole creation groaneth and travaileth in pain together until now. And not only so, but ourselves also, which have the firstfruits of the Spirit, even we ourselves groan within ourselves, waiting for our adoption, to wit, the redemption of our body." Here the presence of the Spirit and the eschatological hope are not simply placed side by side; there is a connection, even a causal connection, between them. The presence of the Spirit within a man urges him to look forward beyond this present conflict, in a self and a world that needs to be "redeemed" or "delivered", to the time when the sons of God will enter upon their glorious liberty and the creation itself be freed from the bondage of corruption. In this connection the expression "the firstfruits" (ἀπαρχή) of

---

[1] Not reckoning the Pastorals.
[2] G. S. Duncan in Moffatt's Commentary, p. xlii.
[3] 1. 21.   [4] 1. 23.   [5] 4. 4, 5.

the Spirit is very significant, and may be compared with 2 Cor. 5. 5, "God, who gave unto us the earnest (ἀρραβών) of the Spirit". On "firstfruits" Sanday and Headlam aptly comment: "The possession of these gifts served to quicken the sense of the yet greater gifts that were to come. Foremost among them was to be the transforming of the earthly or 'psychical' body into a spiritual body." Similarly, on the "earnest" of the Spirit Plummer remarks: "The Spirit inspires the longing and is the security that our longing for the spiritual body, the σῶμα τῆς δόξης, will be satisfied."

Of like significance is the statement in 1 John 3. 2: "Beloved, now are we children of God, and it is not yet made manifest what we shall be. We know that, if he shall be manifested, we shall be like him; for we shall see him even as he is." We note here, first, St. John's use of the word "child" (τέκνον) to denote the relationship of the believer to God. "The idea of τέκνον as it is thus presented by St. John includes the two notions of the presence of the divine principle and the action of human growth. The child is made to share in his Father's nature,[1] and he uses in progressive advance the powers which he has received."[2] St. Paul prefers to use the term "son" (υἱός) for this purpose, because he wishes to emphasize our *status* before God: we are freemen—sons, not slaves. He indicates the idea and need of growth in the Christian disciple by such words as "to increase" (πλεονάζειν) and "to abound" (περισσεύειν), and by the phrase "the fruit of the Spirit". But the "child" (τέκνον) is essentially immature. The Spirit who has made him to share in his Father's nature has implanted in him a seed as concerning which he cannot now see what it will grow to: "it is not yet made manifest what we shall be." That is to say, the implanted "divine principle", like the "firstfruits" or "earnest" of the Spirit, urges the "child of God" to look forward to a goal for redeemed humanity, including himself, which he cannot now see or comprehend in its fulness. Only when the manifestation or Parousia[3] comes to pass shall we attain to that for which we are intended. But the transformation or change which will then take place will not make us *fundamentally* different from what we are at present. "Beloved, *now* are we children of God." Already we

---

[1] Cp. 2 Pet. 1. 4. [2] Westcott, *The Epistles of St. John*, 123.
[3] 1 John 2. 28.

are made to share in our Father's nature; and when we become "like him" it will be to give us manifestly a likeness which we already in some measure, though largely imperceptible to the human eye, possess.

In studying the Johannine writings we are in no danger of forgetting the truth that judgement and eternal life are present facts; but the passage just quoted and not a few others indicate that nevertheless the ideas of a *future* consummation and a *future* judgement are not absent from them, and that these are not, as has been supposed by some, interpolations or inconsistent survivals of primitive Christian thought in a later writer, but rather are integral to a balanced view of the Johannine teaching. We may refer to an excellent treatment of this subject in a recent work.[1]

There is in fact a greater amount of unity as concerning the subject of the kingdom between the Synoptic Gospels on the one hand and the rest of the New Testament on the other than has been commonly admitted. I do not speak of verbal agreement—for that does not exist—but of agreement in fundamental ideas. In the Gospels the kingdom or rule or sovereignty of God is both future and present. It would be manifested completely and finally in the future, but it had already come—in the mind and heart of Jesus. Jesus was the Man whose will was subordinated at every point to the will of God. Nothing found a place in him which was contrary to the divine purpose. In him, therefore, the rule of God found its seat. But even in his case, where there was no question of moral failure or imperfect achievement, the absolute acceptance of the will of God involved a strained looking forward to its accomplishment, inasmuch as a sinful world could be redeemed only through pain and loss. "I have a baptism to be baptized with; and how am I straitened till it be accomplished!"[2] And when through the death and resurrection of Jesus the immanent power of the Spirit came to dwell in his disciples, the very presence of the Spirit caused in them a painful longing for future consummation and deliverance, and all the more because in them, unlike their Lord, the mind of the flesh still retained a place.[3] Thus we are led, not only on theological grounds, but also on those of religious

---

[1] W. F. Howard, *Christianity according to St. John*, chap. v.
[2] Luke 12. 50.   [3] Rom. 8. 18-25.

experience, to the conclusion that possession of the Spirit and eschatological hope are by no means incompatible, but on the contrary connected. Dr. Inge speaks very truly in a passage in his *Christian Mysticism*,[1] in which, criticizing a statement of Reuss, he says: "if he means that such expressions as those referred to in St. John, about eternal life as something here and now, imply that judgement is now, *and therefore not in the future,* he is attributing to the evangelist, and to the whole array of religious thinkers who have used similar expressions, a view which is easy enough to understand, but which is destitute of any religious value, for it entirely fails to satisfy the religious consciousness. The feeling of the contrast between what ought to be and what is, is one of the deepest springs of faith in the unseen."

This quotation from Dr. Inge at once leads us on to seek for and to reach the same conclusion in the study of those who have been masters of the spiritual life and have endeavoured to express in writings what they experienced—the mystics and especially the Christian mystics of all ages. The mystical life is at once a goal and a possession. The ultimate aim of the mystic, on the one hand, is the beatific vision, complete union with God, sometimes expressed by the startling term "deification".[2] And the attainment of this aim is reached by means of definite stages, by a "ladder of perfection" whereby the aspirant climbs gradually to final achievement. Ever since the days of the pre-Christian mystery cults it has been recognized that the soul must pass through the stages of purification and illumination before it can attain to the heavenly vision. Thus not only has the mystic a goal set before him in the "future", but those who are his teachers in the way have left him a definitely marked map of the route and also the guides that he must take upon his upward ascent if he is to be successful. On the other hand, the mystical life is, equally, a possession. The mystic, as the very basis of his being a mystic, possesses God *now*, and more than other men experiences his presence; and, moreover, he claims to do so because his nature is akin to God's and he is made in God's image. Dr. Inge has

---

[1] p. 54 (1913).

[2] So Basil, *De Spiritu Sancto*, 23, speaks of life in the Holy Spirit as "the abiding in God, the being made like unto God, and—the highest point of desire—the becoming God".

made it clear that one of the propositions upon which mysticism rests "is that, since we can only know what is akin to ourselves, man, *in order to know God, must be a partaker of the divine nature.* 'What we are, that we behold; and what we behold, that we are,' says Ruysbroek. The curious doctrine which we find in the mystics of the Middle Ages, that there is at 'the apex of the mind' a spark which is consubstantial with the un-created ground of the Deity, is thus accounted for. We could not even begin to work out our own salvation, if God were not already working in us. It is always 'in his light' that 'we see light'."[1]

These two sides of mysticism, the present possession and the goal, have not always been comprehended or held together by all mystics. Some of them have found in the two an antinomy, an opposition, which they have been unable to resolve, and—like those theologians who contrast absolutely the Holy Spirit and eschatological hope—they have been led to take up an "either-or" position, and to choose between the one and the other. But such has not generally been the case among *Christian* mystics. The richer and more comprehensive character of the Christian revelation of God, with its doctrine of internal distinctions in the Godhead and their manifestation to men in the redemptive acts of Jesus Christ, has provided both an intellectual and a devotional basis on which the two-fold aspect of mysticism can rest. This is well stated by Evelyn Underhill: "Where non-Christian mystics, as a rule, have made a forced choice between the two great dogmatic expressions of their experience, (a) the long pilgrimage towards a transcendent and unconditioned Absolute, (b) the discovery of that Absolute in the 'ground' or spiritual principle of the self; it has been possible to Christianity by means of her central doctrine of the Trinity, to find room for both of them and to exhibit them as that which they are in fact —the complementary parts of a whole."[2] In the next quotation from the same writer the words at the close of it which I have italicized are especially significant for our subject: "*Deus,* whose root means day, shining, the Transcendent Light; and *Theos,* whose true meaning is supreme desire or prayer—the Inward Love—do not contradict, but complete each other. They form, when taken together, an almost perfect definition of that

[1] *Christian Mysticism* (1913), pp. 6f.   [2] *Mysticism,* 105.

Godhead which is the object of the mystic's desire: *the Divine Love which, immanent in the soul, spurs on that soul to union with the transcendent and Absolute Light—at once the source, the goal, the life of created things.*"[1]

This axiom of the mystics, or at any rate of Christian mystics, might be widely illustrated from their writings, but a few quotations from various sources of different ages may suffice:

"What is this which flashes in upon me, and thrills my heart without wounding it? I tremble and I burn; I tremble, feeling that I am unlike him; I burn, feeling that I am like him."[2]

"Dear Father, let my mind thy hallowed seat ascend,
Let me behold the spring of grace and find thy light,
That on thee may fix my soul's well clearèd sight,
Cast off the earthly weight wherewith I am opprest,
Shine as thou art most bright, *thou only calm and rest*
To pious men whose end is to behold thy ray,
Who their beginning art, their guide, their bound, and way."[3]

"Blest night of wandering,
In secret, where by none might I be spied,
Nor I see anything;
Without a light or guide,
Save that which in my heart burnt in my side.
That light did lead me on
More surely than the shining of noontide,
Where well I knew that One
Did for my coming bide;
Where he abode might none but he abide."[4]

"Our Lord said to me, 'I am the ground of thy beseechings: first, it is my will that thou have it; and then I make thee to wish for it; and then I make thee to beseech it, and thou beseechest it. How then should it be that thou shouldest not have thy beseeching?'"[5]

---

[1] *Ibid.*, 103.   [2] Augustine, *Conf.* xi. 9.
[3] Boethius, *Consolation of Philosophy*, iii. 9 (trans. as in Loeb Classical Library). The Latin of the last line is "Principium, uector, dux, semita, terminus idem."
[4] St. John of the Cross (trans. A. Symons, in *Images of Good and Evil*).
[5] Juliana of Norwich, quoted by W. R. Inge, *Christian Mysticism*, 204.

> I give you the end of a golden string,
>   Only wind it into a ball;
> It will lead you in at heaven's gate,
>   Built in Jerusalem's wall.[1]

Perhaps the clearest, and certainly the tersest, expression of this mystical truth is to be found in the words of Pascal, in which the Father says to Jesus on the Cross: "Thou couldest not be seeking me, unless thou hadst already found me."[2]

And—to relate the matter more definitely to the subject of this book—"this discovery of a 'divine' essence or substance, dwelling, as Ruysbroeck says, at the apex of a man's soul, is that fundamental experience—found in some form or degree in all genuine mystical religion—which provides the basis of the New Testament doctrine of the indwelling spirit. . . . In the struggle to describe this experience, the 'spark of the soul,' the point of juncture, is at one moment presented to us as the divine to which the self attains: at another, as that transcendental aspect of the self which is in contact with God."[3]

From a more philosophical point of view, A. S. Pringle-Pattison[4] expresses the same truth: "A purely immanental theory . . . means the denial of the divine altogether as in any way distinguishable from the human, and involves, therefore, the unqualified acceptance of everything just as it is. A theory of pure transcendence, on the other hand, tends to leave us with a 'mighty darkness filling the seat of power,' for only so far as God is present in our experience can we know anything about him at all. It is the immanence of the transcendent, the presence of the infinite in our finite lives, that alone explains the essential nature of man—the 'divine discontent' which is at the root of all progress, the strong sense of doubleness in our being, the incessant conflict of the lower and the higher self, so graphically described by St. Paul as a law in his members warring against the law of his mind. And the more clearly we identify the call of the higher with our true self the more unfeignedly do we recognize the illumination of the divine Spirit. *Deus illuminatio mea*—'In thy light shall we see light'."

[1] William Blake.
[2] "Tu ne me chercherais pas, si tu ne m'avais trouvé": *Pensées*, Section VII: "Le Mystère de Jésus."   [3] Evelyn Underhill, *Mysticism*, 100.
[4] *The Spirit* (ed. B. H. Streeter), p. 22.

Dr. Inge has pointed out that this principle of mysticism which we have been noting is also a doctrine held by most philosophers who maintain that a knowledge of God is possible for men.[1] It is unnecessary and perhaps not quite relevant here to give a detailed proof of his statement. But the point may be well illustrated from an unpublished lecture by Dr. W. R. Matthews, who has kindly given me permission to quote the following passage from it.[2] "The life of the spirit must be considered as one whole, though with distinctive parts. By the life of the spirit, I mean all those activities which are concerned with values going beyond the temporary interests of the individual. Philosophy—the search for truth, and art—the creation and appreciation of beauty, are two forms of the life of the spirit. I want to suggest that at the basis of the whole life of the spirit we can recognize a fundamental intuition which can be described in the phrase, 'the beyond which is within.'

"There is at the basis of the whole life of the spirit the intuition that our consciousness is continuous with a reality that is not wholly other than ourselves. Nay, I should like to go further, and say that we have an intuition that we are continuous with a reality which is akin to ourselves—a beyond which is both within and akin.

"I suggest that in religion this fundamental intuition is fully expressed and reaches a complete realization. It has often been pointed out as a reproach against religion that religion almost invariably expresses its conception of God in anthropomorphic images. This, it seems to me, is certainly no reproach to religion, and is implied in its very nature. If in religion we push this intuition, which is at the basis of every form of the life of the spirit, to its ultimate conclusion—the 'beyond' is so much 'akin' that it may be regarded under the form of personality. It is not merely a passively receptive material for the creative activity of the human mind. It has, on the contrary, a nature which actively responds to our aspirations. Nay, from that Other comes the initiative which stirs my soul out of slumber in order that it may aspire."

[1] *Christian Mysticism*, 7.

[2] From the Donnellan Lectures delivered before the University of Dublin in 1935. The quotation is taken from the report of the final lecture as given in *The Irish Times* of February 1, 1935.

Dr. Matthews is clearly not speaking in this passage of Christianity alone, but of religion in the widest sense of the term; although Christianity by reason of the doctrine of the Incarnation —the perfect manifestation of the character of God in a human life—is itself the supreme example of "the Beyond which is within and akin". Obviously also he is not referring to the sacraments. Yet the sacrament of the Holy Communion—the highest act of Christian worship—provides us with a good illustration of the truth of the general principle.

In this connection we may, first, think of the Sacrament as "proclaiming the Lord's death till he come"—that is to say, as a religious rite which points away from this present order to that which is to come and take its place. In a previous chapter[1] we saw that the New Testament evidence does not justify us in sharply distinguishing the ideas of spiritual feeding on Christ in the Sacrament and of eschatological hope. And this argument has been subsequently supported from another angle by reference to the literature of mysticism; so that we may say that religiously also this sharp distinction is unsound. If, further, we now go on to think of the sacramental presence as that which is "within and akin", and the future manifestation to which the Sacrament points forward as the "Beyond": then, according to this principle for which Dr. Matthews argues, there is no discontinuity between these two ideas; but, rather, the idea of feeding on Christ in the Sacrament is in no way to be placed in opposition to the idea of his Coming to us from a sphere beyond this order of things in a new age. Similarly, *John* is guilty of no incongruity when he says, "He that eateth my flesh and drinketh my blood hath eternal life; and I will raise him up at the last day."[2] The words, as I believe,[3] are not to be limited in their explanation to the Sacrament. Indeed, on the contrary, they are capable of having put into them the whole content of mystical union with Christ. But this includes sacramental feeding; and this saying is only another example, of which we have already found many in the New Testament, of the truth that the ideas of present possession and future consummation are indeed indissolubly connected in the life of the soul.

But, clearly, a more obvious illustration of the "Beyond which is within and akin" is to be found in the relation between the

[1] Pp. 123ff.   [2] John 6. 54.   [3] See pp. 79ff.

indwellingness of the Holy Spirit and the grace received in the Holy Communion. Here again, a tendency to differentiate between these two things is to be noted. The "mystical" and the "sacramental" types are placed in contrast by many, who would say that when we emphasize the abiding presence of Christ in the soul we are thereby disparaging the grace of the Sacrament. In other words, that continuous possession discourages, or tends to discourage, the use of, and belief in, set occasions and definite means of grace. But this by no means follows. In point of fact, churchmen of all schools of thought, however much they may differ among themselves concerning the manner of Christ's presence and its relation to the elements of bread and wine, are agreed that he is present in such a way that we must speak of the grace of the eucharist as a *gift*. And this is true of those who lay stress upon the perpetual presence of the Holy Spirit in the personal life. It is worth while quoting again familiar words on the subject, spoken by a person of definitely evangelical views, Bishop Moule of Durham, at a Conference held in Fulham Palace in 1900: "Such special presence . . . is perfectly mysterious in mode, but absolutely true in fact, no creation of the imagination or emotion, but an object for our faith. I believe that our Lord, so present, not on the Holy Table, but at it, would be seen himself in our presence to bless the bread and wine for a holy use, and to distribute them to his disciples." Similarly, Hooker, who, as we have seen in a previous chapter,[1] clearly relates the spiritual life imparted in the eucharist to the spiritual life immanent in the Christian as a member of Christ, and who, further, says that "the real presence of Christ's most blessed body and blood is not to be sought for in the Sacrament, but in the worthy receiver of the Sacrament", at the same time maintains that "our participation of Christ in this Sacrament dependeth on the co-operation of his omnipotent power which maketh it his body and blood to us."[2] It has been suggested that Hooker's position is inconsistent, or, if not actually so, that the second of the two statements (for example) quoted above qualifies or modifies the first. Such a criticism is really based upon the erroneous view that belief in the reality of the *gift* of the eucharist *demands* the acceptance of a different viewpoint from that of Hooker concerning the presence of Christ in the Sacrament. But

[1] Pp. 141ff. [2] *E.P.* v. 67. 6.

Hooker was in no doubt that the grace of the eucharist was something *given*. He says, "Let it therefore be sufficient for me presenting myself at the Lord's table to know *what there I receive from him*, without searching or inquiring of the manner how Christ performeth his promise."[1] For Hooker the eucharist was essentially grace—that is, fresh spiritual life imparted through reception of the elements; and yet he was too good a theologian not to know that what takes place in the soul at that point where its life meets fresh life from God is a mystery which leaves no place for dogmatism. Just because, as we believe, the Holy Communion takes the highest place in the devotional life of the Christian, it therefore supplies the supreme example of the truth to which the mystics bear witness, when they speak of the apex of a man's soul, the point of juncture, as at once the divine presence to which the self attains, and the higher self in contact with God. This is the "I, yet not I", the seeking for God which is itself the ground of his presence, the Beyond which is within and akin. How this point of contact is made in the Sacrament, as Hooker would say, "it skilleth not" to understand; but we are certainly on insecure ground when we *isolate*[2] the problem, and, through assuming that the eucharist differs from all other means of grace in the manner of its bestowal, fail to see that it is but another example of those high mysteries of which the masters of the spiritual life have to tell. And from this standpoint we see that there is, or need be, no inconsistency in emphasizing that the grace of the Sacrament is something "given", and at the same time affirming that Christ is already present in the soul of the communicant as he approaches

[1] *E.P.* v. 67. 12.

[2] An example of this is to be found in E. J. Bicknell, *A Theological Introduction to the Thirty-nine Articles*, p. 491, note. Bicknell quotes, as qualifying the statement that the real presence of Christ is to be found, not in the Sacrament, but in the worthy receiver of the Sacrament, the further statement of Hooker (v. 77. 1) that "The power of the ministry of God . . . by blessing visible elements . . . maketh them invisible grace." In point of fact, these words of Hooker (as is clear from the context) do not exclusively refer to the Holy Communion, and perhaps do not refer to it at all, but certainly include a reference to Holy Baptism. And this is confirmed by Hooker's words in another place (*E.P.*, v. 67. 6): "If on all sides it be confessed that the grace of Baptism is poured into the soul of man, that by water we receive it although it be neither seated in the water nor the water changed into it, what should induce men to think that the grace of the Eucharist must needs be in the Eucharist before it can be in us that receive it?"

the Sacrament, and that the meeting point lies in what is unseen. Indeed we are true to the teaching of the New Testament and to that of Christian mystics when we affirm that the presence within us of Christ is the very thing which stirs the soul to "seek" him as he "comes" in the Sacrament.

Should this line of thought be considered by any to be esoteric or lacking in plainness, it may not be out of place to point out that it underlies the teaching given to children in the Church Catechism as set forth in the Churches of the Anglican Communion.

Question. What are the benefits whereof we are partakers thereby (i.e., in the Lord's Supper)?

Answer. The strengthening and refreshing of our souls by the body and blood of Christ, as our bodies are by the bread and wine.

The latter half of the answer supplies one of the rare instances in which the Book of Common Prayer lapses in respect of grammar. But, in spite of this, the meaning is quite clear. The implication is that there is already in our souls something akin to that which we receive. We are *strengthened* and *refreshed*. An analogy is sought from bodily sustenance. We do not give material food to a corpse, or to a person so physically weak that he is incapable of receiving or assimilating it. And, conversely, when we partake of food, we seek a renewal of the life that is already within us. The food strengthens us because its nature is such that it corresponds with the nature of our body and can be used and incorporated by the bodily functions. And further, that we have a desire for food is generally a sign of healthy life. Now, whatever other aspects of the eucharist there may be, the symbols of bread and wine suggest that spiritual feeding and renewal is an obvious—if not the most obvious—aspect. In the Holy Communion, therefore, there is a renewal of that already existing spiritual life which, because it is a reality, needs to be strengthened and refreshed. Accordingly, the Holy Communion is not given to the unbaptized, nor—in the Anglican Communion—normally to the unconfirmed. It is intended for those to whom, as members of Christ, has been already given the gift of the Holy Spirit and an increase of the Holy Spirit.

It is worth while noting that the line of thought suggested in the Church Catechism is also found in one of the earliest, if not the earliest, of explicit references to the eucharist outside the New Testament. I refer to chapters 9 and 10 of the *Didache*. "But let none eat or drink of your eucharist except those who have been baptized in the Lord's Name. For concerning this also did the Lord say, 'Give not that which is holy to the dogs.' But after you are satisfied with food, thus give thanks: 'We give thanks to thee, O holy Father, for thy holy Name *which thou didst cause to tabernacle in our hearts*. . . . Thou, Lord Almighty, didst create all things for thy Name's sake, and didst give food and drink for their enjoyment, that they might give thanks to thee; but us hast thou blessed with spiritual food and drink and eternal life through thy Son."

The history of the early centuries of the Church would seem to bear out the truth of this point of view. The fact has been somewhat obscured by theologians, who in treating the subject of the Holy Spirit during that period have concentrated for the most part on the strictly dogmatic aspect of the matter, being chiefly concerned with the abstract question of his Deity and with the terminology employed by the early fathers. While these are important and must be given their due place in the study of the subject, it is admitted that the Church came but slowly to see its way in formulating a clear statement concerning the matter, and that for a time certain writers who were orthodox at heart confused such terms as "Word" and "Spirit" in a bewildering manner. But all this time, in spite of an inadequate intellectual grasp of the subject, the place of the Holy Spirit as the Giver of Life to and in the Church was manifestly acknowledged. Irenæus put it plainly when he said: "Where the Church is, there is also the Spirit of God, and where the Spirit of God is, there is the Church and all grace."[1] This living aspect of the Holy Spirit's work in the early Church—that work in virtue of which it was later clearly seen that he who accomplished it could only be a Person and could only be God—has never been adequately presented by the Christian historian.[2] Yet it is clear that in these early centuries the power of the Holy Spirit enabled the members of the Church, individually and collectively, to win

---

[1] *Hær.* iii. 38. 1 (Harvey).

[2] H. B. Swete's important work *The Holy Spirit in the Ancient Church* is a partial—but only a partial—exception to this.

victories over self and the world so notable that the expansion
and influence of Christianity became a fact with which the world
had to reckon. The source and beginning of this power lay for the
Christian in his Baptism,[1] which marked at once his separation
from a world hostile to the Christian faith and ethic and his entry
upon the new life of the Christian society. Henceforward it was
his privilege and his duty to join Sunday by Sunday in eucharistic
worship and to communicate thereat. This was "at once the
sustenance and the sign of his spiritual fellowship";[2] and in that
visible fellowship and that outward worship he remained until
death, unless excommunicated for apostasy or grave offence.
For about three hundred years after Pentecost, it would appear,
Church membership continued to be a living reality, expressed
in the manner outlined above. "In the first three centuries to be
present at the eucharist virtually meant being a communicant.
The Christian had a personal qualification for being present,
baptism and confirmation. Before receiving these sacraments
he was required to make an explicit statement that he shared
the *faith* of the Church in the revelation and redemption by
Jesus Christ. Without this he could not be of that 'household
of faith' whose domestic worship the eucharist was. It was the
indiscriminate admission to baptism and confirmation of the
infant children of Christian parents when all society began to turn
nominally Christian which was at the root of that decline of lay
communion which set in during the fourth and fifth centuries."[3]
The closing words of this quotation are significant. When
Christianity became nominal, and, as a result and cause of this,
Holy Baptism was administered without due regard to the
obligations involved, the sense of a dedicated Church life was
weakened and a decline in sacramental communion on the part
of the people set in.[4] And as connected with this it is relevant to
refer again[5] to the fact that in the earliest forms of the Epiclesis
the Holy Spirit was invoked upon the elements only, and not upon
the people of God, in whom the Holy Spirit was believed to dwell
already. But "in the fifth century the Holy Spirit was invoked

---

[1] With which Confirmation was closely conjoined.

[2] F. E. Brightman in *The Early History of the Church and Ministry*, 353.

[3] G. Dix, *The Shape of the Liturgy*, 18.

[4] Cp. *ibid.*, p. xii: "the *non-communicant* eucharistic piety which begins in the later fourth century."   [5] See pp. 132ff.

upon the communicants, in some places at any rate, as well as on the elements.''[1] That is to say, the loss of conviction concerning the indwelling presence of the Holy Spirit—a conviction which had been maintained up to the first half of the fourth century—brought with it in the next century an alteration in the form of the Epiclesis. The *lex orandi* followed in due course the *lex credendi*.

The student of Church history is always beset with the dangerous temptation of drawing parallels and analogies between one age and another, and of seeking to heal the wounds of his own generation by applying the remedies that it would now seem clear that past generations in like case lacked. Accordingly, although there are many parallels that we might adduce between the twentieth century and the fifth, and the state of Christianity in them, we must be cautious in assuming that we have only to prescribe the medicine which looking back we now see should have been offered to the Church fifteen hundred years ago. The ''problems'' of each age of the Church are always to some extent new, even as the conditions of its life are always new; else there would be no need for the continued guidance of the Holy Spirit, and a ''deposit'' only of experience drawn from the past would suffice. Nevertheless, we are on safer ground, if, resisting the temptation of commending some particular nostrum which happens to appeal to our individual fancy, we fall back on basic principles. And seeing that ''nominal'' Christianity is, in European lands at any rate, a common feature today as it was in the days of the break-up of the Roman empire under the pressure of barbarian invasions, it can scarcely be a merely academic point of view which postulates as a remedy a return to the New Testament conception of a society formed and dwelt in by the Holy Spirit, with all the obligations as well as privileges that membership in such a society involves. This will necessitate also a return to the conception of the place which Holy Baptism occupied in the primitive Church, forgetfulness of which led to the decay of Church life in the later fourth and the fifth centuries. The remedy for the present state of things is not to be achieved by appealing to the inner circle of Christians to communicate more frequently, however desirable that may be in itself; and certainly not by teaching Church people that Church

[1] E. G. C. F. Atchley, *On the Epiclesis of the Eucharistic Liturgy and in the Consecration of the Font*, 199f. See also G. Dix, *op. cit.*, 296.

membership begins at Confirmation (as it is now administered) rather than Baptism. The words of F. D. Maurice, which he uttered, seemingly, in advance of his own times, give us our starting-point today: "I cannot but think that the reformation in our day, which I expect to be more deep and searching than that of the sixteenth century, will turn upon the Spirit's presence and life, as that did upon the Justification by the Son."[1]

Unfortunately, the very crisis and dangers of our day prevent some from perceiving that the remedy lies here, or at any rate from laying emphasis upon it. Reactions due to fear may be as harmful in the intellectual life as psychologists tell us they are in the emotional life. At any rate it seems clear that theology has suffered in recent years from so violent a reaction that as a result it can scarcely be in a healthy condition. Some of our theologians, including an undue proportion of the younger among them, borrowing perhaps unconsciously ideas from totalitarian political systems, are presenting the Christian faith mainly if not solely as something to be received on authority (but it is not clearly defined what the "authority" is). This crisis-theology, with its emphasis upon transcendence, given-ness and "other-ness", leaves little or no room for the ideas of "reception" or "response" on the part of man; and there is a tendency to leave this out of consideration as if it were irrelevant. And, strangely enough, we are told that this is "biblical theology" or a return to it. But in point of fact the doctrine of the Holy Spirit, which it may not be out of place to describe as an important element in "biblical theology", preserves in their due balance and proportion the ideas of transcendence and immanence, both of which are essential in any system of Christian theology which is going to last or to convince and satisfy the mind and conscience. The Holy Spirit is "given" and also "received"; he is "from above" and at the same time abides "within"; he is supernatural, yet works through the natural faculties; he "creates", but uses the old material;[2] he brings heavenly illumination, nevertheless "beareth witness with our spirit".[3]

---

[1] Quoted in *The Spirit* (ed. B. H. Streeter), p. viii.
[2] Cp. 2 Cor. 5. 17: "If any man is in Christ, he is a new creature: the old things are passed away; behold, they are become new" (R.V.). The "received text" (A.V.) has "behold, all things are become new."   [3] Rom. 8. 16.

But it is just this balance or reconciling of opposites which it is difficult to maintain at a time like the present. The heresy of what is called "humanism", together with its manifest and disastrously concrete results in human affairs, has like all heresies proved injurious also in the reactions it has set up among those who reject it. Similarly, in the second century the grave peril with which the Church was faced by Gnosticism—some think it the gravest peril that the Church ever encountered—resulted in a stiffening and rigidity in the doctrine and organization of the Church, which resulted in an inadequate place being left for the life of the Holy Spirit within the Church; and as against this even the excesses of Montanism were evidences of a reaction not altogether to be deplored. It would be a tragedy if at a time such as this, when a conviction concerning the presence of the Holy Spirit in the Church and in each of its members is sorely needed if belief in a divine society and in the value of the individual is to be preserved, our theologians should allow themselves to be pressed towards a purely transcendental aspect of our Faith, which will not only be one-sided, and therefore practically erroneous, but will also fail to convince "them that are without", and will lead some among the rank and file of Christians to an easy acquiescence in what is irrational or obscurantist.

The remedy for this is a return to "Biblical Theology" in the proper sense of the term—that is, to a more inclusive grasp of the many-sided aspects of the Faith, as set forth in Scripture, not to any of them in isolation. As we have noted, the doctrine of the Holy Spirit combines in one these various elements; and with this thought in view the words of Christ take on for us fresh meaning: "When he, the Spirit of truth is come, he will guide you into all truth."[1] The Church, therefore, depends on the Holy Spirit not only for power to go forward in its life as a redeemed society, but also for the capacity to retain an inclusive grasp of "the much-variegated wisdom of God".[2] In the Holy Spirit the Church is, potentially, enabled to see the truth concerning the redemption of man under all its aspects—that is, to "see it steadily and see it whole". In this connection the teaching of the early Greek fathers on the Holy Spirit as the illumination of the intellect is important.

[1] John 16. 13.
[2] Eph. 3. 10: ἡ πολυποίκιλος σοφία τοῦ θεοῦ.

N

The return to Biblical Theology is, therefore, not a return to an emphasis upon the Cross rather than on the Incarnation, or to transcendence and apocalyptic rather than immanence and possession of the Spirit, or to the society rather than the individual, or to the sacraments rather than unmediated sources of grace. All these elements or truths are to be found in the New Testament, which indeed has a unity, but has also manifold variety contained within this unity. Too often an attempt by scholars to demonstrate that unity has been accompanied by an unconvincing accommodation of its several aspects one to another. The true method of such adjustment is to be found by reference to him who not only is the Inspirer of those who wrote the record of the revelation of Christ, but also is the Life in whom all the operations of the Church are carried on. And it is because the Church, being "of men" as well as "of heaven", has never had, at any rate since the earliest days, an adequate apprehension of what life in the Spirit involves, that its history has been marked by expansion and decay, action and reaction, reformation and counter-reformation. We are thinking at the moment of its intellectual life or grasp of truth; and in this, just as much as in its practical and moral life, the above-mentioned changes have been a feature. Basil in his treatise, *On the Holy Spirit*,[1] remarks that the action of the ecclesiastical place-hunters of his day "pushed aside the dispensation of the Holy Spirit". This dispensation has also been "pushed aside" by theologians and their camp-followers, although not of course with the same moral obliquity. Isolation, partiality, and undue emphasis have been pursued at the expense of comprehensiveness and "wholeness".

An attempt has been made in this book to treat one subject with reference to "the dispensation of the Holy Spirit". And this subject has been chosen because perhaps of all theological subjects it has suffered most from being treated in isolation; and since it is a subject which is intimately connected with the visible life of the Church and its several members, the practical as well as the intellectual results of this isolation have been manifestly unfortunate—if that is not too mild a term.

This book is written in the conviction to which the writer is committed as a member of the Anglican Communion that "Holy Scripture containeth all things necessary to salvation."

[1] Chap. 77.

He believes that men do not require to discover new spiritual truths. They rediscover them in the Bible, and so make them new for themselves. And, conversely, he holds that doctrines which cannot be proved from Holy Scripture have turned out to be harmful, both theoretically and practically, in the life of the Church. And since he further believes in the progressiveness of revelation he holds that the Bible is a fount of ever fresh spiritual truth, and this is so because the Church lives under the "dispensation" of the Holy Spirit, who enables those members of the Church who seek them to find truths which are "given" and yet "akin" in those records which above all other records reveal the mind of the Spirit.

Accordingly no further apology need be made for the amount of attention given to the New Testament background to the doctrine of the Holy Communion. This background, as we have seen, is twofold, historical and doctrinal. Sometimes it would seem that those who are anxious to emphasize what the Holy Communion means and has meant in the faith and experience of the Church become restive when a return is made to the evangelical accounts of the Institution and to the details of those accounts, in so far as they supply us with a more or less clear picture of what actually happened. But this impatience appears to us unreasonable and even inconsistent. One of the distinctive features of the eucharist, and that which fastened its observance on Christians as a religious duty, is that it is rooted in history. Further, the meaning of the sacramental gifts is acknowledged by all faithful Christians to rest upon the words of Christ used concerning them at the Last Supper. Indifference, therefore, to a study of the accounts of the Last Supper cannot be logically the position of those who are foremost in interpreting the observance of the Sacrament as an act of obedience to a divine command to the Church.

No doubt it is disconcerting for those who have been brought up in a certain liturgical tradition to be asked to consider afresh whether they must modify opinions perhaps unconsciously entertained through the use of a rite which does not adequately express some point of importance that may be deduced from the Gospel accounts of the Last Supper. Readiness to do so will largely depend on whether or no they accept the position, which the writer of these pages accepts, that the members of the Church must always be prepared to correct their views in accordance with such fresh light as a further study of the Holy Scriptures may reveal.

For example, a recent work on liturgiology speaks of "those modern theorists who are fond of repeating that the so-called words of institution at the Last Supper are really words of administration".[1] On this, more than one observation may be made. To many—to all, we should hope—Christians the Gospel accounts of the Last Supper are ancient records of a peculiarly sacred character. It is not clear, therefore, why those whose aim it is to go back to these ancient records should be described as "modern". Again, in spite of many differences in the various accounts of the Supper, the order of actions of the Lord at its most solemn moment—namely, the institution of the Sacrament—stands out plainly. Therefore, it is again not clear why those who point out a simple fact—that it was when distributing or administering the bread and the cup that the Lord spoke certain words—should be styled "theorists". But there is a great deal more in the question than that. It is not simply that the Lord said certain words at a particular moment in the Supper, and did not say them at some other moment—although it cannot be unimportant for a Christian to secure as accurate a knowledge as possible of what actually happened at the Supper, especially when, as in this case, the accounts are consistent. The thing that is really significant is that the words, "This is my body", "This is my blood", as used by our Lord, brought the sacramental gifts into relation with persons,[2] and—we may add—persons who already stood in a relation of peculiar intimacy with him who spoke them.

The question of the most satisfactory form of a liturgical prayer of consecration is of importance, but a question, as it would seem, which will always cause differences of opinion among experts. I merely wish to indicate here that when a prayer of consecration entirely obscures the above-mentioned fact, and leads the congregation to suppose that the elements are consecrated apart from their use as the means of conveying a spiritual gift to the communicants, something much more is at stake

[1] G. Dix, The Shape of the Liturgy, 137.
[2] Hooker clearly perceived this, and pointed out what he thought might be deduced from the fact: E.P., v. 67. 6.

than a liturgical tradition, however valuable or even sacred that may be.[1]

But the background of the New Testament teaching on the Holy Communion is not only historical; it is also doctrinal or theological. And there is no opposition or conflict between these two aspects. We may pass from the Gospels through *Acts* to the Epistles and experience in the transition no sense of break or continuity in the "setting" in which the Sacrament is placed. The accounts of the Last Supper speak of a fellowship enriched and made even more intimate by him who is its centre and source. It is throughout the scene of a Person in his relationship with persons; and that relationship is indicated, as we should expect in an historical account, by a series of actions. In the Epistles the dominant note is, again, a fellowship; nevertheless, now no longer a fellowship grouped round the visible form of Jesus, but a fellowship founded on things unseen. The doctrine of the Holy Spirit provides the intellectual basis for the existence of this society; yet it is not to be regarded as an abstract idea, but the explanation of a fact—the concrete fact of the new fellowship connected historically with the old, for it is still the fellowship of *Jesus*, even as the Holy Spirit who forms it is the Spirit of Jesus. And again, even as the disciples in the Upper Room were frail and unstable followers of their Master, and in need of strengthening, so also the members of the new society, even in the days of its first glow and fervour, were weak and imperfect examples of their high calling. Special means of strengthening they needed also; and accordingly, in addition to the doctrine of the Holy Spirit, but included in it, emerges the doctrine of the Holy Communion; which by means of a recitation of the historical facts of its Institution, connected faith with history, and assured those who had to face the difficulties and temptations of daily life of help in time of need from One who had himself endured to the end. And, once again, in the Upper Room the Lord had looked beyond the end of his earthly life and bidden his disciples fix their hopes upon him as he would be when death was conquered. So also, the members of the new society were conscious that, though on earth, their citizenship was in heaven. However great

[1] J. A. Robinson, *Giving and Receiving*, 82, says of the Western tradition that "it fails to do justice to the conditioning command which limits the effectual character of the Sacrament to its prescribed use as food and drink."

the joy of their fellowship in the Spirit with their Lord and with one another, however manifold the streams of grace by which their pilgrimage was refreshed, they knew that never in this world could they see of the travail of their soul and be satisfied. For that they must look beyond the things of sense and the times of refreshing here to a land of clearer vision where sacraments shall cease. "Verily I say unto you, I will drink no more of the fruit of the vine, until that day when I drink it *new* in the kingdom of God."[1] "As often as ye eat this bread, and drink the cup, ye proclaim the Lord's death till he come."[2]

[1] Mark 14. 25.   [2] 1 Cor. 11. 26.

INDEX I

REFERENCES AND CITATIONS

(a) OLD TESTAMENT AND APOCRYPHA

INDEX

INDEX

INDEX

INDEX

INDEX

(c) EARLY CHRISTIAN LITERATURE

INDEX

INDEX II
REFERENCES AND CITATIONS
MODERN WRITERS

INDEX

PRINTED IN GREAT BRITAIN BY
BILLING AND SONS LTD.
GUILDFORD AND LONDON
G8668